HEALING AND
MENTAL HEALTH
FOR NATIVE AMERICANS

D0059624

CONTEMPORARY NATIVE AMERICAN COMMUNITIES
Stepping Stones to the Seventh Generation

Acknowledging the strength and vibrancy of Native American people and nations today, this series examines life in contemporary Native American communities from the point of view of Native concerns and values. Books in the series cover topics that are of cultural and political importance to tribal peoples and that affect their possibilities for survival, in both urban and rural communities.

SERIES EDITORS:
Troy Johnson
American Indian Studies
California State University, Long Beach
Long Beach, CA 90840
trj@csulb.edu

Duane Champagne
Native Nations Law and Policy Center
292 Haines Hall, Box 951551
University of California, Los Angeles
Los Angeles, CA 90095-1551
champagn@ucla.edu

BOOKS IN THE SERIES
1. *Inuit, Whaling, and Sustainability*, Milton M. R. Freeman, Ingmar Egede, Lyudmila Bogoslovskaya, Igor G. Krupnik, Richard A. Caulfield and Marc G. Stevenson (1999)
2. *Contemporary Native American Political Issues*, edited by Troy Johnson (1999)
3. *Contemporary Native American Cultural Issues*, edited by Duane Champagne (1999)
4. *Modern Tribal Development: Paths to Self Sufficiency and Cultural Integrity in Indian Country*, Dean Howard Smith (2000)
5. *American Indians and the Urban Experience*, edited by Susan Lobo and Kurt Peters (2000)
6. *Medicine Ways: Disease, Health, and Survival among Native Americans*, edited by Clifford Trafzer and Diane Weiner (2000)
7. *Native American Studies in Higher Education: Models for Collaboration between Universities and Indigenous Nations*, edited by Duane Champagne and Jay Stauss (2002)
8. *Spider Woman Walks This Land: Traditional Cultural Properties and the Navajo Nation*, Kelli Carmean (2002)
9. *Alaska Native Political Leadership and Higher Education: One University, Two Universes*, Michael Jennings (2004)
10. *Indigenous Intellectual Property Rights: Legal Obstacles and Innovative Solutions*, edited by Mary Riley (2004)
11. *Healing and Mental Health for Native Americans: Speaking in Red*, edited by Ethan Nebelkopf and Mary Phillips (2004)
12. *Rachel's Children*, Lois Beardslee (2004)
13. *Contemporary Education Issues in the Northern Cheyenne Indian Nation: The Role of Family, Community and School in Educational Performance*, Carol Ward (2004)
14. *A Broken Flute*, Doris Seale and Beverly Slapin (2004)

HEALING AND MENTAL HEALTH FOR NATIVE AMERICANS

Speaking in Red

EDITED BY
ETHAN NEBELKOPF
AND MARY PHILLIPS

ALTAMIRA PRESS
A Division of Rowman & Littlefield Publishers, Inc.
Walnut Creek • Lanham • New York • Toronto • Oxford

ALTAMIRA PRESS
A division of Rowman & Littlefield Publishers, Inc.
1630 North Main Street, #367
Walnut Creek, CA 94596
www.altamirapress.com

Rowman & Littlefield Publishers, Inc.
A wholly owned subsidiary of The Rowman & Littlefield Publishing Group, Inc.
4501 Forbes Boulevard, Suite 200
Lanham, MD 20706

PO Box 317
Oxford
OX2 9RU, UK

British Library Cataloguing in Publication Information Available

Library of Congress Cataloging-in-Publication Data

Healing and mental health for Native Americans : speaking in red / edited by Ethan
    Nebelkopf and Mary Phillips.
        p. cm. — (Contemporary Native American communities ; v. 11)
    Includes bibliographical references and index.
    ISBN 0-7591-0606-1 (cloth : alk. paper) — ISBN 0-7591-0607-X (pbk. : alk. paper)
    1. Indians of North America—Mental health. 2. Indians of North America—Health and
hygiene. 3. Indians of North America—Services for. I. Nebelkopf, Ethan. II. Phillips, Mary,
1972– III. Series.

RC451.5.I5H43 2004
362.2'08997—dc22   2003027985

Printed in the United States of America

∞™ The paper used in this publication meets the minimum requirements of American
National Standard for Information Sciences—Permanence of Paper for Printed Library
Materials, ANSI/NISO Z39.48-1992.

CONTENTS

Part II: Innovations in Mental Health 43

Part III: Building Healthy Communities 75

Part IV: Traditional Ceremonies and Healing 107

Acknowledgments

THE FOLLOWING ARTICLES are reprinted by permission from the *Journal of Psychoactive Drugs*, volume 35, number 1, entitled "Morning Star Rising: Healing in Native American Communities," published January–March 2003 by Haight-Ashbury Publications, 612 Clayton Street, San Francisco, California:

"The Historical Trauma Response among Natives and Its Relationship to Substance Abuse: A Lakota Illustration" by Maria Yellow Horse Brave Heart.

"A Behavioral Health Approach among the Yup'ik and Cup'ik Eskimo" by Phoebe Mills.

"Community Readiness: The Journey to Community Healing" by Pamela Jumper-Thurman, Barbara A. Plested, Ruth W. Edwards, Robert Foley, and Martha Burnside.

"Mobilizing Communities to Reduce Substance Abuse in Indian Country" by Bernard Ellis.

The following articles are abridged or updated versions of articles that appeared in the *Journal of Psychoactive Drugs*, volume 35, number 1, published by Haight-Ashbury Publications, 612 Clayton Street, San Francisco, California, and are reprinted by permission:

"Reducing Substance Abuse in American Indian and Alaska Native Communities: The Healthy Nations Initiative" is an abridged version of "Healthy Nations: Reducing Substance Abuse in American Indian and Alaska Native Communities" by Tim Noe, Candace Fleming, and Spero Manson.

"Substance Abuse Treatment at Friendship House: Transformation and Culture" is an abridged version of "Cultural Connection and Transformation: Substance Abuse Treatment at Friendship House" by Yvonne Edwards.

"Urban Trails: A Holistic System of Care for Native Americans in the San Francisco Bay Area" is an updated version of "Holistic System of Care for Native Americans in an Urban Environment" by Ethan Nebelkopf and Janet King.

"Aiming to Balance: Native Women Healing in an Urban Behavioral Health Care Clinic" is an updated version of "The Women's Circle Comes Full Circle" by Karen Saylors.

"Substance Dependency among Homeless American Indians in Oakland and Tucson" is an abridged version of "Substance Dependency among Homeless American Indians" by Susan Lobo and Margaret Mortensen Vaughan.

Introduction: Speaking in Red

ETHAN NEBELKOPF AND MARY PHILLIPS

IN THE 500 YEARS since the arrival of Europeans in North America, Native Americans have experienced genocide, forced assimilation, involuntary relocation, and displacement. As a result of these events, a profound benchmark in treatment for intergenerational trauma has been accepted in the mental health field for Native Americans. Substance abuse, mental illness, and violence are a self-perpetuating vicious cycle in many Native American communities. American Indians make up less than I percent of the U.S. population, yet American Indians lead all ethnic groups in alcohol and drug dependence.

Eliminating health disparities and increasing access of Native Americans to critical substance abuse and mental health services have become priorities for both American Indian leaders and public officials. Ways that are relevant and sensitive to the needs of diverse populations are greatly needed as alternatives to dominant-culture approaches that do not work. For example, the Red Road to Recovery, a model developed by Gene Thin Elk, a Lakota elder, has helped thousands of people to walk in balance and heal as a member of a family and village. The Wellbriety Movement combines wellness with sobriety, a combination that is catching on in urban areas and on the reservations.

Healing and Mental Health for Native Americans: Speaking in Red offers insights into the problems encountered and solutions practiced by Native Americans today. This collection provides a nexus from tradition to innovation, restoring to health the pains of heart and mind. While substance abuse and mental health problems among Indian people remain significant, these chapters present approaches that open the gates for healing. Wisdom is voiced by our best educators, researchers, and clinicians in the Native community who have committed their life's work to changing the health care system to heal Indigenous people.

Working with this core group of professionals, we have gathered these compelling stories that give hope to a people ravaged by destruction. Too many of our families, mothers, fathers, and young people have been exposed to the devastating effects of incompetent systems of care within community or public institutions. In these pages we reveal discoveries about what our ancestors could not fight and what their moral codes would not allow them to believe could break our sacred ties. The voices of our authors point the way to working within both the walls of Western medicine and the circles of traditional healers, opening the book of history for change.

We are honored to devote this latest addition to the series *Contemporary Native American Communities: Stepping Stones to the Seventh Generation* to documenting these breakthroughs. We hope to communicate to the reader that with good intention, creative thought, and hard work, even the most devastated communities can change for the better.

We express our gratitude to Helen Waukazoo (Navajo), executive director of Friendship House Association of American Indians of San Francisco, and to Martin Waukazoo (Lakota), chief executive officer of the Native American Health Center. We also thank the staff of the Family & Child Guidance Clinic of the Native American Health Center and the staff of Friendship House. We are grateful to the editors of the *Journal of Psychoactive Drugs*, the publication in which many of these articles first appeared, who gave us permission to reprint the articles. The editorial committee of the Family & Child Guidance Clinic of the Native American Health Center consisted of Mary Phillips (Omaha/Laguna Pueblo), Nelson Jim (Navajo), Sandra Beauchamp (Mandan/Hidatsa/Arikara), Angelena Tsosie (Navajo), and Karen Saylors.

Blending together the many diverse strands has been challenging but rewarding. Most of all we thank our authors, who worked over and above the call of duty to create *Healing and Mental Health for Native Americans*; without their help this tapestry would never have been woven.

The blanket is split between rural versus urban, traditional versus modern, storytelling versus science, full-blood versus mixed ancestry. While most of the chapters are framed in scientific terms, many look at prayer as a foundation for healing. How do we bind the threads into wholeness? Yet not despondent, we acknowledge our ability to choose to live full lives as cultural beings. We are healing wounds through urgently needed changes in the way we treat our sick—spiritually, traditionally, ceremonially, and scientifically—in rural areas, on reservations, and in the cities.

Today, elements from a wide variety of tribes are practiced in urban areas, reflecting an intertribal culture adapted to modern-day life, a culture in which humor, food, and knowing who you are and not pretending to be someone else attract individuals and families into the healing community. For instance, the Native American community in the San Francisco Bay Area is multitribal, multiethnic, and multiracial. The community is dispersed throughout the Bay Area. It is defined in nongeographical terms. Nonprofit, community-based organizations are nodes for community interaction, and storytelling remains a basis for communicating and sharing information in these organizations.

Organizations leading the pursuit to secure mental health services for Native Americans have seen episodic transformations in leadership, funding, community tolerance, and intolerance. Holistic health is not new to Indian country. It is the inner source of many Indian families who stay connected to each other on and off the reservation. A web of life has no separation of reservation borderlines or health clinic service areas. Survivors of the forced acculturation tactics inflicted on Native people throughout U.S. history have eked out, between traditional and modern ways, a coexisting life moving us toward new knowledge and strong leadership to remedy the tragic health disparities of Native people.

Friendship House is a community-based, nonprofit residential substance abuse program in San Francisco whose treatment philosophy is based on the Red Road. As Executive Director of Friendship House, Helen Waukazoo has dedicated her life to healing, starting with herself, as well as teaching and upholding the traditional values of the American Indian. In 1997, the board of directors of Friendship House had a vision of building a new, state-of-the-art alcohol and drug-abuse treatment facility for Indian people in San Francisco. They had no money, no site, and no experience implementing a project of this magnitude. In December 2000, Friendship House obtained funding from the mayor's office and purchased a site in the Mission District of San Francisco to build the Friendship House Healing Center, an eighty-bed treatment facility. In September 2002, a ground-breaking ceremony was held at the site. During the ceremony, Helen Waukazoo, from the Navajo Nation, shared her feelings:

> I've been so emotional since I got here today. It's been a long ride, let me tell you. I am so happy to be here this morning, to see many of our people, outsiders, and people who supported us being here to celebrate something we have been dreaming and planning for the last ten years. I have gotten so many hugs. I am such a cry-person. I cried every time someone hugged me, and it's because I am really happy. My heart is so full of joy today. It's all about happiness today that the tears are flowing.
>
> On this journey we have faced many difficulties. There are people who told us, 'You are a nonprofit organization. You are not going to make it. How are you going to do it?' Prayer is important. I want to thank those who have been praying for us. That's what we need every day. Prayer is the main part of what we do here. I rely on someone much higher than any human being, and that's the Creator. I give him thanks today, for my life, the strength that I have, the vision, the hope for our people. For we as Indian people are very intelligent people and strong people, and if we want to make something happen, we are going to do it. We have to do it. We have to do it together.

HEALING SUBSTANCE ABUSE I

I was angry, judgmental, spiritually bankrupt. I was the worst type of Indian. The outside was defining who I was. I finally got serious about recovery, working the twelve steps and eventually staying clean and sober for my family and for myself. My efforts today are an attempt to repay what they gave me twenty years ago.

I do not want my own family and my grandchildren to go through it, but I would not exchange the experience of recovery for a million dollars, for all I've learned from it. It taught me lessons, including the fact that it is not what happens to you in life, but how you handle it. You look first for the good things, such as the lessons, and then you decide how you are going to come out on the positive side of it.

It must not be forgotten that our old ones aspired and dreamed, created and struggled, and cared for one another. This generation and future generations must remember that their greatest legacy is the teaching that everyone has healing gifts to build our common decency and wholeness. Our community has grown emotionally and psychologically and has embraced both who we are and where we came from. We are healed of the spiritual diseases such as anger and jealousy that held us back ten to fifteen years ago.

—MARTIN WAUKAZOO, LAKOTA

IN THIS PART WE FOCUS on Native cultural practices and their effectiveness in both substance abuse treatment and prevention. The Takini Network, founded by Maria Yellow Horse Brave Heart, addresses the psychosocial context of historical trauma among the Indian people and has developed specific interventions to ameliorate this trauma and grief through education and traditional ceremonies. Part I also includes a chapter by Tim Noe, Candace Fleming and Spero Manson on the Healthy Nations Initiative. They describe the strategies and outcomes of a Robert Wood Johnson Foundation program to combat substance abuse in fourteen American Indian and Alaska Native communities.

Many Native American people want to identify and maintain traditional beliefs and values while they participate in the contemporary world. Successful prevention efforts incorporate the notion of bicultural identity in practice, employing interventions tailored to the community and strengthening participants' ability to walk in two worlds. Finally, Yvonne Edwards describes what Friendship House graduates report as the most important elements of their recovery from alcohol and drugs. Martin Waukazoo graduated from Friendship House in 1980.

The Historical Trauma Response among Natives and Its Relationship to Substance Abuse
A Lakota Illustration

2

MARIA YELLOW HORSE BRAVE HEART

> *I feel like I have been carrying a weight around that I've inherited. I have this theory that grief is passed on genetically because it's there and I never knew where it came from. I feel a sense of responsibility to undo the pain of the past. I can't separate myself from the past, the history and the trauma. It has been paralyzing to us as a group.*
>
> —A LAKOTA/DAKOTA WOMAN (BRAVE HEART AND DEBRUYN 1998)

HISTORICAL TRAUMA (HT) is cumulative emotional and psychological wounding, over the lifespan and across generations, emanating from massive group trauma experiences. The historical trauma response (HTR) is the constellation of features in reaction to this trauma. The HTR may include substance abuse as a vehicle for attempting to numb the pain associated with trauma. The HTR often includes other types of self-destructive behavior, suicidal thoughts and gestures, depression, anxiety, low self-esteem, anger, and difficulty recognizing and expressing emotions. Associated with HTR is historical unresolved grief that accompanies the trauma; this grief may be considered impaired, delayed, fixated, and/or disenfranchised (Brave Heart 1999a and b, 1998; Brave Heart-Jordan 1995).

Historical trauma theory emerged from more than twenty years of clinical practice and observations as well as preliminary qualitative and quantitative research. This theory describes massive cumulative trauma across generations rather than the more limited diagnosis of post-traumatic stress disorder (PTSD), which is inadequate in capturing the influence and attributes of Native trauma (Brave Heart 1999a and b; Robin, Chester, and Goldman 1996). General trauma literature (van der Kolk, McFarlane, and Weisaeth 1996) and Jewish Holocaust literature (Yehuda

1999; Fogelman 1998, 1991) support the theoretical constructs underpinning the concept of HT, specifically the HTR features and their intergenerational transfer. Native-specific literature calls for the need to develop precise culturally based trauma theory and interventions (Manson et al. 1996; Robin, Chester, and Goldman 1996). In addition to culturally congruent trauma theory and interventions, a consideration of Native history and the continuing transfer of trauma across generations is critical in developing prevention and intervention strategies that will be effective for Native Peoples.

This chapter examines the relationship between the HTR and substance abuse and explains HT theory and the HTR, delineating its features. Implications for substance abuse prevention will be suggested, including interventions aimed at ameliorating the intergenerational transfer of the HTR (which compounds the transfer of substance abuse across generations).

The Lakota Illustration

Although the Lakota traditionally had no mind- or mood-altering substances, alcohol was introduced, and now the Lakota, like other Native communities, suffer from psychosocial problems such as extremely high levels of substance abuse, violence, and suicidal behavior. For Native females the mortality rate is 24 percent and for Native males, 35 percent; both rates are significantly higher than that for all races in the United States, 10.3 percent (IHS 1997b). Alcoholism, suicide, and homicide death rates are higher for Native youth than for youth in the population in general. Native premature death rates are higher than those for African Americans, with 31 percent of Native premature deaths occurring before forty-five years of age (AAIHS 1999; IHS 1997a). In the Indian Health Service for the Aberdeen Area (which includes mostly the Lakota and Dakota/Nakota reservations), the age-adjusted mortality rate is 1,426.2 deaths per 100,000, almost 3.6 times the national average of 513.3 deaths per 100,000 (AAIHS 1999).

For the Lakota and Dakota/Nakota reservations, alcoholism mortality rates are almost 29 times higher than for the United States as a whole (AAIHS 1999). Suicide rates for the Aberdeen Area are the second highest in the Indian Health Service area, exceeded only by Alaska. Further, homicide rates in the Aberdeen Area are 1.5 times greater than the all-Indian rate and 2.2 times higher than the U.S. rate for all races. Other mortality and morbidity rates are elevated among the Lakota. For example, the tuberculosis death rates on the Lakota and Dakota/Nakota reservations are more than six times the national average and almost three times the rate for all Indians (IHS 1997a and b).

High mortality rates from alcoholism, suicide, homicide, and poor health conditions suggest elevated substance abuse as well as mental health risks and needs. Further, the high incidence of death exposes surviving community members to frequent traumatic deaths and the accompanying grief. Oppression, racism, and low socioeconomic status, in addition to elevated mortality rates, place Native peoples at higher risk for traumatic loss and trauma exposure (Brave Heart 1999b; Manson et al. 1996; Robin, Chester, and Goldman 1996; Holm 1994). On some Lakota reservations, the age-adjusted mortality rate is almost 3.6 times the national average (AAIHS 1999). With unemployment soaring as high as 73 percent on some Lakota reservations, nearly 50 percent of the reservation population lives below the poverty level (BIA 1998; IHS 1997a and b).

These modern psychosocial problems are superimposed on a background of historically traumatic losses across generations. The historical losses of Native peoples meet the United Nations definition of genocide (Brave Heart and De-Bruyn 1998). For example, Lakota (Teton Sioux) history includes massive traumatic group experiences (Brave Heart and DeBruyn in press; Brave Heart 1998) incorporating (a) the 1890 Wounded Knee Massacre; (b) war trauma, prisoner of war experiences, starvation, and displacement; (c) the separation of Lakota children from families and their placement in compulsory (and often abusive) boarding schools (Tanner 1982); and (d) the tuberculosis epidemic, in which more than one-third of the Lakota population died between 1936 and 1941 (Hoxie 1989). Forced assimilation and cumulative losses across generations, involving language, culture, and spirituality, contributed to the breakdown of family kinship networks and social structures. This historical legacy and the current psychosocial conditions contribute to ongoing intergenerational trauma.

Historical unresolved grief, a component of the HTR, may be exacerbated by the quality of attachment traditional among the Lakota, as distinct from European American connections. The extent of emotional attachment to family is manifested in the traditional mourning practices among the Lakota (Brave Heart 1998). Bereaved close relatives would cut their hair and sometimes their bodies as external manifestations of their grief, suggesting a deep attachment to the lost relative. Some Lakota traditionally would "keep the spirit" of the deceased for one year before releasing the spirit, thereby permitting time to adjust to the loss. At the end of an appropriate mourning time, traditional grief resolution included a "wiping of the tears" ceremony. However, with the U.S. policy of 1881 outlawing the practice of Native ceremonies, many Natives were forced to either abandon ceremonies or practice indigenous spirituality in secret, thereby impairing traditional mourning resolution. With the rapid succession of massive traumatic losses, Native grief became unresolved and impaired.

It is our way to mourn for one year when one of our relations enters the Spirit World. Tradition is to wear black while mourning our lost one, tradition is not to be happy, not to sing and dance and enjoy life's beauty during mourning time. Tradition is to suffer with the remembering of our lost one and to give away much of what we own and to cut our hair short. Chief Sitting Bull was more than a relation. He represented an entire people: our freedom, our way of life—all that we were. And for one hundred years we as a people have mourned our great leader. We have followed tradition in our mourning. We have not been happy, have not enjoyed life's beauty, have not danced or sung as a proud nation. We have suffered remembering our great chief and have given away much of what was ours. And tens of thousands of Lakota Sioux have worn their hair short for a hundred years, and blackness has been around us for a hundred years. During this time the heartbeat of our people has been weak, and our lifestyle has deteriorated to a devastating degree. Our people now suffer from the highest rates of unemployment, poverty, alcoholism, and suicide in the country (Blackcloud, quoted in Brave Heart-Jordan 1995).

This eloquent testimony to the existence of genocide across generations frames the question regarding the modes of transfer across generations. The trauma may manifest itself among Indian youth as alcohol use, which is more prevalent than in the general U.S. population: 96 percent for Indian males and 92 percent for Indian females by the twelfth grade for lifetime use (Oetting and Beauvais 1989). Not only are the frequency and intensity of drinking greater and the negative consequences more prevalent and severe, but the age at first involvement with alcohol is younger for Indian youths (Beauvais et al.—see Brave Heart and DeBruyn in press; Moran 1999a and b). Alcohol remains the drug of choice, although inhalant and marijuana use are prevalent. Intergenerational transfer of the HTR, as well as the existence of other risk factors for substance abuse among Native youth, is suggested by these findings. Also, there may be a correlation of substance use with impaired Native parenting resulting from HT, specifically boarding school trauma.

The legacy of traumatic history, specifically regarding boarding schools, has negatively impacted Lakota and other Native families. The HTR is complicated by socioeconomic conditions, racism, and oppression. Risk factors for substance abuse, violence, mental illness, and other family problems among Native people may be exacerbated by the HTR. Generations of untreated HT victims may pass on this trauma to subsequent generations. Having undermined the fabric of Native families, boarding schools have deprived these families of traditional Lakota parenting role models, impairing their capacity to parent in an indigenous healthy cultural milieu.

Parental and other intergenerational boarding school experiences negatively impact protective factors against substance abuse, such as parental competence, parental emotional availability and support, and parental involvement with a child's schooling. Parents raised in boarding schools, who are most likely to have been victims of punitive (or what is sometimes referred to as "boarding school style") discipline, may be more likely to have experienced trauma as children—at a minimum, the separation from family. This legacy is perceived as negatively impacting parental interaction with children and contributing to risk factors for youth substance abuse (Morrissette in Brave Heart 1999a). Boarding school survivor parents lack healthy traditional Native role models of parenting within a culturally indigenous normative environment. This lack places parents at risk for parental incompetence. Traumatic childhood experiences may result in emotional unavailability of parents for their own children. The legacy of a lack of control over choices about education, the school environment, and negative boarding school experiences across generations places Lakota and other Native parents at greater risk for insufficient involvement in the education of their offspring.

Intergenerational trauma is clearly illustrated in this testimony given by a forty-three-year-old Lakota male recovering alcoholic:

> I never bonded with any parental figures in my home. At seven years old, I could be gone for days at a time and no one would look for me. . . . I've never been in a boarding school. I wished I [had] because all of the abuse we've talked about happened in my home. If it had happened by strangers, it wouldn't have been so bad—the sexual abuse, the neglect. Then I could blame it all on another race. . . . And yes, [my parents] went to boarding school (Brave Heart 1999a).

Risk Factors for Native Youth

The degree of trauma exposure for children is impacted by the quality of parenting. Greater lifetime trauma exposure is increased by substance abuse (Segal in press). The risk for substance abuse, as well as trauma exposure, increases when children are subjected to nonnurturing and ineffective parental disciplinary practices; absence of family rituals; alcohol-related violence; parental psychiatric problems such as depression; sibling alcohol use; and stressful life events such as verbal, physical, and sexual child abuse perpetrated by a family member (Brave Heart and DeBruyn in press; Brave Heart 1999a). A lack of effective Native parenting role models and the lack of nurturing, as well as the presence of abuse in boarding schools, have resulted in parents who are uninvolved, nonnurturing, punitive, and authoritarian to varying degrees. Consequences of the boarding school legacy and spiritual oppression—poor spiritual foundations, weak Native identity, and poor family affiliation—are associated with Indian youth alcohol and other substance abuse (Oetting and Beauvais 1989).

In contrast to the substance abuse risk factors, positive family relations with supervision, monitoring, and antidrug family norms serve as protective factors against youth substance abuse (Nye, Zucker, and Fitzgerald 1995). Protective family factors include high parental involvement, bonding with family and social groups that value nonuse of alcohol and other substances, external social support, positive discipline methods, and spiritual involvement. Parental encouragement of children's dreaming and setting goals about their life's purpose, an important protective factor (Brave Heart and DeBruyn in press; Brave Heart 1999a), is a challenge for Native parents who carry a legacy of disempowerment and oppression. This legacy, coupled with the prohibition against the open practice of Native spirituality, historically has, to varying degrees, deteriorated the capacity of Native people to set life goals, dream about the future, and find their spiritual purpose.

Intergenerational Post-traumatic Stress Disorder

Childhood exposure to trauma, often associated with parental substance abuse, influences perceptual and emotional experiences of childhood events; these effects persist into adulthood. Substance abuse is implicated in parental neglect and abuse and is related to emotional problems and sexual victimization of offspring among Alaska Native females (Segal in press).

Risk factors for post-traumatic stress disorder (PTSD) have been studied among descendants of Jewish Holocaust survivors. Yehuda (1999) identified well-designed studies demonstrating vulnerability among children of Holocaust survivors for the development of PTSD. Yehuda's research found that adult children of survivors had a greater degree of cumulative lifetime stress, despite a lack of statistically significant differences in the actual self-reported number of traumatic events or in the degree of trauma exposure (Brave Heart and DeBruyn in press). This finding implies that there is a propensity among offspring to perceive or experience events as more traumatic and stressful; children of Holocaust survivors with a parent having chronic PTSD were more likely to develop PTSD in response to their own lifespan traumatic events. The trauma symptoms of the parents, rather than the trauma exposure per se, are the critical risk factors for offspring manifesting their own trauma responses.

A significant proportion of traumatic events reported by children of Holocaust survivors was related to being a descendant of survivors. On the Antonovsky Life Crisis Scale, the incidence of both lifetime and current PTSD was significantly higher among Holocaust descendants (31 percent and 15 percent, respectively) than among the comparison groups (Yehuda 1999). PTSD prevalence among American Indians and Alaska Natives is 22 percent, which is substantially higher than the 8 percent prevalence rate for the general population; American Indian veterans also have significantly higher PTSD rates than both African Americans and the general population, attributed at least in part to higher rates of trauma exposure (DHHS

2001). These rates are considerable, even though PTSD nomenclature inadequately represents Native trauma (Robin, Chester, and Goldman 1996), specifically historical trauma. Culture may impact symptom presentation and assessment and may skew the number of American Indians meeting the PTSD criteria, despite the pervasiveness of trauma exposure (Manson et al. 1996). In addition to elaborating HT theory, the Takini Network (a Native nonprofit organization) promises to advance further understanding of the HTR, refine its assessment, and capture a more accurate picture of Native trauma across generations. The Takini Network is developing HTR assessment tools and evaluating the effectiveness of HT interventions.

In addition to the Jewish Holocaust literature, the experiences of Japanese American descendants of World War II internment camp survivors also manifest intergenerational trauma response features (Nagata 1998, 1991). According to this literature, descendants carry internal intuitive representations of generational trauma, and these internal representations become the organizing concepts in their lives and perpetuate trauma transfer to successive generations (Danieli 1998; Nagata 1991). Among African Americans, oppression and racism exacerbate PTSD (Allen 1996). Trauma exposure increases with lower socioeconomic status and shorter life expectancy, both factors for African Americans; darker skin color negatively impacts socioeconomic status (Hughes and Hertel—see Brave Heart 1999b). Native peoples have similar risk factors for trauma exposure. Native mortality and substance abuse rates, their high degree of trauma exposure (Manson et al. 1996), and the impairment of traditional grief resolution practices may result in Native people's becoming *wakiksuyapi* (memorial people), carrying internalized ancestral trauma and unintentionally passing it on to their children (Brave Heart and DeBruyn in press; Brave Heart 2000, 1998; Wardi in Brave Heart 2000).

Historical Trauma and Substance Abuse

Substance abuse and dependence may co-occur with PTSD; the traumatized individual attempts to self-medicate to reduce the emotional pain. First-degree relatives of trauma survivors with PTSD manifest a higher prevalence of substance use disorders as well as mood and anxiety disorders. Suicide attempts among children of substance abusers appear to be more prevalent than among the general population of the United States. Another possible manifestation of intergenerational trauma transfer, childhood sexual abuse reported among boarding school survivors, is a significant risk factor for substance abuse as well as depression and anxiety disorders. Substance abuse and depression are both prevalent among Natives and are correlated with PTSD. High trauma exposure is also significant among Natives (Brave Heart and DeBruyn in press; Brave Heart 1999b; Robin et al. 1996; Yehuda 1999; Manson et al. 1996; Segal in press).

Both prevention and treatment need to focus on ameliorating the HTR and fostering a reattachment to traditional Native values, which may serve as protective factors to limit or prevent both substance abuse and further transmission of trauma across generations. For the Lakota, children are *wakanheja*—sacred (*wakan*) spirits returning to earth; parents are caretakers of these sacred beings, which is a sacred responsibility. Rekindling or imparting these values through intervention and prevention activities promises to promote improved parenting skills and parent-child relationships. Improved relationships across generations may serve as protection against both substance abuse and the transfer of the HTR. The focus on helping parents heal from HT and improve parenting skills is one type of HT intervention delivered to Lakota parents by the Takini Network (Brave Heart 1999a).

An emphasis on traditional culture may also mitigate substance abuse. The Lakota traditionally utilized no mood- or mind-altering substances. Even tobacco use was foreign to the Lakota, who used *cansasa*—a healthy natural substance with no mood-altering or physically damaging effects—rather than tobacco. Most Native groups who did use certain psychoactive substances limited that use to ceremonies or certain prescribed times. A Native culture that traditionally fosters extensive familial and social support networks also offers protection against substance abuse. Native ceremonies often require discipline and commitment, delay gratification, and provide Native children with healthy role models of skills needed in refusal behavior and healthy defenses against substance use.

One model useful in both prevention and intervention programs is the Historical Trauma and Unresolved Grief Intervention (HTUG). This model, developed by the Takini Network, has been recognized as an exemplary model by the Center for Mental Health Services. The model has been validated through both preliminary quantitative and qualitative research and evaluation and has been documented in peer-reviewed journals as well as other publications. Group trauma and psycho-educational interventions, which seek to restore an attachment to traditional values, manifest promising results for the Lakota. HTUG promises efficacy for addressing risk and protective factors for substance abuse for Lakota children and families as well as for manifesting potential in halting the transfer of trauma across generations. HTUG is perceived by respondents as highly relevant for the Lakota population (Brave Heart and DeBruyn in press; Brave Heart 2001, 2000, 1999a and b, 1998).

HTUG focuses on ameliorating the cumulative trauma response through intensive psycho-educational group experiences. Intervention goals are congruent with PTSD treatment: A sense of mastery and control is transmitted (van der Kolk, McFarlane, and Weisaeth 1996) within a traditional, retreat-like setting (i.e., the Black Hills, sacred to the Lakota), providing a safe, affectively containing milieu. Participants in the HTUG model are exposed through audiovisual materials to content that stimulates historically traumatic memories; this is done in order to provide opportunities for cognitive integration of the trauma as well as for the affective cathartic working through necessary for healing. Small and large group processing provides occasions for increasing capacity to tolerate and regulate emotions, for trauma mastery, and for at least short-term amelioration of the HTR. Traditional prayer and ceremonies, incorporated throughout the intervention as feasible, afford emotional containment and increased connection to indigenous values and a pretraumatic Lakota past (Brave Heart 2001, 1998; Brave Heart-Jordan 1995). Purification ceremonies have been observed as having a curative effect in PTSD treatment (Silver and Wilson 1988).

Preliminary research on the HTUG model and its integration into parenting sessions indicates that it promotes (a) a beginning of trauma and grief resolution, including a decrease in hopelessness as well as an increase in joy, (b) an increase in positive Lakota identity, (c) an increase in protective factors and a decrease in risk factors for substance abuse, (d) perceived improvement in parental relationships with children and in family relationships across generations, and (e) perceived improvement in parenting skills, family connections, and sensitivity to one's children. The Takini Network is developing research on longer-term benefits of the HTUG model and has expanded its application to other tribes in New Mexico, North Carolina, Idaho, Montana, Oklahoma, Alaska, Washington, and California. Additional research focuses on both the efficacy of HT interventions and the qualities and degree of the HTR across tribes. Plans are currently underway to develop an HTR assessment instrument and further exploratory studies.

HT and the HTR are critical concepts for Native Peoples. Increasing understanding of these phenomena and their intergenerational transmission should facilitate preventing or limiting their transfer to subsequent generations. Continued research must include not only (a) evaluation of the effectiveness of HT interventions but also (b) further study and assessment of the HTR and its relationship with substance abuse and (c) investigation of the method of its transfer to descendants. Sharing knowledge across massively traumatized groups can facilitate increased understanding of the HTR and the implications for prevention and treatment. A beginning formal process of such sharing took place during the Takini Network–sponsored conference titled Models of Healing Indigenous Survivors of Historical Trauma: A Multicultural Dialogue among Allies, held in September 2001 (just prior to September 11). During this four-day event, indigenous survivors from Native groups in Canada, Hawaii, Alaska, and the other parts of North, Central, and South America exchanged experiences and healing models with international trauma experts and clinicians from (a) the Jewish Holocaust survivors community, (b) descendants of Japanese Americans interned during World War II,

(c) African American descendants of slaves, and (d) Latino survivors of colonization. A follow-up conference was held in September 2003, in an effort to help each community heal from genocide by continuing knowledge exchange, dialogue, and recognition of common features of all survivors of massive group trauma. The hope is also that we can unite to prevent genocide in the future.

Notes

Please address all correspondence to Maria Yellow Horse Brave Heart, Takini Network, 1818 West Fulton Street, Suite 101, Rapid City, S. Dak., 57702. "The Historical Trauma Response among Natives and Its Relationship to Substance Abuse: A Lakota Illustration" is an abridged version of "The Historical Trauma Response among Natives and Its Relationship to Substance Abuse: A Lakota Illustration" by Maria Yellow Horse Brave Heart, Ph.D., L.C.S.W., which appeared in the *Journal of Psychoactive Drugs* 35 (1). Reprinted by permission of Haight-Ashbury Publications, 612 Clayton Street, San Francisco, California.

Aberdeen Area Indian Health Service (AAIHS). *Aberdeen Area Population Release #34: Indian Health Service (Census). Population Estimates for Fiscal Years 1998–2007.* Aberdeen, S.Dak.: Indian Health Service, 1999.

Allen, I. M. "PTSD among African Americans." In *Ethnocultural Aspects of Posttraumatic Stress Disorder,* ed. A. J. Marsella, M. J. Friedman, E. T. Gerrity, and R. M. Scurfield. Washington, D.C.: American Psychological Association, 1996.

Brave Heart, M. Y. H. "The Return to the Sacred Path: Healing the Historical Trauma Response among the Lakota," *Smith College Studies in Social Work* 68 (3) (1998): 287–305.

———. "Oyate Ptayela: Rebuilding the Lakota Nation through Addressing Historical Trauma among Lakota Parents," *Journal of Human Behavior and the Social Environment* 2 (1/2) 1999(a): 109–126.

———. "Gender Differences in the Historical Trauma Response among the Lakota," *Journal of Health and Social Policy* 10 (4) (1999b): 1–21.

———. "Wakiksuyapi: Carrying the Historical Trauma of the Lakota," *Tulane Studies in Social Welfare* 21–22 (2000): 245–266.

———. "Culturally and Historically Congruent Clinical Social Work Assessments with Native Clients and Culturally and Historically Congruent Clinical Social Work Interventions with Native Clients." In *Culturally Competent Social Work Practice: Practice Skills, Interventions, and Evaluation,* ed. R. Fong and S. Furuto. New York: Longman Publishers, 2001.

Brave Heart, M. Y. H., and L. M. DeBruyn. "The American Indian Holocaust: Healing Historical Unresolved Grief," *American Indian and Alaska Native Mental Health Research* 8 (2) (1998): 56–78.

Brave Heart, M. Y. H., and L. M. DeBruyn. "The Historical Trauma Response among Natives: The Lakota Example." In *Historical Trauma within the American Experience: Roots, Effects, and Healing,* ed. M. Y. H. Brave Heart, L. DeBruyn, B. Segal, J. Taylor, and R. Daw. New York: Haworth Press, in press.

Brave Heart-Jordan, M. Y. H. "The Return to the Sacred Path: Healing from Historical Trauma and Historical Unresolved Grief among the Lakota" (Ph.D. diss., Smith College School for Social Work, 1995), abstract in *Dissertation Abstracts International* 56/09: 3742A. Copyright held by the author; for copies, contact Takini Network, 1818 West Fulton Street, # 101, Rapid City, S. Dak. 57702.

Bureau of Indian Affairs (BIA). *Labor Force Report.* Aberdeen, S. Dak.: Bureau of Indian Affairs, 1998.

Danieli, Y., ed. *International Handbook of Multigenerational Legacies of Trauma.* New York: Plenum Publishing, 1998.

Department of Health and Human Services (DHHS). *Mental Health: Culture, Race and Ethnicity, A Supplement to Mental Health: A Report of the Surgeon General.* Rockville, Md.: DHHS, 2001.

Fogelman, E. "Mourning without Graves." In *Storms and Rainbows: The Many Faces of Death,* ed. A. Medvene. Washington, D.C.: Lewis Press, 1991.

———. "Therapeutic Alternatives for Holocaust Survivors and the Second Generation." In *The Psychological Perspectives of the Holocaust and of Its Aftermath,* ed. R. L. Braham. New York: Columbia University Press, 1998.

Holm, T. "The National Survey of Indian Vietnam Veterans." *American Indian and Alaska Native Mental Health Research* 6 (3) (1994): 18–28.

Hoxie, F. E. *A Final Promise: The Campaign to Assimilate the Indians, 1880–1920.* New York: Cambridge University Press, 1989.

Indian Health Service (IHS). *Regional Differences in Indian Health.* Washington, D.C.: U.S. Department of Health and Human Services, 1997a.

———. *Indian Health Focus: Youth.* Washington, D.C.: U.S. Department of Health and Human Services, 1997b.

Manson, S., J. Beals, T. O'Nell, J. Piasecki, D. Bechtold, E. Keane, and M. Jones. "Wounded Spirits, Ailing Hearts: PTSD and Related Disorders among American Indians." In *Ethnocultural Aspects of Posttraumatic Stress Disorder,* ed. A. J. Marsella, M. J. Friedman, E. T. Gerrity, and R. M. Scurfield. Washington, D.C.: American Psychological Association, 1996.

Moran, J. "Family Strengthening Project." Unpublished manuscript, 1999a.

———, "Preventing Alcohol Use among Urban American Indian Youth: The Seventh Generation Program," *Journal of Human Behavior in the Social Environment* 2 (1,2) (1999b).

Nagata, D. "Intergenerational Effects of the Japanese American Internment. Clinical Issues in Working with Children of Former Internees." *Psychotherapy* 28 (1) (1991): 121–128.

———. "Transgenerational Impact of the Japanese-American Internment." In *International Handbook of Multigenerational Legacies of Trauma,* ed. Y. Danieli. New York: Plenum Publishing, 1998.

Nye, C., R. Zucker, and H. Fitzgerald. "Early Intervention in the Path to Alcohol Problems through Conduct Problems: Treatment Involvement and Child Behavior Change," *Journal of Consulting and Clinical Psychology* 63 (1995): 831–840.

Oetting, E. R., and F. Beauvais. "Epidemiology and Correlates of Alcohol Use among Indian Adolescents Living on Reservations." In *Alcohol Use among U.S. Ethnic Minorities.* NIAAA Research Monograph 18. Rockville, Md.: U.S. Public Health Service, 1989.

Robin, R. W., B. Chester, and D. Goldman. "Cumulative Trauma and PTSD in American Indian Communities." In *Ethnocultural Aspects of Post-Traumatic Stress Disorder*, ed. A. J. Marsella,
M. J. Friedman, E. T. Gerrity, and R. M. Scurfield. Washington, D.C.: American Psychological Press, 1996.

Segal, B. "Personal Violence and Historical Trauma among Alaska Native Pre-Teen Girls,
and Adolescent Girls and Women in Treatment for Substance Abuse." In *Historical
Trauma within the American Experience: Roots, Effects, and Healing*, ed. M. Y. H. Brave Heart,
L. M. DeBruyn, B. Segal, J. Taylor, and R. Daw. New York: Haworth Press, in press.

Silver, S. M., and J. P. Wilson. "Native American Healing and Purification Rituals for War
Stress." In *Human Adaptation to Extreme Stress: From the Holocaust to Viet Nam*, ed. J. P. Wilson,
Z. Harele, and B. Hahana. New York: Plenum Press, 1988.

Tanner, H. "A History of All the Dealings of the United States Government with the
Sioux," unpublished manuscript prepared for the Black Hills Land Claim by order of
the United States Supreme Court, on file at the D'Arcy McNickle Center for the History of the American Indian, Newberry Library, Chicago, Ill.; 1982.

Van der Kolk, B. A., A. C. McFarlane, and L. Weisaeth, eds. *Traumatic Stress: The Effects of
Overwhelming Experience on Mind, Body, and Society*. New York: Guilford Press, 1996.

Yehuda, R., ed. *Risk Factors for Posttraumatic Stress Disorder*. Washington, D.C.: American Psychiatric Press, 1999.

Reducing Substance Abuse in American Indian and Alaska Native Communities
The Healthy Nations Initiative

3

TIM NOE, CANDACE FLEMING, AND SPERO MANSON

Then two men among them became sick and grew weaker day by day. The people didn't do anything for them because no one knew then about illnesses and how to cure them. The One Who Made the Earth said, "Why don't you do something for those two men? Why don't you say some words over them?" But the people had no knowledge of curing ceremonies. Four men among the people happened to be standing one to the east, one to the south, one to the west, and one to the north. The One Who Made the Earth spoke to one of these men, telling him, "Everything on earth has power to cause its own sickness, make its own trouble. There is a way to cure all of these things." Now this man understood that knowledge was available.

—WHITE MOUNTAIN APACHE (ERDOES AND ORTIZ 1984)

BY THE EARLY 1990S, substance abuse problems among American Indian and Alaska Native (AI/AN) communities were well documented (Segal 1994; Dick, Manson and Beals 1993; Kettl and Bixler 1993; Mail and Johnson 1993; Beauvais and Segal 1992; Young 1991; Beauvais et al. 1989; Edwards and Edwards 1988; Okwumabua and Elias 1987; Welte and Barnes 1987; Yates 1987; Beauvais and LaBoueff 1985; Oetting et al. 1980; Cockerman 1975). A broad range of solutions was proposed including education, social skills enhancement, stress reduction, and regulatory approaches (Heath 1992; May 1992; Wolf 1992; Mail 1989; Gilchrist et al. 1987). Many authors argued that comprehensive, community-based strategies offer the only effective long-term solution to substance abuse problems in AI/AN communities (Beauvais 1992; Dorpat 1992; Levy 1992; May 1992; Wolf 1992; Edwards and Edwards 1988; Beauvais and LaBoueff

1985). In response, the Robert Wood Johnson Foundation (RWJF) announced in 1992 that it would award $13.5 million for an initiative called Healthy Nations: Reducing Substance Abuse among Native Americans, or HNI (Brodeur 2002).

The program was designed to provide grants to support the development of community-wide efforts to combat substance abuse, integrating public awareness campaigns, prevention programs, and facilitation of services for treatment, after-care, and support. Particular emphasis was placed on prevention of and early intervention in the use of alcohol, illegal drugs, and tobacco among youth. Incorporation of traditional cultural values was also encouraged as a key component of the HNI programs.

Unlike most funding agencies, which come into Native communities with their own prescriptions for what people should do, the RWJF invited the communities to find their own solutions—to use their natural wisdom in deciding how to address substance abuse. Each community was encouraged to develop its own models and strategies based on its unique strengths and traditions.

In December 1993, the foundation announced the tribes and Native organizations that received funding. The fifteen grantees were the Central Council of Tlingit and Haida Indian Tribes of Alaska, in Juneau, Alaska; the Cherokee Nation of Oklahoma, in Tahlequah, Oklahoma; the Cheyenne River Sioux Tribe of the Cheyenne River Reservation, in Eagle Butte, South Dakota; the Confederated Salish and Kootenai Tribes of the Flathead Reservation, in Pablo, Montana; the Confederated Tribes of the Colville Reservation, in Nespelem, Washington; the Confederated Tribes of the Warm Springs Reservation, in Warm Springs, Oregon; the Eastern Band of Cherokee Indians of North Carolina, in Cherokee, North Carolina; the Friendship House Association of American Indians, in San Francisco, California; the Minneapolis American Indian Center, in Minneapolis, Minnesota; the Norton Sound Health Corporation, in Nome, Alaska; the Seattle Indian Health Board, in Seattle, Washington; the United Indian Health Services, in Eureka, California; and the White Mountain Apache Tribe of the Fort Apache Indian Reservation, in Whiteriver, Arizona.

The Healthy Nations grantees developed and successfully implemented a broad range of creative and interesting community-based activities. For example, the Seattle Indian Health Board developed technology-focused youth mentoring projects with the Boeing Corporation, Microsoft, and the American Indian Academy of Science and Engineering. The Minneapolis American Indian Center's Healthy Nations program instituted a large and well-attended recreational project and successfully implemented a Native youth mentoring program. The Cherokee Nation of Oklahoma actively engaged up to 1,000 members in increasing physical activity and healthy lifestyles as well as instituting a school-based health-promotion curriculum, smoking cessation classes, and cultural heritage projects.

Friendship House Association of American Indians sponsored sports, youth gatherings, parenting projects, an after-school drop-in project, an annual youth conference, and annual family-focused sobriety celebrations. Norton Sound Health Corporation instituted a Village-Based Counselor program to provide much-needed behavioral health services to its seventeen remote villages. Most of the grantees incorporated traditional healing practices such as sweat lodges and talking circles into their community's treatment and aftercare options. In addition, many of the grantee communities utilized traditional language and arts and crafts projects as aftercare activities. More information regarding the types of activities implemented by each grantee can be obtained by referring to the Healthy Nations website at www.uchsc.edu/ai/hni.

It is often difficult to assess the ultimate impacts of comprehensive community-based programs (Baldwin 1999; Furlong, Casas and Corral 1997; Gabriel 1997; Morrissey et al. 1997; Saxe et al. 1997; Yin and Kaftarian 1997; Boruch 1996; Braithwaite 1994; Cook, Roehl, and Trudeau 1994; Goodman and Wandersman 1994; Kim et al. 1994; Kaftarian and Hansen 1994; Murray and Wolfinger 1994; Pentz 1994; Cook and Campbell 1979). Typically, behavioral changes are sought to determine if the program has made an impact. For example, if the goal is to reduce substance abuse in a community, the only way to determine success is either to conduct expensive surveys of community members to determine their level of use before (baseline) and after (posttest) the program or to consider social indicators of change, such as reductions in drunk-driving arrests, a measurable reduction in drug-related crime, alcohol-linked traffic fatalities, or school dropout rates.

Statistical indicators are most frequently used to gauge the success or failure of substance abuse interventions. If a program does not lead to a measurable reduction in drug-related crime, alcohol-linked traffic fatalities, or school dropout rates, often it is considered a waste of money and effort. However, in order to determine if change has occurred in the community, several other important results can be considered, such as interest generated, engagement, community capacity enhancement, and policy as well as institutional changes. These key outcome indicators create a hierarchy of results that are strongly associated with community change (Cohen and Kibel 1993; Capra and Steindl-Rast 1991).

This hierarchy of results (see figure 3.1) is a set of increasingly difficult accomplishments that must be realized on the way toward the ultimate result (community impact). In rare cases, a single program may be sufficiently potent to pass through several stages in the hierarchy and produce an impact. It is more likely that a succession of complementary programs, each building on the results of prior ones, is necessary to reach the ultimate impact, that is, reducing substance abuse and its sequelae.

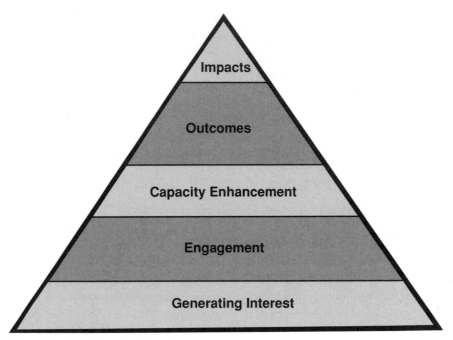

Figure 3.1.   The hierarchy of results.

A key effect, which is considered to be at the low end of the hierarchy of results, is generating interest, that is, getting people to attend activities, meetings, and events in order to gain exposure to a no-use message and healthy alternative activities. The numbers of community members who actively participate in program-sponsored activities represent an appropriate indicator of a program's ability to generate interest.

Engagement means gaining the commitment of key people to work toward bringing about change in their organization or community. For example, an elected tribal government official's attendance at a planning meeting held by a local coalition working to reduce underage drinking would be an interest-building result. Engagement is a higher-level result than generating interest; getting the same tribal official to become an active member of the coalition and to advocate its agenda at a council meeting would be an example of engagement.

The next level of change in this hierarchy is capacity enhancement. This refers to changes in practices of individuals and groups in organizations, partnerships, or communities-at-large as such practices relate to addressing substance abuse. Key types of capacity enhancement results include policy changes and institutional changes. Has the tribal government (or Native organization) passed resolutions addressing substance abuse? (Such resolutions might call for smoke-free buildings, drug-testing for tribal employees, stricter driving under the influence [DUI] laws and minors-in-possession laws, liquor-licensing changes, or changes in training or certification requirements for employees.)

Outcomes are the next level in the hierarchy of results. Outcomes are specific, observable changes in the behavior of members of the population that lead to healthier or more productive lifestyles and away from problem-causing actions. A desirable outcome related to alcohol misuse could be a reduction in the number of intoxicated patrons leaving bars as a result of changes in bar policy. The ultimate results of programs are impacts, the highest level of program results in the hierarchy. Impacts are measurable changes in social indicators used to gauge the levels of problem occurrence. Examples of impacts are a reduction in alcohol-linked auto accidents, an increase in the percentage of the school population who are not regular users or abusers of drugs, and a decrease in drug-related violent crimes.

In order to determine if these types of results have occurred in the HNI grantee communities, the authors had discussions with HNI staff and community members during site visits and reviewed record data. The following is an assessment of the extent to which the Healthy Nations grantee programs were able to accomplish change with regard to (1) generating interest, (2) increasing engagement, and (3) enhancing capacity. Finally, an assessment of each grantee program's sustainability success is provided.

Generating Interest

The number of community members who actively participated in HNI-sponsored activities represents one measure of how successful HNI was in generating interest.

The HNI grantees obviously increased interest in the subject of substance abuse in their local communities. This is evidenced by the fact that they implemented, on average, 710 activities and events at each site over the six- to seven-year life of their programs. All of these activities were well attended, with an average of 10,000 children, adolescents, adults, and elders served annually by each grantee.

Increasing Engagement

To assess engagement, the authors looked at HNI grantees' success in engaging key people to address substance abuse in the community, specifically through recruiting and utilizing volunteers (many of whom were tribal leaders/officials). In addition to thousands of people attending HNI-sponsored activities and events each year, the grantees also successfully engaged many of these people in implementing substance abuse programs. This is a significant accomplishment given that engagement is a higher-level result in the hierarchy and is more likely to lead to significant community change. The HNI grantees spurred people to "do something" and to become proactive in the fight against substance abuse.

Enhancing Capacity

Capacity enhancement, or changes in practices of individuals and groups in organizations, partnerships, or communities, can take many different forms, such as policy changes, institutional changes, and human capital development. These types of changes represent key indicators that a community's capacity to address substance abuse has been enhanced. The HNI grantees made significant accomplishments with regard to capacity enhancement. Many of the grantees instituted key local policy and institutional changes during the six-year HNI implementation period. For example:

The Norton Sound Health Corporation changed corporate alcohol policy to require zero tolerance of abuse by employees and board members and to ban alcohol use at corporate functions. It also earmarked a higher percentage of money for prevention activities, enhanced the relationship between the substance abuse program and the courts through commitments from judges to mandate treatment for alcohol abusers, and created a training institute in Nome to train Village-Based Counselors.

The Cherokee Nation of Oklahoma implemented a drug-testing policy for tribal employees, established a smoke-free workplace for tribal employees, prohibited the sale of alcohol in convenience stores within the tribal jurisdictional area, provided training for tribal employees in identifying substance abusers, incorporated substance abuse curricula in the schools, changed school policies regarding substance-abusing Native youth, and increased from three to twelve the staff assigned to substance-abuse-prevention activities.

The Confederated Salish and Kootenai Tribes of the Flathead Reservation likewise accomplished a long list. It created and implemented a minors-in-possession court diversion program, developed an employee assistance program and a drug-testing policy for tribal employees, implemented a smoke-free-workplace policy for tribal employees, created a zero-tolerance policy for alcohol and drug use in a tribal alternative school, created a tribal DUI program, developed a hepatitis C prevention program, created an intensive outpatient program for chronically unemployed substance abusers, and established a juvenile diversion department in every community.

The Cheyenne River Sioux Tribe passed a tribal resolution mandating Lakota language classes be taught in tribal schools; permitted youth to use gym facilities for midnight basketball; established higher fines for DUI and public intoxication; created antigang programs; implemented a no-smoking policy for public buildings; established youth centers in sixteen communities, developed a wrap-around services system to get youth providers to work together; and created a cultural immersion program for students in kindergarten through sixth grade.

The White Mountain Apache Tribe of the Fort Apache Reservation changed school policy to allow health promotion and disease prevention educators in the classroom, set a new policy providing treatment rather than termination for tribal employees with alcohol or drug abuse problems, established a fitness policy within the education department that allows employees to take an additional thirty minutes at lunch to exercise, started a parenting program, and created a drug-testing policy for tribal employees. Teachers are now required to complete a certain number of hours of substance-abuse curriculum. Liquor distributors are no longer allowed to sponsor youth athletics programs.

For the Eastern Band of Cherokee, many restaurants are now smoke free, police officers at events now screen with Breathalyzers at the door, a juvenile drug court has been established, counseling and support group services are now offered for juvenile offenders, and student services programs and support groups are now provided in the schools. Also, the Eastern Cherokee Chief walked in the Sobriety Walk, increasing public support for this type of event.

The Seattle Indian Health Board toughened its policies in regard to alcohol and drug use. No drinking is allowed on paid travel, and no smoking on the board's premises. Staff positions for prevention programs have increased from two to twelve. Microsoft developed a mentoring program that connected its staff with Native youth. The Seattle Area Government Services Agency created a computer donation program to provide computers for the Native tech center, and an Indian heritage curriculum was developed and is being implemented by several schools.

The Colville Business Council (Tribal Council) of Confederated Tribes of the Colville Reservation passed resolutions calling for a number of innovations: increased substance-abuse treatment services for tribal employees; a multiculturally relevant substance abuse treatment center offering both inpatient and outpatient services; increased knowledge and appreciation of tradition, cultural language, values, and history for Indian students; a reservation-wide youth council to represent tribal youth before the Colville Business Council; prohibition of alcohol and drugs at tribally sponsored activities; and the assignment of top priority to reducing substance abuse on the reservation.

Not only did Healthy Nations grantees successfully facilitate local policy and institutional change; they also enhanced capacity through an increase in human capital. The personnel (both volunteer and paid) who worked for the local HNI grantee institutions gained valuable experience, skills, and knowledge, especially in key areas such as strategic planning, public speaking, conference planning, meeting facilitation, and discussion-group leadership. Many staff subsequently assumed leadership positions in the local area after leaving the HNI. Obviously, many of these individuals would not have received this valuable experience and would not have progressed to their current positions if not for the opportunities provided by the HNI program. The initiative has undeniably enhanced the competence of local human capital and as a result has increased the community's capacity to effectively address social problems.

Sustainability

Achieving sustainability is one of the most important outcomes of community-based programs, especially in Native communities. As one program leader stated, "We have a responsibility to our program recipients. They've had so many losses in their lives, and [if we] come in for a year or two or three and give them hope, only to have the program go away, we've just caused another loss and further hopelessness in their lives." Almost all Healthy Nations grantees sustained at least a portion of their activities; some sustained all. Grantees used a variety of creative strategies to accomplish this objective, as illustrated in the following examples:

1. Existing tribal/organizational departments incorporated the activities: An existing department within the tribal government or organization (e.g., Health and Human Services) took ownership of one or several program activities and integrated the activities into its service delivery system.
2. Community groups took ownership: A volunteer community group (existing or newly formed) took ownership of an activity. It raised the funds needed for supplies and volunteers to facilitate the implementation of the activity.
3. Grants and contracts were secured: In some cases, a grant was secured to continue or expand entire programs. Several grants were secured to continue specific activities. Also, activities were shifted to another funding source. In one case, for example, a Center for Substance Abuse Prevention grant was used to continue a mentoring activity, and an Office of Juvenile Justice and Delinquency Prevention grant was used to continue a violence-prevention activity.
4. An organization or government adopted programs wholesale: A tribal government or other organization used tribal/organizational funds to sustain the program, specifically, to support staffing and program activities for a given length of time.

5. Tribes or organizations collaborated with the community: A tribal government or other parent organization continued to provide staffing for community mobilization efforts (to create and sustain community action groups), but the community assumed ownership of the activities, raised funds for the activities, and facilitated their implementation.
6. Tribes or organizations used an endowment model: A tribe or organization provided funds for community programs. Community groups submitted proposals for programs, received funding based on merit or innovation, and facilitated the implementation of the activities.
7. Groups adopted a fee-for-services model: A tribe or Native organization institutionalized an activity and charged a fee to all those who participated in order to cover operating expenses.

Summary

The Healthy Nations programs have (1) increased interest in substance abuse prevention and treatment by increasing the number of individuals who attend program-sponsored events and activities; (2) actively engaged key people in the implementation process by recruiting and using them as program advocates and volunteers; (3) enhanced community capacity by increasing the number of activities and trained personnel and resources allocated to their programs; (4) influenced policy changes regarding how the community and its organizations and institutions address substance abuse issues; and (5) created the necessary infrastructure to institutionalize and sustain programs. Therefore, it appears that significant community change has been accomplished. Of course, some programs were more successful than others. Commonalities among the most effective programs point to several characteristics that appear to increase the likelihood of success. Specifically, effective programs:

- Maintained consistent and effective leadership. Programs that experienced significant turnover within key program personnel often realized substantial setbacks in implementation success.
- Incorporated a culture-focused approach. Culture became "the program" for the most effective grantees instead of culture as an "add on."
- Achieved community ownership and "buy in." Effective programs stressed that community members should be involved at all levels of planning and implementation and incorporated the perspective of "doing with" the community instead of "doing for" the community.
- Developed creative and entrepreneurial approaches. "Thinking outside of the box" was often a characteristic of the most successful programs.
- Developed comprehensive efforts. Programs that sought to impact as many community systems as possible (e.g., schools, families, peers,

neighborhoods, and tribal organizations) were repeatedly the most effective.

- Established effective collaboration. Programs that established effective collaborative linkages across service organizations and successfully combined resources and talents were more effective.

The Healthy Nations initiative has clearly demonstrated that local American Indian and Alaska Native communities do indeed have the insight, wisdom, and strength to successfully address substance abuse if necessary resources are available. As a result of their experience with this initiative, which is ongoing in many communities despite the end of RWJF funding, the local grantees have exponentially increased their capacity to address the problem. A grassroots movement was initiated that continues to build momentum and strength. New heroes emerged from within the community; in addition to leaders who implemented activities as part of their position within the formal service structure, Indian and Native citizens of all ages and walks of life stepped forward to help plan and implement programs. The movement extends across diverse Indian and Native communities as well. Due to the HNI's high national profile, many are eager to understand the experiences of the HNI grantee communities and to apply that knowledge as deemed relevant.

The RWJF took a chance and invested venture capital in the future of AI/AN communities. Its investment is reaping wonderful rewards both for the grantee communities and for the foundation itself. Yet there is still a lot of work to be done. The RWJF is examining how it can continue to invest in the future of AI/AN communities. Also, the local grantee communities will work diligently to sustain the efforts that began as a result of the initiative, and they will continue to draw upon their internal strengths and knowledge to find solutions to local substance abuse problems.

Notes

Please address correspondence to Timothy Noe, M. Div., University of Colorado Health Sciences Center, Division of American Indians and Alaska Native Programs, 4455 E. 12th Ave., Box A011–13, Aurora, CO, 80045–0508. "Reducing Substance Abuse in American Indian and Alaska Native Communities: The Healthy Nations Initiative" is an abridged version of "The Healthy Nations Initiative: Reducing Substance Abuse in American Indian and Alaska Native Communities," by Tim Noe, M. Div., Candace Fleming, Ph.D., and Spero Manson, Ph.D., which appeared in the *Journal of Psychoactive Drugs* 35 (1). Reprinted by permission of Haight-Ashbury Publications, 612 Clayton Street, San Francisco, California.

Baldwin, J. A. "Conducting Drug Abuse Prevention Research in Partnership with Native American Communities: Meeting Challenges through Collaborative Approaches," *Drugs and Society* 14 (1–2) (1999): 77–92.

Beauvais, F. "Comparison of Drug Use Rates for Reservation Youth, Non-Reservation Indian and Anglo Youth," *American Indian and Alaska Native Mental Health Research* 5(1) (1992): 13–31.

Beauvais, F., and S. LaBoueff. "Drug and Alcohol Intervention in American Indian Communities," *International Journal of Addiction* 20 (1985): 139–171.

Beauvais, F., E. R. Oetting, W. Wolf, and R. W. Edwards. "American Indian Youth and Drugs, 1976–87: A Continuing Problem," *American Journal of Public Health* 79 (1989): 634–636.

Beauvais, F., and B. Segal. "Drug Use Patterns among American Indian and Alaska Native Youth: Special Rural Populations," *Drugs and Society* 7(1/2) (1992): 77–94.

Boruch, R. *Conducting Randomized Experiments.* Thousand Oaks, Calif.: Sage, 1996.

Braithwaite, R. L. "Challenges to Evaluation in Rural Conditions," *Journal of Community Psychology* Special Issue (1994): 188–200.

Brodeur, P. "Programs to Improve the Health of Native Americans." In *To Improve Health and Health Care, Volume V: The Robert Wood Johnson Foundation Anthology,* ed. S. Issacs and J. Knickman. San Francisco: Jossey-Bass, 2002.

Capra, F., and D. Steindl-Rast. *Belonging to the Universe.* New York: HarperCollins, 1991.

Cockerman, W. C. "Drinking Attitudes and Practices among Wind River Indian Reservation Youth," *Journal of the Study of Alcohol* 36 (1975): 321–326.

Cohen, A. Y., and B. M. Kibel. *The Basics of Open-Systems Evaluation.* Rockville, Md.: DHHS, 1993.

Cook, R., J. Roehl, and J. Trudeau. "Conceptual and Methodological Issues in the Evaluation of Community-Based Substance Abuse Prevention Coalitions: Lessons Learned from the National Evaluation of the Community Partnership Program," *Journal of Community Psychology* Special Issue (1994): 155–169.

Cook, T. D., and D. T. Campbell. *Quasi-Experimentation: Design and Analysis Issues for Field Settings.* Boston: Houghton-Mifflin, 1979.

Dick, R. W., S. M. Manson, and J. Beals. "Alcohol Use among Male and Female Native American Adolescents: Patterns and Correlates of Student Drinking in a Boarding School," *Journal of Studies on Alcohol* 54(2) (1993): 172–177.

Dorpat, N. "Community Development as Context for Alcohol Policy," *American Indian and Alaska Native Mental Health Research* 4 (1992): 82–84.

Edwards, E. D., and M. E. Edwards. "Alcoholism Prevention/Treatment and Native American Youth: A Community Approach," *Journal of Drug Issues* 18 (1988): 103–114.

Erdoes, R., and A. Ortiz. *American Indian Myths and Legends.* New York: Pantheon Books, 1984.

Furlong, M. J., J. M. Casas, and C. Corral. "Changes in Substance Use Patterns Associated with the Development of a Community Partnership Project," *Evaluation and Program Planning* 20(3) (1997): 299–305.

Gabriel, R. M. "Community Indicators of Substance Abuse: Empowering Coalition Planning and Evaluation," *Evaluation and Program Planning* 20 (1997): 3, 335–343.

Gilchrist, L. D., S. P. Schinke, J. E. Trimble, and G. T. Cvetkovich. "Skills Enhancement to Prevent Substance Abuse among American Indian Adolescents," *International Journal of the Addictions* 22 (1987): 869–879.

Goodman, R. M., and A. Wandersman. "FORECAST: A Formative Approach to Evaluating Community Coalitions and Community-Based Initiatives," *Journal of Community Psychology* Special Issue (1994): 6–25.

Heath, D. B. "Alcohol Policy Considerations in American Indian Communities: An Alternative View," *American Indian and Alaska Native Mental Health Research* 4 (1992): 64–70.

Kaftarian, S. K., and W. B. Hansen. "Improving Methodologies for the Evaluation of Community-Based Substance Abuse Prevention Programs," *Journal of Community Psychology* Special Issue (1994): 3–5.

Kettl, P., and E. O. Bixler. "Alcohol and Suicide in Alaska Natives," *American Indian and Alaska Native Mental Health Research* 5(2) (1993): 34–45.

Kim, S., C. Crutchfield, C. Williams, and N. Hepler. "An Innovative and Unconventional Approach to Program Evaluation in the Field of Substance Abuse Prevention: A Threshold-Gating Approach Using Single System Evaluation Designs," *Journal of Community Psychology* Special Issue (1994): 61–73.

Levy, J. E. "Commentary," *American Indian and Alaska Native Mental Health Research* 4 (1992): 95–100.

Mail, P. D. "American Indians, Stress, and Alcohol," *American Indian and Alaska Native Mental Health Research* 3 (1989): 7–26.

Mail, P. D., and S. Johnson. "Boozing, Sniffing, and Toking: An Overview of the Past, Present, and Future of Substance Use by American Indians," *American Indian and Alaska Native Mental Health Research* 5(2) (1993): 1–33.

May, Philip A. "Alcohol Policy Considerations for Indian Reservations and Bordertown Communities," *American Indian and Alaska Native Mental Health Research* 4(3) (1992): 5–59.

Morrissey, E., A. Wandersman, D. Seybolt, M. Nation, C. Crusto, and K. Davino. "Toward a Framework for Bridging the Gap between Science and Practice in Prevention: A Focus on Evaluator and Practitioner Perspectives," *Evaluation and Program Planning* 20(3) (1997): 367–377.

Murray, D. M., and R. D. Wolfinger. "Analysis Issues in the Evaluation of Community Trials: Progress toward Solutions in SAS/STAT MIXED," *Journal of Community Psychology* Special Issue (1994): 140–154.

Oetting, E. R., R. Edwards, G. S. Goldstein, and M. A. Garcia-Mason. "Drug Use among Adolescents of Five Southwestern Native American Tribes," *International Journal of the Addictions* 15(3) (1980): 439–445.

Okwumabua, J. O., and D. J. Elias. "Age of Onset, Periods of Risk, and Patterns of Progression in Drug Use among American Indian High School Students," *International Journal of the Addictions* 22(12) (1987): 1269–1276.

Pentz, M. A. "Adaptive Evaluation Strategies for Estimating Effects of Community-Based Drug Abuse Prevention Programs," *Journal of Community Psychology* Special Issue (1994): 26–51.

Saxe, L., E. Reber, D. Hallfors, C. Kadushin, D. Jones, D. Rindskopf, and A. Beveridge. "Think Globally, Act Locally: Assessing the Impact of Community-Based Substance Abuse Prevention," *Evaluation and Program Planning* 20 (1997): 3, 357–366.

Segal, B. "Urban–Rural Comparisons of Drug-Taking Behavior among Alaskan Youth," *International Journal of the Addictions* 29 (1994): 8, 1029–1044.

Welte, J. W., and G. M. Barnes. "Alcohol Use among Adolescent Minority Groups," *Journal on the Study of Alcohol* 48 (1987): 319–326.

Wolf, A. "Commentary on Alcohol Policy Considerations for Indian Reservations and Bordertown Communities," *American Indian and Alaska Native Mental Health Research* 4 (1992): 71–76.

Yates, A. "Current Status and Future Directions of Research on the American Indian Child," *American Journal of Psychiatry* 144 (1987): 1135–1142.

Yin, R. K., and S. J. Kaftarian. "Introduction: Challenges of Community-Based Program Outcome Evaluations," *Evaluation and Program Planning* 20(3) (1997): 293–297.

Young, T. J. "Native American Drinking: A Neglected Subject of Study and Research," *Journal of Drug Education* 21 (1991): 65–72.

Substance Abuse Treatment at Friendship House
Transformation and Culture

4

YVONNE EDWARDS

T HE MOST SUCCESSFUL substance abuse treatment programs for Native Americans not only treat symptoms but also embody Native American values and identity (Spicer 2001; LaFromboise, Trimble, and Mohatt 1990; Shaffer 1990; Landers 1989; May 1986). When an individual has a problem in a functional, healthy Native American community, all the people in the community look at it as their collective problem. Family, kin, and friends become an interlocking network that may observe the individual's behavior, draw him (or her) out of isolation, and integrate that person back into the social life of the group (LaFromboise 1988).

Many Native American substance abuse counselors believe that the incorporation of cultural and spiritual values into treatment programs is the *only* lasting solution to the substance abuse problems of North American Indians (Beauchamp 1997). The traditional healing practices of Native Americans have developed over several thousand years and survived the intrusion of European cultures. Native American healing practices still exist today, frequently supplementing Western healing methods (Jilek 1971). Native healing systems involve not only having faith in herbal medicines but also believing in and exercising the values and traditions that shape and guide the system and are at the core of traditional Native culture (Trimble et al. 1984).

Green (1983) coined the term *retraditionalization* to describe a return to traditional cultural forms. LaFromboise, Trimble, and Mohatt (1990) posit that retraditionalization can promote cultural and individual self-esteem. According to White (1994), hundreds of pilot programs in prisons over the last twenty years have demonstrated that sweat ceremonies and other traditional spiritual practices offer Native American prisoners the "best chance at renewal, healing, and rehabilitation," especially when these are offered together with regular cultural programs and Native-styled Alcoholics Anonymous (AA) programs.

The Friendship House Association of American Indians in San Francisco provides a residential substance abuse treatment program that combines traditional Native American values with Western psychology to rehabilitate its clients. The retraditionalization process is embedded in the treatment philosophy of this program, which focuses on the strengths of Indian people rather than their problems. Friendship House is a six-month substance abuse treatment program for Native Americans, although clients from other cultural backgrounds are accepted into the program when room is available. The treatment facility is a two-story Victorian house in the Mission District of San Francisco. At the time the interviews were conducted (1998–1999), the residential program had the capacity to treat ten women and twenty men. The outpatient aftercare program included support groups, individual and family counseling, instruction, and employment and educational referrals.

Native Americans with substance abuse problems are referred to treatment at Friendship House by other Indian health programs in California, Nevada, Alaska, Washington, Oregon, Arizona, and New Mexico. Many of the clients are ordered to treatment by the courts or upon release from prison. Clients are also referred to Friendship House by Indian reservation clinics, by family members, and by former program participants. Some clients refer themselves. There is usually a six-month waiting list for court-ordered referrals. Once in the program, paroled clients are carefully monitored by parole officers.

Treatment consists of a ninety-day residential program and a ninety-day aftercare program. The residential program includes an initial thirty days that are highly structured, intensive, and restricted. During this period, the clients cannot send or receive telephone calls or personal mail and cannot leave the building unaccompanied. Residents share a room with others and are required to attend all groups, classes, and individual counseling sessions. They are expected to help prepare the community meals and clean the common areas.

The Friendship House program integrates several treatment modalities: (a) individual and group counseling; (b) codependency group work; (c) alcohol, drug, and HIV/AIDS education; (d) Red Road to Recovery class, based on the work of Gene Thin Elk (1993), focusing on the foundations of Native American culture, traditions, and spirituality, and (e) AA and Narcotics Anonymous (NA) 12-Step meetings.

This chapter investigates the transformational experiences of Native Americans during the course of their retraditionalization and treatment for drug and alcohol dependence. Twelve graduates of the residential treatment program at Friendship House in San Francisco were interviewed about the nature and quality of their healing experiences in this particular program, which provides a comprehensive matrix of Native American medicine as well as Western models of psychological treatment. The purpose of this study was to understand and document the experience of substance abuse recovery from the perspective of the Native Americans in treatment. Twelve distinct themes emerged from the data analysis.

The main question asked in the interview was "Can you describe some of the transformational (healing) experiences you had at Friendship House?" After the participant described an experience, the following questions were asked about each experience:

1. How did it feel?
2. Did anything unusual happen at that moment?
3. Who or what sparked this feeling?
4. How long did it last?
5. What happened in your body during this experience?
6. What did you think about?
7. Was there a spiritual realization connected with this experience?
8. How did this experience affect your recovery?

In analyzing the data, the criterion for identifying these experiences as transformational was that they made an important difference in the client's mental, spiritual, emotional, or physical well-being. In the end, those experiences formed the basis of the analysis. In the next phase, a content analysis was applied to the transcripts to find concepts in the data that reflected mental, physical, spiritual, and emotional experiences. Each of the concepts was analyzed by its properties (frequency, extent, duration, and intensity) and dimensions (often-never, more-less, high-low, and long-short). Then each concept was compared to every other concept by properties and dimensions, and similar concepts were grouped into categories of experience. These categories were compared with each other until themes emerged that were present to varying degrees in every interview. The following twelve themes emerged, listed in descending order of the number of transformational experiences that were included under each theme:

1. Feeling cared for
2. Spiritual experiences
3. Insight
4. Making a commitment
5. Empowerment and self-esteem
6. Releasing emotional pain
7. Remorse

8. Reconnecting to traditional values
9. Forgiveness
10. Relief
11. Safety
12. Gratitude

Theme 1: Feeling Cared For

The experience of being cared for by others can be a powerful transformational experience, and it was cited by the participants in this study more than any of the other transformational themes. In the case of substance abusers, feeling cared for supports and reinforces their self-love and allows them to risk experiencing the difficult feelings that were previously masked by drugs and alcohol. Some of the participants in this study had intense experiences of feeling cared for and nurtured by their counselors. For example, Cynthia said about her counselor: "Emma is very nurturing, she's like the mother I never had." Dana had a similar response to Emma: "I love her," she said; "she reminds me of my mom in certain ways."

Part of feeling cared for involves sensing empathy from others. Leonard, who had been beaten as a child, felt cared for by other members of his men's group when they shared stories of their own childhood abuse: "The healing part came," he said, "when I was getting feedback, and I was very surprised when three other clients raised their hands and said they had had a similar experience to mine, just about that age, too. One guy came over to me, and we just cried on each other's shoulder."

Theme 2: Spiritual Experiences

Eight people reported transformational experiences that they referred to as spiritual experiences. Four others reported transformational experiences that included some aspect of a mystical experience. Clinton released a lot of emotional pain in an Inner Child group. Clinton said, "In that exercise I got to speak up for myself, and it felt good. . . . The high I was reaching for in drinking and doing methamphetamines was that same high; I got that same high feeling." He added, "That night I woke up, and I could hear this song. . . . I recognized it as being one of our high (sacred) dance songs. . . . It has to do with cleaning up the evil in our part of the world. Since I was a little kid, I've always wanted a song, and a song had never come to me until that night at Friendship House."

Linda's experience of belonging and connectedness occurred during a celebration. She said, "I was singing the Honor song with Emma. . . . I don't know what it is about the drums. . . . I just kept crying; I think I felt connected to that home, and I belonged, I truly belonged somewhere. I'll reach out and touch the next person's hand that I'm there with. I feel a real connection. I don't know if that's the spirits or what."

Carmen said, "The house is very spiritual; there's good feelings and good healing in that house. The house has a lot of good spirits and a lot of power behind that to heal you, not just the help that you get there. It's the house itself, too." Linda said, "I think it's the process of how the house is so Indian orientated, and you have all this energy from all these American Indians and all the spirit, and I think that house is so blessed and so sacred."

Theme 3: Insight

Five clients said they gained insight about certain triggers that have caused them to relapse in the past. Carmen developed insight about how she blamed the Creator for problems of her own doing. She felt extreme remorse for losing her children to adoption because of her substance abuse. She said, "In reality it was my own fault; it wasn't the Creator doing it to me. . . . All I would have had to do was stop using, and I would have gotten my kids back."

Leonard developed insight about how his drinking affected his children. "I would just go out and drink, and I'd be selfish and self-centered, and . . . seeing what I've seen in that house and hearing some of the issues from the other clients, also some of the abandonment issues they've had, . . . helped me as a father. . . . to kind of see where my children might be at with me."

Theme 4: Making a Commitment

Many of the clients entered treatment without a clear commitment to their recovery. Yet commitment is often related to staying with a difficult course of action. Therefore, many people commit and recommit to treatment all along the way. While all twelve interviewees made a commitment to their recovery to varying degrees, six people said there were moments when they made a commitment that was transformational for them. Clients made commitments to themselves and to others to do the things asked of them in treatment.

A particularly important transformational experience was the commitment to honesty. When Marilyn entered treatment for the second time, she said, "I had to be honest; I had to be totally different from how I was the first time." Marilyn also had a transformational experience that she called a "reality check" about the need for honesty. She said, speaking of a client who left the program and died of an overdose, "She knew the Big Book back and forth, but she wasn't working an honest program. I looked through her diary when she died, and she was in a lot of pain."

Theme 5: Empowerment and Self-Esteem

Four people had eight transformational experiences that included new feelings of empowerment and/or self-esteem. Marilyn overcame fear of her older brother who had sexually abused her. She said, "I took my power back from him. With this empowerment, I don't have to doubt my feelings." Three clients reported experiences of empowerment when they accomplished difficult tasks. For example, Cynthia confronted her peers about their gang-related activity that frightened her. She said to Emma, "I can't believe that I just did that. . . . Usually I'll be the little mouse. Now I'm the mouse that roared."

Theme 6: Releasing Emotional Pain

Addicts in early recovery often do not know that they have feelings, because they have been covered up by drugs and alcohol. A major focus of treatment at Friendship House is to help clients get back in touch with their feelings so that the healing process can begin. The release of emotional pain is part of this process. Seven interviewees reported a total of eight transformational experiences that had to do with releasing emotional pain. Jim said, "There was a lot of rage. . . . I could hurt somebody. I just sat there gritting my teeth, trembling for . . a good fifteen minutes while everybody responded to what I had said. . . . It felt good to let it go because I didn't hurt anymore." Anthony grieved about the loss of his mother and grandparents. He said, "I went through the whole thing of kind of spilling my guts and crying. . . . Actually reliving it was kind of like letting it out . . . of my system."

Theme 7: Remorse

Four interviewees reported transformational experiences in which they felt remorse about hurting themselves or other people. Clients who were parents reported feelings of remorse about how they treated their children. Marilyn felt remorse for not taking care of her children when she was using heavily. Carmen talked about losing all of her children to adoption because of her addiction. She said, "The reality was that I lost my kids and my homes and everything behind all that. . . . I hold a lot of guilt and pain and shame behind it, not being there for my kids."

Theme 8: Reconnecting to Traditional Values

Linda reconnected to the traditional values that she had been cut off from during her years of using drugs. She said, "There was a celebration going on, and . . . I felt connected to that home, and I belonged, I truly belonged somewhere. . . . I can feel . . . that feeling of belonging and connection, through the sound and the people, and being able to sing a song and never hear it, and follow right along with it." Linda is Native American, but she was raised Catholic. Her experience with the drumming helped her reconnect to the Indian part of herself. She said, "I have my abalone shell, I have my altar with my eagle feather. . . . I incorporate the American Indian thing because I go to sweats, I smudge . . . I talk to the Grandfather, I talk to the Creator, and I pray the Catholic way. I integrate it all, and I think it's really neat that I can do that."

Carmen learned about Native spiritual values. She said, "I learned a lot from the cultural classes. In recovery you need to respect yourself, other people, the plants, the animals, the whole earth. You learn to respect yourself, love yourself, and everything else follows."

Theme 9: Forgiveness

Three clients reported transformational experiences of forgiveness. These clients said they experienced feelings of forgiveness toward abusive parents and other family members. Marilyn said, "Now I believe that my parents had to come to a point in their life where they turned their life over to the care of God . . . and were forgiven for stuff that they did." Marilyn told her father, "Dad, it's not about blame, it's about forgiveness. The Creator is able to forgive for anything that I've done wrong, and I'm able to forgive anybody who done anything wrong to me." Anthony wrote a "Dear Mom" letter and read it during a process group. He said, "[I] also wrote that I forgave her for drinking and being physically abusive." He felt remorse for selling drugs to family members but implied that they had forgiven him. Anthony said, "I think my aunt was proud of me, she wasn't mad at me at all . . . and . . . she's saying, 'I forgive you.'"

Theme 10: Relief

The experience of relief feels like the removal or lightening of something oppressive, burdensome, painful, or distressing. Marilyn said, "It felt so good, like tons had been lifted off you, and I experienced that a whole lot of times in recovery." Anthony said, "I felt kind of a burden off of my shoulders . . . like my head was clear, like fog in the morning . . . clears up in the afternoon when the sun comes out." Linda described a transformational experience in which she realized she could create a different life for herself. She said, "It really washed in over me, and when I breathed, it was like something just lifted off me."

Theme 11: Safety

Feeling safe is an important theme among all of the participants in the study. Everyone expressed the need to feel safe in treatment, and several of the complaints about the program concerned instances in which individuals did not feel safe. Leonard said, "I knew that it would be a safe place for me, especially in talking about some of my feelings and stuff that I wouldn't share with anyone else, so I went to the Friendship House." While discussing a very powerful and emotional group he participated in, Leonard added, "I know that those guys felt totally at peace and at home with everybody else, and safe enough to cry like that."

The safety of confidentiality is important to clients. Jim said, "It was better knowing that I'm safe and there's not a whole group of people like I went through before. It's confidential; it makes it easier for me to just say what I'm feeling, what happened. I'm not scared to say it again." Marilyn said, "I think a lot of it had to do with being in a safe environment like the treatment center—everybody is working for the same goal—and the bonding that went on there!"

Theme 12: Gratitude

The twelve interviewees had successfully completed three months of treatment at Friendship House and gained many new insights, behaviors, and healing experiences, including the experience of freedom from their addictions. Jim said, "I don't have to use, I don't have to get drunk to find that blissful feeling. . . . I give Friendship House a lot of thanks for that." Jennifer said, "I was really grateful to Friendship House staff and counselors that they accepted me."

Program Elements

Many Native American treatment programs aim at healing the soul wounds of Native Americans (Duran and Duran 1995; Manson et al. 1996). Three main elements of the Friendship House program emerged in the data analysis: (a) the retraditionalization process; (b) trauma work; and (c) the use of AA's philosophy for treating addictions. These healing processes were both educational and experiential, intertwining within the safe environment of Friendship House.

The retraditionalization process teaches clients about Native American values and traditions in classes such as "The Red Road" and "Native American Family Values." Clients receive this spiritually based knowledge experientially by participating in talking circles, sweat lodge ceremonies, and Friendship House celebrations, and through their personal relationships with the Native American staff members and the visiting Medicine people, who embody traditional Native American values. Retraditionalization was most linked to the themes of spiritual experience, empowerment, and self-esteem, and reconnecting to traditional values. A positive result of this process is that clients may develop pride in their new identities as Native Americans. This gives them a spiritual identity that they previously lacked.

The substance abuse treatment at Friendship House filters AA's philosophy through a Native American perspective, which includes belief in a Higher Power

(Creator). The other two main principles that Friendship House has adapted from the 12-Step program are surrender of control and identification as an addict. The clients at Friendship House learn these principles through written assignments that relate to the twelve steps and through attendance at AA or NA meetings at Friendship House and in the larger community of San Francisco. The themes most related to the substance abuse element of treatment include making a commitment, insight, release of emotional pain, remorse, and forgiveness.

Trauma work at Friendship House includes education about historical Native American traumas and the effects of the European cultural invasion on the lives of many generations of Native Americans. Trauma work usually occurs as clients participate in intense groups, such as the Inner Child Group, the Men's Group, the Women's Group, and the Process Group. One of the goals of trauma work is to help clients to change their identity from victim to survivor. The themes most related to trauma work include feeling cared for, spiritual experience, making a commitment, releasing emotional pain, relief, and safety.

The results of this study show that the participants reported healing experiences related to childhood trauma and that the various types of group sessions were conducive to the resolution of their traumas. An experiential healing process in substance abuse treatment for Native Americans is especially important for the resolution of their childhood traumas. Clients must first feel safe and cared for by others in the treatment community. Transformational experiences that seem to produce the most complete resolution of childhood trauma are those in which there is a spontaneous flow of feelings such as fear, grief, anger, remorse, forgiveness, empowerment, gratitude, and relief. It seems clear that Native American substance abuse treatment programs should adopt an integrated treatment model to serve clients with a substance abuse disorder and a coexisting psychological disorder such as post-traumatic stress disorder (PTSD), as well as historical trauma. Therefore, identifying, diagnosing, and treating trauma, both childhood and historical, should become an integral part of substance abuse treatment programs for Native Americans.

Notes

"Substance Abuse Treatment at Friendship House: Transformation and Culture" is an abridged version of "Cultural Connection and Transformation: Substance Abuse Treatment at Friendship House," by Yvonne Edwards, Ph.D., which appeared in the *Journal of Psychoactive Drugs* 35 (1). Reprinted by permission of Haight-Ashbury Publications, 612 Clayton Street, San Francisco, California.

Beauchamp, S. "Healing Alcoholism in Indigenous People," *Social Work Perspectives* 8(1) (1997): 35–40.

Duran, E., and B. Duran. *Native American Postcolonial Psychology*. Albany: State University of New York Press, 1995.

Green, R. *Native American Women: A Contextual Bibliography*. Chicago: Newberry Library Center for the History of the American Indians Bibliographical Series, 1983.

Jilek, W. "From Crazy Witch Doctor to Auxiliary Psychotherapist: The Changing of the Medicine Man," *Psychiatric Clinic* 4 (1971): 200–220.

LaFromboise, T. "American Indian Mental Health Policy," *American Psychologist* 43 (1988): 388–397.

LaFromboise, T., J. Trimble, and G. Mohatt. "Counseling Intervention and American Indian Tradition: An Integrative Approach," *Counseling Psychologist* 18(4) (1990): 628–654.

Landers, S. "Programs for Indians Draw on Tribal Customs," *American Psychological Association Monitor* (November 1989): 32.

Manson, S., J. Beals, D. Bechtold, T. O'Neil, J. Piaseki, E. Keane, and M. Jones. "Wounded Spirits, Ailing Hearts: PTSD and Related Disorders among American Indians." In *Ethnocultural Aspects of Posttraumatic Stress Disorder*, eds. A. Marsella, M. Friedman, E. Gerrity, and R. Scurfield. Washington, D.C.: American Psychiatric Association, 1996.

May, Philip A. "Alcohol and Drug Misuse Prevention Programs for American Indians: Needs and Opportunities," *Journal of Studies on Alcohol* 47(3) (1986): 87–95.

Shaffer, P. "A Tree Grows in Montana: Indians Turn to Old Ways to Meet New Challenges," *Utne Reader* January/February (1990): 54–60.

Spicer, P. "Culture and the Restoration of Self among Former American Indian Drinkers," *Social Science and Medicine* 53(2) (2001): 227–236.

Thin Elk, Gene. "Walking in Balance on the Red Road," *Journal of Emotional and Behavioral Problems* 2 (1993): 3.

Trimble, J., S. Manson, N. Dinges, and B. Medicine. "American Indian Conception of Mental Health: Reflections and Directions." In *Mental Health Services: The Cross-Cultural Context*, eds. P. Pedersen, N. Sartorius, and A. Marsella. Honolulu: University of Hawaii Press, 1984.

White, T. "Living Up to Our Nation's Highest Laws: The Need to Extend Native Religious Rights to Prisoners," *Shaman's Drum* (summer 1994): 6–11.

INNOVATIONS IN MENTAL HEALTH   II

Today our Native American people need guidance and healing from generational crises and abuses that happened in the residential Indian boarding school during their lifetime, during their parents' lifetime, during their parents' parents' lifetime. Much of it began when our Native American children were institutionalized at a very young age, and from that time on our people had to heal as a result. Some of us don't ever heal, because it is not dealt with. We were taught how not to be parents, because they took our children away from us. They taught us that it was bad to be an Indian, and some of us have believed that all our lives.

Our number one rule is to love one another. This is part of the Wolf Society ritual. We discipline our body, mind, soul, and spirit. This is followed by respect for one another. Respect for self and each other was the number one law. Respect means giving high honor and high esteem to yourself and to other human beings that cross your path.

I have been sober twenty-nine years and am a survivor of Indian boarding schools. Holistic Wellness through Native American culture is treatment for all negative ailments of the four aspects of life: Mind, Body, Soul, and Spirit. Culture equals Treatment.

—ANDY CALLICUM, MOWACHAHT (NOOTKA)/QUINALT

MENTAL HEALTH PROGRAMS serving diverse populations must incorporate an understanding of culture, beliefs, and culture-specific family interactions into their design. Achieving cultural competence is a process that involves adaptations at policy-making, administrative, and practice levels to make sure that any system of care is sensitive and responsive to the unique needs of the population served. We are particularly honored to document the healing journey taking place in the urban Native American community of the San Francisco Bay Area. Ethan Nebelkopf and Janet King describe a holistic system of care developed by Native Americans in the Bay Area. It incorporates holistic concepts with Native culture. Phoebe Mills shows how traditional healing methods are integrated into Western approaches among the Yup'ik (Eskimo). Sandra Beauchamp describes family relationships in relation to social history among the Mandan, Hidatsa, and Arikara.

Urban Trails $\qquad$ 5
A Holistic System of Care for Native
Americans in the San Francisco Bay Area

ETHAN NEBELKOPF AND JANET KING

T HE NATIVE AMERICAN HEALTH CENTER (NAHC) is a community-based, nonprofit urban Indian organization that has provided medical and social services in the San Francisco Bay Area since 1972. Currently, NAHC provides medical care, mental health services, dental care, substance abuse treatment, outreach, and HIV/AIDS care.

Since 1989, the Family and Child Guidance Clinic (FCGC) of NAHC has provided outpatient mental health and substance abuse counseling for Native Americans in San Francisco and Oakland. The FCGC offers help to Native Americans with substance abuse and mental health problems. The program uses a holistic approach based on cultural values as a foundation for a healthy community. Services include individual, group, and family counseling; case management; talking circles; risk reduction counseling; psychosocial assessment; relapse prevention; wellness education; education in positive parenting; cultural activities; and traditional healing.

The Youth Center of the Native American Health Center bridges the gaps among Native youth, family, and community. In 1989, the youth program pioneered a curriculum for HIV/AIDS prevention that incorporates substance abuse and HIV/AIDS prevention education with empowerment education (Marquez and White Rabbit 1992; Mangum et al. 1994). The Youth Center was identified as a model program in *Alcohol and Drug Prevention Education for American Indian Youth in California*, a report for the California Department of Alcohol and Drug Programs (Zahnd et al. 1999).

Urban Indian Profile
The Native American population within the San Francisco Bay Area is very diverse. It consists of members of over 100 American Indian and Alaska Native

tribes. There are nearly 80,000 Native Americans, including those who report that they identify with one or more other races as well, in the San Francisco Bay Area, comprising San Francisco, Alameda, Contra Costa, Marin, and San Mateo counties. The San Francisco Bay Area has one of the largest concentrations of American Indians living in urban areas in the United States (Nebelkopf, Phillips, and King 2001; U.S. Census 2000).

While most people have the perception that American Indians live primarily on reservations, the majority actually live in urban settings. Many of these urban Indians are third- or fourth-generation city dwellers, the descendants of those who first came to urban areas during the federal government's relocation program in the 1950s and early 1960s. The Bureau of Indian Affairs did not deliver on its promises of transition assistance, and relocation created a chronically disenfranchised urban Indian population. Funding for urban programs is problematic because federal resources are targeted to tribes. Nevertheless, the corrosive effects of cultural alienation, alcoholism, poor health services, unemployment, and inadequate housing are slowly being overcome (Fixico 2000).

In a pilot study funded by the Indian Health Service, clinical files of 200 clients who received outpatient treatment at NAHC FCGC were reviewed. The findings revealed that 85 percent had a history of alcohol abuse and 73 percent had a history of drug abuse. When diagnostic information consistent with American Psychiatric Association guidelines was reviewed, 64 percent of the clients were found to have diagnoses of substance disorders, 58 percent had anxiety disorders, and 50 percent had mood disorders, indicating many clients with dual diagnoses of substance abuse and mental illness (Duran and Yellow Horse-Davis 1996).

A 1999 study of American Indians admitted to the emergency department of San Francisco General Hospital found that the majority of admissions were men between twenty-one and sixty-four years of age, and 34 percent were homeless. Drug- and alcohol-related diagnoses accounted for 28 percent of all admissions diagnoses (Caruso 1999). In a study of high-risk Native women in Oakland, 41 percent reported feeling afraid about being beaten or threatened by a sexual partner during the preceding twelve months. Also, 21 percent reported having been forced to have sex by a sexual partner during the past twelve months (Klein et al. 1997).

Native American youth in the San Francisco Bay Area are at high risk for alcoholism, substance abuse, mental illness, HIV/AIDS, and juvenile delinquency. This population includes youth who are children of substance abusers; youth involved in the juvenile justice system; members of low-income families; teenage parents; youth living in foster care; gay, lesbian, bisexual, transsexual, and questioning youth; and homeless youth.

San Francisco has the highest percentage of American Indians with AIDS of all metropolitan areas (Satter 1999). Because of the stigma attached to HIV/AIDS on reservations and in tribal communities, Native Americans with this disease come from all across the United States to the Bay Area to receive services (Vernon 2001).

Lack of Resources for Urban Indians

The United States abounds with disparities in the availability of health services to ethnic and racial groups (Surgeon General 1999). Many people are not aware that the federal government has specific responsibilities toward Native Americans, because by treaty Native Americans are recognized as sovereign nations. This unique status must be taken into account in the provision of services (Weaver 1998). Resources for urban Indian programs are even more meager than those for tribes. To make matters worse, only a small proportion of Indian Health Service funding goes to urban programs even though more than half of the Indian population in the United States lives in urban areas.

As in many cities, the dominant system of care in the Bay Area is highly centralized, with the locus of control firmly established in state and county bureaucracies. The language used in mental health meetings—utilization, capitation, and reimbursement—is suited more to insurance professionals and accountants than to mental health professionals or consumers of services. The system is neither community based nor family centered. The mainstream system of care has been designed around the needs of the funding agencies instead of the needs of the clients. Managed care does not recognize that effective services must acknowledge individual differences and cultural identities.

Circle of Care

The strategic planning process has proceeded for a decade among Native American organizations in the San Francisco Bay Area. In 1986, Dr. Gerald Hill conducted a community needs assessment funded by the Robert Wood Johnson Foundation. An analysis of 550 surveys of American Indian community members indicated that medical care, employment, dental care, substance abuse, mental health, housing, family services, health education, and traditional healing were perceived as major unmet needs (Hill 1987).

In 1993, seven American Indian agencies signed a Memorandum of Understanding to participate in the Community Mobilization Project. The mission of the Community Mobilization Project was "to set in motion a process of change that would facilitate the efforts of urban American Indians to create the structure and means necessary to reach their social, cultural, economic, and political goals as they perceive and define them."

The Community Mobilization Project had a powerful impact. It marked the first time that community members came together to assess needs, set priorities, secure resources, and develop plans for social and economic development. Community visioning meetings, town hall meetings, task forces, focus groups, conferences, and workshops built a sense of unity among the major stakeholders and resulted in a strategic plan for social and economic development for Native Americans in the San Francisco Bay Area.

In 1998, the Native American Health Center was awarded a three-year planning grant through the Circle of Care initiative of the federal Center for Mental Health Services (CMHS) to develop a system of care for Native American children and their families in the San Francisco Bay Area. The national Circle of Care initiative supported Native communities in designing local systems of care rooted in cultural values (Manson 2000; Novins et al. 2000).

A system of care is a child-centered, family-focused, coordinated, community-based, and culturally competent approach to providing access to a coordinated network of mental health and other necessary services to meet the multiple and changing needs of children with serious emotional disturbances and of their families. Families are full participants in the planning, implementation, and evaluation of services (Stroul and Friedman 1986).

The system-of-care model is not new to Indian country. In the Navajo Nation, the K'e Project utilizes a system of care based on Navajo traditional healing approaches, which understand the family as central to a child's health and well-being and view the child's mental, behavioral, and emotional health as intricately connected to the social, economic, and spiritual health of the family and the community (Simpson et al. 1998).

The best evidence of success of the system-of-care model for the Native American population is documented in *Cultural Strengths and Challenges in Implementing a System of Care Model in American Indian Communities* (Cross et al. 2000). It highlights five American Indian programs funded through the Child Mental Health Initiative. These programs utilize a unique blend of Western and Native traditions. Family members and children are actively involved in all aspects of planning, carrying out, and evaluating the system of care and individualized care plans.

The Native American community in the San Francisco Bay Area adopted a model developed by FCGC for a holistic system of care for Native Americans in an urban environment (Nebelkopf et al. 2001). This model has been instrumental in obtaining federal resources to fund various elements in this model through collaborative efforts with urban Native American agencies in the San Francisco Bay Area. Our Circle of Care was designed to achieve four objectives:

1. Promote a unifying and enduring sense of urban Indian community identity, pride, and cohesion based on common traditional Native values and beliefs
2. Build leadership skills and capacity among Indian families and community-based organizations that serve the Indian community
3. Produce a strategic plan for implementing a system of care that links treatment with prevention, substance abuse, and mental illness
4. Obtain resources to implement our emerging community-based system of care

The strategic planning process provided a rich opportunity for community participation at all levels of system design and implementation. Significant input came from agency directors, agency staff, parents, consumers, youth, community members, traditional healers, and clients in our programs. The community needs assessment utilized focus groups, talking circles, community visioning meetings, and interviews with key stakeholders. The strategic plan articulates the principles and components in an integrated system of health care that links mental health, substance abuse, medical treatment, HIV/AIDS, and social services. Native American culture is the foundation for this model.

The strategic plan made the following recommendations in the areas of program development, mental health reform, family advocacy, youth leadership, and wellness education:

1. Develop cultural competency training for public officials
2. Develop mental health programs that strengthen the family
3. Support advocacy efforts of parent groups
4. Ensure that parents and family members play an essential role in implementation of new programs
5. Incorporate HIV/AIDS prevention into mental health and substance abuse programs
6. Expand leadership training opportunities for youth
7. Work with juvenile justice officials to develop programs for Indian youth

Holistic Model

In the holistic model developed by FCGC and used for the Circle of Care (see figure 5.1), mental illness, substance abuse, HIV/AIDS, homelessness, poverty, crime, and violence are symptoms of historical trauma, family dysfunction, and spiritual imbalance. The Bay Area Native community reached a consensus to focus on *solutions* rather than *problems*. These solutions consist of exemplary practices that have been piloted in our Circle of Care: youth empowerment, leadership training, self-help, higher education, communication skills, affordable housing, good nutrition, community mobilization, economic development, wellness education, positive parenting, traditional medicine, and a value system based on Indian culture.

At the center of the holistic model is a small circle, Creator. The harmonious relationship of the basic elements of fire, air, earth, and water depicted in the next concentric circle is essential for balance. Within human beings, these elements are manifested in spirit, thought, emotions, and the body. When these elements are out of balance, symptoms arise. Social institutions that impact the individual include the school system, the criminal justice system, managed health care, mental health services, welfare, and housing.

Prevention and treatment are inextricably linked in our model. Treatment programs include mental health, substance abuse, family therapy, Western medicine, and Native medicine. Prevention includes alcohol, tobacco, and other drug education; HIV/AIDS prevention; domestic violence prevention; and wellness education.

The holistic system of care is based upon the assumption that urban Indian people prefer to receive services from Indian organizations. The community identified several principles as a foundation for the system of care:

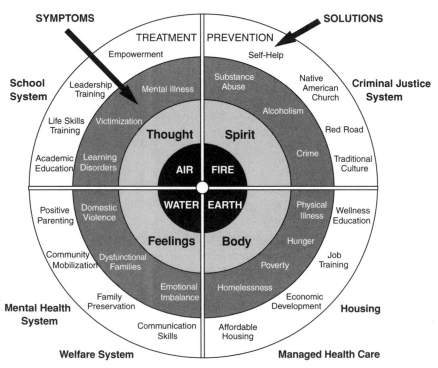

Figure 5.1.   Holistic system of care for Native Americans in an urban environment

- We do not "treat" people; we teach them to help themselves.
- We do not use the label *mentally ill*; we see these people as our most vulnerable and needy community members.
- We emphasize prevention as well as treatment.
- We encourage our most vulnerable members to participate in community activities with everyone else.
- We discourage labeling and scapegoating of our most vulnerable members.
- We seek resources to build our own programs because mainstream programs have a poor track record in helping Native families and their children.
- We build linkages between substance abuse and mental health services.
- We encourage empowerment and self-help, discourage entitlement and victimization.
- We encourage consumer input in our system of care.
- We support a community-based methodology that includes professionals, traditional healers, and peer support in a "wrap-around," team approach to care.

Collaboration among the Native American organizations in the Bay Area enabled the development and implementation of the holistic model. The Friendship House Association of American Indians (FH) and American Indian Public Charter School (AIPCS) played key roles in the community's growth. The California Board of Education granted charter school status to the American Indian Public Charter School in 1996 as a result of the strategic planning efforts of the Community Mobilization Project. Currently the Charter School serves 200 students in grades six through nine. The Family and Child Guidance Clinic places staff on site at the Charter School for outreach; case management; individual counseling; substance abuse and HIV/AIDS prevention; and an after-school program that includes an organized athletic program, traditional arts and crafts, tutoring, and video production.

The Need for Cultural Competency Training

The California Department of Mental Health requires county mental health agencies to devise a cultural competency plan to improve services and reduce disparities for multicultural and multilingual populations in California. At FCGC, cultural competency was a goal and a responsibility long before it was a state mandate. Cultural competency has been an objective in many of our proposals to increase capacity and improve mental health services for the Native American community. We have been conducting cultural competency training for cities and counties since long before the term *cultural competency* was coined.

In the year 2002, FCGC conducted three cultural competency training sessions for the Alameda County Juvenile Probation Department, one for Alameda County's adolescent case management team, and one for Alameda County Public Health Nurses. FCGC staff represented Native American issues on numerous multicultural panels at conferences sponsored by other agencies. FCGC cohosted Paths to the Future: An American Indian Child Welfare Symposium at San Francisco State University, attended by more than 400 people. Each semester FCGC makes presentations at the California School of Professional Psychology; California State University, Hayward; and the University of California, Berkeley.

In 2003, FCGC sponsored a forum to inform non–Native American service communities about mental health issues facing Native families. FCGC staff served as guest editor for a special edition of the *Journal of Psychoactive Drugs* entitled "Morning Star Rising: Healing in Native American Communities." A well-publicized roundtable discussion was held at the city hall with Alameda County social service and health agency directors to explore the issues raised in this publication.

The many ways Native Americans are misunderstood are addressed in our cultural competency training. Native American history with the United States is reviewed to explain the contemporary psychosocial issues facing Native Americans today as a result of that history. Stereotypes about Native Americans are replaced with accurate information. Interview strategies are suggested to help providers identify Native Americans during the intake process engaged in by public agencies. Two prominent stereotypes that persist today are that few Indians are left and that the ones who remain live in remote areas or on reservations. These two stereotypes are some of the reasons Native Americans do not get identified in the intake process of social service agencies. In addition, many Native Americans have a generalized distrust of government officials. In recent history Native Americans have been forced to participate in government-sponsored programs and policies that have had devastating effects on Indian individuals, families, communities, and culture. These include removal from ancestral lands; downsizing of land to small plots called reservations, which are too small for Native Americans to subsist on using traditional cultural methods; education in boarding schools, in which young children are not raised by their parents but by military-style boarding school matrons; relocation from reservations to cities; and the outlawing of Native American customs and culture. These negative experiences have caused Native Americans not to readily identify themselves to government officials as Native: Invisibility became a survival tactic to avoid participating in the demeaning programs designed to destroy Native American culture.

As a result of our cultural competency training sessions at Juvenile Probation, Alameda probation officers now report higher numbers of Native American youth on their caseloads. Prior to our training, the officers often reported no Native American youth in their system.

Another reason Native Americans are not truly reflected in data collected by social service agencies is that Native Americans are often counted as *other*, the catchall category for populations with too few members to be specified. Our training has been helpful in correcting the misconception that few Native Americans live in the San Francisco Bay Area.

Getting a more accurate count of Native American youth in the juvenile probation system was a big accomplishment. In general, Native Americans are not routinely identified in many social service systems, or they are misidentified as members of other ethnic groups. This misclassification of Native Americans in system-of-care data has been a big problem for Native American community-based organizations that need data to show need and justify the funding for redressing disparities.

Implementing a Holistic System of Care

The strategic plan stressed the simultaneous planning and implementation of pilot projects based on the holistic model, thus positioning the urban Indian community to take advantage of the unprecedented funding opportunities made available through the Substance Abuse and Mental Health Services Administration (SAMHSA) Treatment Capacity Expansion/HIV Services programs in 1999–2002. These funds were a major breakthrough in acquiring resources to meet the needs of urban Indians because Indian Health Service funding has been dwindling.

An extremely fortuitous occurrence for the implementation of our strategic plan was the release of *Changing the Conversation: The National Treatment Plan Initiative* by SAMSHA/Center for Substance Abuse Treatment (CSAT) (2000). This initiative articulated a new vision of reducing stigma, integrating services, developing intersystem linkages, and increasing access to services, all of which are embodied in our holistic system of care. A second major thrust for implementation of our strategic plan was the release of *Mental Health: Culture, Race and Ethnicity* by the Surgeon General (2001). This document revolutionized the field of mental health by stressing (1) the essential importance of culture in designing mental health programs for people of color and (2) the value of community-based programs as an alternative to the psychiatric model.

Issues of cultural competency, community involvement in the planning process, integrated services, and the linkages across systems were built into SAMHSA's funding announcements as a result of these new federal initiatives to support community-based services. With the holistic model as a central foundation of this system of care, the Native American community crafted specific programs to meet the specifications for SAMHSA's requests for proposals. Thus a

$300,000 planning grant for the Circle of Care was parlayed into $25 million for implementation of specific projects (1998–2004) based on the strategic plan.

The holistic system of care for Native Americans in an urban environment emphasizes solutions; fosters linkages among providers, Indian and non-Indian; and includes community education and outreach. Events are designed monthly and seasonally to develop community cohesion. Community members look forward to participating in prosocial, clean-and-sober events. These events combat fragmentation, isolation, and alienation and give everyone a sense of being part of a therapeutic community that is larger than any one individual—a community that is culturally and spiritually based.

Notes

This work was supported by Center for Mental Health Services grants SM52258 (Circle of Care), SM56051 (Urban Trails), and SM53893 (Native Circle); Center for Substance Abuse Treatment grants TI 12205 (Native American Women's Circle) and TI1314 (Native Youth Circle); Center for Substance Abuse Prevention grant SP 10154 (Urban Native Youth); and Health Resources and Services Administration Special Projects of National Significance (SPNS) grant H97 HA 00251. The publication's contents are solely the responsibility of the authors.

"Urban Trails: A Holistic System of Care for Native Americans in the San Francisco Bay Area" is an abridged version of "Holistic System of Care for Native Americans in an Urban Environment," by Ethan Nebelkopf, Ph.D., and Janet King, which appeared in the *Journal of Psychoactive Drugs* 35 (1). Reprinted by permission of Haight-Ashbury Publications, 612 Clayton Street, San Francisco, California.

Caruso, J. M. "A Demographic and Clinical Comparison of American Indian Emergency Department Patients with Emergency Department Patients of Other Ethnicities at San Francisco General Hospital." M.D. thesis, M.D. with thesis program, the University of California, San Francisco, 1999.

Cross, T., K. Earle, Holly Echo-Hawk-Solie, and K. Manness. *Cultural Strengths and Challenges in Implementing a System of Care Model in American Indian Communities.* Rockville, Md.: NICWA, CMHS, 2000.

Duran, E., and S. Yellow Horse-Davis. *Final Research Report: Evaluation of Family and Child Guidance Clinic Hybrid Treatment Model, Indian Health Service Grant to Urban Indian Health Board, Inc.* Oakland, Calif.: Native American Health Center, 1996.

Fixico, D. *The Urban Indian Experience in America.* Albuquerque: University of New Mexico Press, 2000.

Hill, G. *Human Service Needs of Urban Native Americans.* Oakland, Calif.: Robert Wood Johnson Foundation, 1987.

Klein, D., D. Williams, J. Witbrodt, and B. Kolodny. *The Women's Circle: Toward Healthier Relationships.* Oakland, Calif.: Native American Health Center and Public Health Institute, 1997.

Mangum, A., A. Green-Rush, and V. Sanabria. *HIV Prevention with Native American Youth*. Oakland, Calif.: Centers for Disease Control, 1994.

Manson, S. "Mental Health Services for American Indians and Alaska Natives: Need, Use, and Barriers to Effective Care," *Canadian Journal of Psychiatry* 48 (2000): 617-624.

Marquez, C., and R. Whiterabbit. "HIV Prevention Education with Native American Youth." In *HIV Prevention in Native Communities*, ed. A. Green-Rush. Oakland, Calif.: Centers for Disease Control, 1992.

Nebelkopf, E., M. Phillips, and J. King. *Strategic Plan: A Holistic Model for a System of Care for Native Americans in the San Francisco Bay Area*. Oakland, Calif.: Native American Health Center, 2001.

Novins, D., C. Fleming, J. Beals, and S. Manson. "Commentary: Quality of Alcohol, Drug and Mental Health Services for American Indian Children and Adolescents," *American Journal of Medical Quality* 15 (2000): 4.

Ogunwole, A. *American Indian and Alaska Native Population: 2000*. Census 2000 Brief, Department of Commerce. Washington, D.C., 2002.

Satter, D. *Literature Review of Culturally Competent HIV/AIDS Prevention for American Indians and Alaska Natives*. Los Angeles, Calif.: UCLA Center for Health Policy Research, 1999.

Simpson, J., N. Koroloff, B. Friesen, and J. Gac. *Promising Practices in Family Provider Collaboration, Systems of Care, Promising Practices in Children's Mental Health*. Portland, Oreg.: Portland State University, 1998.

Stroul, B., and R. Friedman. *A System of Care for Children and Youth with Severe Emotional Disturbances*. Washington, D.C.: National Technical Assistance Center for Children's Mental Health, 1986.

Substance Abuse and Mental Health Services Administration/Center for Substance Abuse Treatment (SAMHSA/CSAT). *Changing the Conversation, Improving Substance Abuse Treatment: The National Treatment Plan Initiative*. Rockville, Md.: U.S. Department of Health and Human Services, 2000.

Surgeon General. *Mental Health: A Report of the Surgeon General*. Rockville, Md.: DHHS, 1999.

———. *Mental Health: Culture, Race and Ethnicity*. Rockville, Md.: DHHS, 2001.

Vernon, Irene. *Killing Us Quietly: Native Americans and HIV/AIDS*. Lincoln: U. of Nebraska Press, 2001.

Weaver, H. "Indigenous People in a Multicultural Society: Unique Issues for Human Services," *Social Work* 43 (1998): 203-211.

Zahnd, E., D. Klein, R. Clark, and A. Brown. *Alcohol and Drug Prevention Education for American Indian Youth in California: Final Report*. Berkeley, Calif.: California Department of Alcohol and Drug Programs (Public Health Institute), 1999.

Joining and Sustaining Yup'ik and Cup'ik Healing with Behavioral Health Treatment

6

PHOEBE A. MILLS

THE YUP'IK AND CUP'IK of southwestern Alaska are striving toward a goal common to many Native communities, healing from historical trauma, and have developed ways to incorporate traditional healing practices into mainstream behavioral health treatment. These efforts to honor and incorporate traditional ways have resulted in the Village Sobriety Project (VSP), a program federally funded by a three-year Center for Substance Abuse Treatment (CSAT) grant (from 1999 to 2002) administered by the Behavioral Health Department of the Yukon-Kuskokwim Health Center (YKHC) in Bethel, Alaska. Cultural activities were incorporated in the treatment activities and documentation and were successfully reimbursed by Medicaid.

For many centuries the Yup'ik and Cup'ik people have lived in a remote arctic environment of the tundra, an area that is presently known as the delta of the Yukon and Kuskokwim Rivers (Y-K delta) in southwestern Alaska. The Yup'ik and Cup'ik (C/Yup'ik) people's traditional lifestyle and survival, including spirituality, housing, food gathering, child rearing, and artwork, became intricately interwoven with their surroundings. However, with the arrival of, and at times harsh influences of, Russians and Europeans, the C/Yup'ik people experienced tragedies that shook their balance and foundation. These tragedies included the loss of masses of C/Yup'ik and other indigenous people of the North American continent due to exposure to foreign diseases and the notion, inculcated in boarding schools and by missionaries, that their traditional ways were of no good.

In present times, many C/Yup'ik are finding a new balance between the two worlds of traditional C/Yup'ik lifestyles and mainstream Western culture. Contemporary C/Yup'ik culture is often a mix of these two worlds. However, while some find health in balancing the influences of the two worlds, communities still struggle with the long-lasting effects of historical trauma—the cumulative emotional, spiritual, and other wounds across generations.

Alaska Natives comprise 16.8 percent of Alaska's population, and over half of Alaska Natives are Eskimos, including Yup'ik, Cup'ik, and Inupiat (Office of Women's Health 2002). The Alaska Division of Alcoholism and Drug Abuse (1998), in a study of residential and outpatient treatment programs, found that Alaska Natives comprised 45 percent of residential program clients and 28 percent of outpatient program clients. Western approaches to substance abuse treatment for Native people have not always been effective (CSAT 1999). They do not address historical trauma in Native people and tend to focus on individual deficits. In southwestern Alaska, before the VSP, behavioral health treatment services among the C/Yup'ik were approached solely from the Western framework, operating with mainstream tools such as the American Psychiatric Association's *Diagnostic and Statistical Manual*, fourth edition, cognitive therapy, rational-emotive therapy, play therapy, and art therapy. However, a balanced treatment of American Indians and Alaska Natives needs to focus on their resiliency and strengths (Jones-Sparck 1993). Many Native people throughout the world have returned to ancestral teachings and found that "within the culture is all that is needed for healing" (CSAT, forthcoming; DHHS 2001).

The Process Used for Incorporating Traditional Healing

The VSP was preceded by a five-year CSAT demonstration grant (from 1994 to 1999) with the title "Chemical Misuse and Treatment Recovery Services" (CMTRS). CMTRS' work laid much of the foundation for VSP. One premise addressed in CMTRS' incorporating traditional modalities into behavioral health treatment is that by validating the use of these traditional C/Yup'ik activities in treatment, the ancestors of the C/Yup'ik people and their wisdom for living a healthy life are validated. Another premise is that if Western modalities can utilize play and art in therapy, then traditional cultural activities can be considered just as valid in formal treatment.

CMTRS program staff used focus groups in three targeted C/Yup'ik villages and gathered information that identified twenty-seven traditional activities that could be incorporated in substance abuse treatment. Some of the twenty-seven modalities identified include pissuryaq (hunting), aqevyigsuq/at'sasuq (berry picking), neqsuq-kuvyiiluuni (fishing), kaluukaq (to hold a feast, potlatch, ceremony), qugtaq (gathering wood), eqiurtauq (chopping wood), cuilqerluni (tundra walk), makiirag (gathering edible and medicinal plants), maqiq (steambath), and caliinguaq (traditional arts and crafts).

In October 1999, shortly after CMTRS ended, YKHC joined substance abuse services with mental health services to create a behavioral health department. Shortly thereafter, the VSP began and commenced incorporating the twenty-seven traditional modalities into behavioral health treatment services and constructing the foundation to begin billing Medicaid for traditional healing. The VSP grant focused on two Bering Sea coastal Yup'ik villages, Hooper Bay and Scammon Bay, and a Bering Sea coastal Cup'ik village, Chevak. The VSP staff included seven village counselors (all local Native village members and two of whom were elder counselors); the project supervisor, located in Scammon Bay; and the village clinician and project director, located in Bethel. Bethel serves as a hub for many services for the surrounding fifty-eight villages in the Y-K delta of southwest Alaska, and the headquarters of the YKHC (i.e., the offices administering the VSP) are located there. Bethel is approximately 150 miles from the three target Bering Sea villages of VSP. The majority of the fifty-eight Y-K delta villages are Yup'ik and Cup'ik Eskimo villages.

Treatment Documentation and C/Yup'ik Culture

The VSP implemented cultural practices not only in the kinds of services offered to the client but in the treatment documentation. The VSP intake assessment addressed areas found in most behavioral health intake assessments, such as personal and family history of substance abuse issues, mental health issues, incarceration, and suicidal ideation. However, VSP also added a cultural assessment, consisting of a one-page questionnaire with seventeen questions that asked the interviewees to rate their agreement/disagreement with statements such as:

- Understanding my Yup'ik/Cup'ik culture is important to me.
- I know who my relatives are in the community.
- I am proud of being Yup'ik/Cup'ik.
- I would like to use Yup'ik/Cup'ik practices in my treatment program.

There were two open-ended questions in the cultural assessment:

1. What traditional/cultural modalities would you like to use in your treatment?
2. What traditional/cultural practices or methods would you like to learn?

The answers to these questions were used to guide the identification of traditional modalities that would best suit each individual in treatment. The treatment plan consisted of six domains: need/problem, goal, modality, objective/plan of actions, duration, and dates for activity. Table 6.1 shows an example of how one may be filled out for an individual whose overall goal for treatment was to be able to get along better with family and to have less tension in the home.

When the treatment plan was reviewed every three months, the counselor used information from the cultural assessment to guide the choice of possible treatment modalities for the client, who chose how to incorporate traditional modalities into treatment.

In treatment, a client chose to what extent he or she would like to incorporate traditional modalities into treatment. Depending on the treatment plan, a client may have attended an anger management group one day and later in the week may have spent a few hours berry picking on the tundra. Each activity tied into a goal in the treatment plan in order to qualify for reimbursement from Medicaid. And in this way, both Western and traditional C/Yup'ik modalities were validated.

Treatment Activities and C/Yup'ik Culture

The counselor frequently attended the traditional activities with the client. Some traditional modalities were more appropriate than others for certain treatment goals.

For example, tundra walks can be a helpful because a walk on the tundra out in nature and away from the village is an ideal time for personal reflection and stress relief. A tundra walk is a traditional cultural practice by the C/Yup'ik and provides a traditional mental health treatment. Elders frequently remind others to always be aware of the land and one's surroundings. This awareness is an important survival tool in C/Yup'ik culture. While the tundra is generally very flat, each area has its unique shapes. An example of growing in awareness of the tundra might be learning what direction the first cold wind blew when it felled the frozen grass that year. In the event of a whiteout, a lost person with that knowledge could dig to the grass below the snow and observe the direction it pointed, thus becoming oriented to the direction of the village. Thus, tundra walks can be therapeutic in a Western way and in a C/Yup'ik way.

Sustaining Traditional Healing in Behavioral Health Treatment

One of the primary goals for sustaining the activities of the VSP following its completion was to obtain Medicaid reimbursement for the village behavioral health services, including reimbursement for the traditional healing activities used. Local village wellness counselors were interviewed by the village clinician to identify what correlations existed between traditional healing activities and the definitions of services reimbursable by Medicaid. A matrix was drawn (table 6.2) illustrating which traditional modalities fell under which Medicaid service categories.

Table 6.1. Example of a Treatment Plan Using Traditional Modalities

Need/Problem	Goal	Modality	Objective/Plan of Action	Duration	Dates
Anger outbursts every night (7 times a week)	Reduce anger outburst from 7 times a week to once a week	A) Traditional B) Western	A-1) Tundra walk 3 times a week A-2) Seal Bladder Festival B-1) Anger management group once a week B-2) Individual counseling once a week	A-1) 3 months A-2) 3 days B-1) 3 months B-2) 3 months	A-1) Aug–Oct A-2) Sept 6–8 B-1) Aug–Oct B-2) Aug–Oct

Table 6.2. Matrix of C/Yup'ik Traditional Modalities and Applicable Medicaid Service Categories

Traditional Modalities	Western Modalities					
	Rehabilitation Treatment Services	Intensive Outpatient Services	Care Coordination	Individual Counseling	Family Counseling	Group Counseling
Pissuryaq (hunting)	X	X		X		
Aqevyigsuq/at'sasuq (berry picking)			X		X	
Neqsuq-kuvyiilluuni (fishing)	X	X		X		
Kaluukaq (to hold a feast, potlatch, ceremony)					X	X

Additionally, the village counselors became certified in their positions, first as substance abuse counselors and then with additional certifications. Weekly supervision took the form of a teleconference case review that all counselors attended and the village clinician supervised. The village clinician also traveled monthly to each of the three villages, spending on average half of each month in the villages and half in Bethel. In her travels, she would also supervise and sign treatment plans and do training for the village counselors.

In summary, to establish the process of obtaining Medicaid reimbursements for traditional modalities, some of these basic steps were followed:

1. Program staff of CMTRS, together with elders and the community, identified appropriate "traditional modalities for treatment," i.e., activities from the local, traditional culture that promote healthy living in a traditional way.
2. Program staff gathered information on what components of Medicaid services were reimbursable in their field (substance abuse, mental health).
3. Program staff correlated traditional modalities with appropriate Medicaid service components, receiving guidance from the local village counselors.
4. Program staff ensured that services being delivered satisfied Medicaid requirements; for example, traditional modalities were written into treatment plans, and staff documented the required licenses and certifications.

A Positive Approach

While more work can be done to further incorporate traditional modalities into treatment for Native peoples and further facilitate healing for Native peoples, the VSP is a positive approach to advocating for, and sustaining, a more holistic and appropriate method of substance abuse and mental health service delivery. The VSP was funded as a Targeted Capacity Expansion grant under the CSAT as a Rural, Remote, and Culturally Distinct site. The CSAT is in the process of publishing an official report on this and similar projects entitled *Pathways to Healing: The Center for Substance Abuse Treatment's Rural, Remote, and Culturally Distinct Populations Program*. The report, forthcoming in 2004, will include quantitative evaluation data and qualitative reporting on the projects.

Notes

Please address correspondence and reprint requests to Phoebe A. Mills, MSW, National Indian Child Welfare Association, 5100 SW Macadam Ave., Suite 300, Portland, OR

97206; for information on the VSP, contact Ray Watson, Project Director, VSP, at Ray_Watson@ykhc.org or 907–543–6300. "Joining and Sustaining Yup'ik and Cup'ik Healing with Behavioral Health Treatment" is an abridged version of "Incorporating Yup'ik and Cup'ik Eskimo Traditions into Behavioral Health Treatment," by Phoebe A. Mills, M.S.W , which appeared in the *Journal of Psychoactive Drugs* 35 (1). Reprinted by permission of Haight-Ashbury Publications, 612 Clayton Street, San Francisco, California.

Alaska Division of Alcoholism and Drug Abuse. *Chemical Dependency Treatment Outcome Study*. Department of Health and Social Services, 1998. http://www.health.hss.state.ak.us/dbh/PDF/substance%20abuse/NewStrdsExecSmry.PDF (accessed August 20, 2002).

Center for Substance Abuse Treatment (CSAT). *Cultural Issues in Substance Abuse Treatment*. Rockville, Md.: Department of Health and Human Services (DHHS), 1999.

———. *Pathways to Healing: The Center for Substance Abuse Treatment's Rural, Remote, and Culturally Distinct Populations Program*. Rockville, Md.: DHHS, forthcoming.

DHHS. *Mental Health: Culture, Race, and Ethnicity—A Supplement to Mental Health: A Report of the Surgeon General*. Rockville, Md.: DHHS, 2001.

Jones-Sparck, L. *Cup'ik People and the State of Alaska: Implications for Culturally Relevant Policies and Practices*. Fairbanks: University of Alaska-Fairbanks Kuskokwim Campus, 1993.

Office of Women's Health, Department of Health and Human Services. *Overview of Region X*. Rockville, Md.: DHHS, 2002. http://www.4woman.gov/owh/reg/10/overview.htm (accessed August 20, 2002).

Mandan and Hidatsa Families and Children 7
Surviving Historical Assault

SANDRA BEAUCHAMP

T HE HEALTH OF THE FAMILY SYSTEM is of extreme importance to the health of the individual throughout life. The resiliency of the infant is predicated upon a high-quality interaction with the principal caregivers, and the effects of this interaction are expressed throughout the individual's life (Letourneau 1997). Unfortunately, the all-important nurturing environment for children has been lost intergenerationally in many Native American families.

The Native American community has a high incidence of familial pathology due to the historical devastation of the family unit (Nebelkopf and Phillips 2003). Indigenous children were forcibly removed from family homes by the government in an attempt to assimilate the Nations into the dominant society. This policy was reinforced throughout the twentieth century (Josephy 1991). Neglect or social deprivation was most often cited in removing the children. The reasons denied a cultural explication of the situation of the child, and judgment was most often made through a dominant-culture perspective, disregarding what might be a norm in the Native community. For example, a child may have been left with a relative for a period of time, and this might have been construed as neglect under dominant-culture social work standards. However, living with an extended family member is a cultural norm in the Indian community—and the extended family includes many relatives and even clan members who may have little blood relation. Or perhaps the social worker viewed with disfavor the permissive attitudes under which a child was reared. This type of Indian child rearing is normal in a culture that reveres its elders and children. Children also were frequently removed because of alcoholism of the parent, but rarely was a child removed for physical abuse (U.S. Bureau of Indian Affairs 1997).

The Native American community suffered through the generations the tribal and family splits that occurred throughout the nineteenth and well into the twentieth century (Josephy 1991). Much has been written about the "Indian Wars" and the fallout from that time. However, some Plains Nations never warred with the U.S. Government, and those Nations included the Mandan, Hidatsa, and Arikara. Family systems of the Mandan and Hidatsa Nations will be examined through a historical review of the literature of the many explorers, missionaries, and others who visited and a few who ultimately stayed with the tribe.

First Contact

At the time of first contact with the colonizers, the Mandan and Hidatsa lived in earth lodges built on the bluffs overlooking the Missouri River and its tributaries in what is now North Dakota. The family relationship was built on a matrilineal clan system that provided the children with many caretakers. The residence of a newly married couple was *matrilocal*, meaning the husband moved into the wife's family lodge upon the marriage. The Mandan and Hidatsa Nations had a sororal polygamy system that allowed the men to marry their wife's sisters (Wilson 1983). The adult female offspring, their spouses, and their children also occupied the home.

The woman built the home and tanned hides from the animals killed in the hunt. From the hides she made footwear, clothing, and other items necessary to the household. She owned the home, the gardening equipment, the colts, and the mares. She sang sacred songs while she hoed in the gardens, located in the fertile bottomlands of the valley (Meyer 1977).

The men owned their weapons, clothing, tools, and the stallions and geldings. They took care of the horses, hunted, and protected the village. Games and contests of strength, endurance, and, later, horsemanship kept the men fit and kept up their skills, which were needed for the survival of the tribes. The issue of who owned what was important only should a marriage not last (Catlin 1973).

The children of the Mandan and Hidatsa were never disciplined by their parents. In the clan system, a child was a member of the mother's clan, and all other members of that clan were sisters and brothers to the child. The father's clan members were identified as clan fathers if they were male and as clan aunts if they were female. The clan fathers were called in if the boys needed disciplining, and the clan aunts corrected the girls (Wilson 1983).

When girls were ten to twelve years old, they began learning the duties of a woman. Their gardening duties included helping to build a platform, sometimes under a tree that was intentionally left in a field when it was planted, and they stood there and sang songs. It was believed that corn had souls and liked being sung to. The singing also served to keep the birds away (Wilson 1983).

In 1832, George Catlin, an artist, visited the Mandan and described the lifestyle of this Nation. He portrayed large earth lodges that housed twenty to forty people comfortably. He commented on the cleanliness of the lodges, with ground "swept so clean . . . that they have almost a polish and would scarcely soil the whitest linen." He also described the people "reclining in the most picturesque attitudes and groups, resting on their buffalo robes and beautiful mats of rushes" around a kettle of buffalo meat hanging over the fire, which was laid "in a hole of four or five feet in diameter . . . sunk a foot or more below the surface and curbed with stone" (Catlin 1973).

Catlin indicated that most white people thought the Indigenous People were very serious and without humor, and he wrote to dispel that notion. He pointed out that laughter was heard throughout the day as games were played and people "cavorted," and in the lodges families could be heard sharing stories and jokes as they passed around a pipe. Catlin further stated:

> Yet they are free from, and independent of, a thousand cares and jealousies, which arise from mercenary motives in the civilized world; and are yet far ahead of us (in my opinion) in the real and uninterrupted enjoyment of their simple natural faculties. They live in a country and in communities, where it is not customary to look forward into the future with concern, for they live without incurring the expenses of life, which are absolutely necessary and unavoidable in the enlightened world; and of course their inclinations and faculties are solely directed to the enjoyment of the present day, without the sober reflections on the past or apprehensions of the future.

The families had clearly delineated duties in the care of the children. The family and clan system in which the children were disciplined, nurtured, and educated was tightly woven and assured that should something happen to the parents, the children would always be cared for.

Introduction of Alcohol

Fur traders introduced alcohol to the Mandan, Hidatsa, and Arikara to enhance the traders' chances of receiving valuable goods for little money, and they eventually traded alcohol directly for those goods. The Native population's socialization into drinking to drunkenness began with the traders and was supported by the government. Later government policies prohibiting drinking in the Native population fostered a binge-drinking pattern of use: the fear of having the bottle taken away encouraged drinking alcohol as quickly as possible after purchasing it. Alcohol was one of the great contributors to the crippling health, cultural, and spiritual problems in each of the tribes that would become the Three Affiliated Tribes

(Mandan, Hidatsa, and Arikara). Traders, agents, and politicians cooperated with the fur companies in these destructive exchanges that still reverberate in today's families (Meyer 1977).

As a direct result of the disruption of the family unit and the indoctrination by boarding schools, which demanded a denial of culture and self, substance abuse has become the leading problem of Native families today (Brave Heart 2003; Meyer 1977; Nebelkopf and Phillips 2003).

Smallpox

In 1837, the Mandan population was devastated by the third in a series of small-pox epidemics. George Catlin (1973) estimated that approximately 2,000 people lived in two tribal villages he visited in 1832. After the third strike of smallpox, that population was reduced to approximately 130 people. The Hidatsa also lost more than half their population. Four Bears, the highly esteemed chief of the Mandan, lay dying of smallpox, cursing the white man:

> I do not fear Death my friends. You know it, but to die with my face rotten, that even the Wolves will shrink with horror at meeting me, and say to themselves, that is the Four Bears, the friend of the Whites—listen well what I have to say, as it will be the last time you will hear me. Think of your wives, children, brothers, sisters, friends, and in fact all that you hold dear, are all dead, or dying, with their faces all rotten caused by those dogs, the Whites. Think of all that my friends, and rise up all together and not leave one of them alive: The Four Bears will act his part (Meyer 1977).

Smallpox was not the only disease to decimate the tribes. Tuberculosis, influenza, and other diseases that rarely killed the Europeans had a devastating impact and further reduced the population of the three tribes. In 1845, the Mandan and Hidatsa joined together in one village for protection from much larger enemy nations; a few years later, the Arikara joined them (Jaimes 1992).

Assimilation

In the United States, the Natives had lost one-half of all Native languages by the turn of the twentieth century, largely through the influences of the government and mission boarding schools. The U.S. government supported the complete disintegration of the family, clan, and tribal and communal land systems and the near destruction of tribal languages and spiritual and cultural practices of the Indigenous People. For example, testimony before Congress in 1871 affirmed, "We see nothing about Indian nationality or Indian civilization which should make its preservation a matter of so much anxiety to the Congress or to the People of the

United States" (Deloria 1985). The tribal community developed a high incidence of familial pathology due to the historical devastation of the family unit. The rations that kept the tribes from starving were often stolen and sold by the agents who were responsible for their distribution, forcing more children into boarding schools, where they would be fed, clothed, and housed.

Between 1865 and 1870, at Fort Berthold, Mahlon Wilkinson, an agent, was required to get the signature of the chief, White Shield, as proof he dispensed the rations and trade goods to the tribes. He did not disperse the rations and goods, and the chief refused to sign papers indicating he had. The agent then removed him as chief and appointed a younger man, who then signed (Meyer 1977).

The Native American program of the Hampton Institute was created as a result of the assimilationist policies of the government. Indian Commissioner Edgar M. Marble stated, "The opportunity for teaching Indian children how to live as well as how to read and think is found only in the boarding school" (Engs 1999). In line with these policies, many children were removed by the soldiers and taken away to boarding school. Some parents chose to hide their children. Others were compliant due to appalling living conditions, starvation, and the inability to care for their children in a hostile environment (Beauchamp 1998). Some of the children were removed and taken to schools without their parents' having any knowledge of where they had been taken (Case and Case 1977).

To rid students of heathen ways, schools emphasized a policy of conversion to Christianity. Tribal member Poor Wolf encouraged his daughters to go to school. This led to his own conversion to Christianity when his daughters encouraged him. He was the first elder to be converted to Christianity, eleven years after the missionaries first arrived. When his daughters returned home after three years, Poor Wolf was ashamed of still living in his earth lodge and sent his daughters back to school, this time at Santee (Case and Case 1977).

On April 14, 1878, the first prospective students of the Mandan, Hidatsa, and Arikara Nations were introduced to the Hampton Institute by Lt. Richard Henry Pratt, a United States Army officer who had commanded African American troops in the Civil War. Pratt was also responsible for the educational philosophy of "Kill the Indian and save the man." Because of this belief, Native Americans at Carlisle boarding school and the boarding schools to follow had their hair shorn and their clothing replaced with that of the dominant culture. They were punished if they spoke their language or engaged in any activity that bespoke their culture (Engs 1999). Reba Walker, a Mandan and Hidatsa elder, recently wrote in a Sunday School bulletin:

I am a Mandan, my father is Hidatsa, and I speak Hidatsa. I attended a mission boarding school where acculturation was emphasized. After-school activities had none of our cultural aspects, and if we wanted to replicate life in our own communities, we did so secretly. When all was quiet and we thought the matrons were asleep, we'd reenact our home and family rituals in our own tribal languages. Language is how culture is passed from one generation to the next. It is no wonder that so much of our culture is lost, what with so many generations having learned "culture" at a boarding school.

Only seven of the first thirteen Native students at Hampton Institute were full-blood Indians. Religious instruction was immediately imposed upon the students. They were also given gardening tools, and instruction in agriculture began upon their arrival at the school. One agent, William Courtenay, of Fort Berthold, stated:

> Indians are essentially conservative and cling to old customs and hate all changes. Therefore the government should force them to scatter out on farms, break up their tribal organization, dances, ceremonies, and tomfoolery; take from them their hundreds of useless ponies which afford them the means of indulging in their nomadic habits, and give them cattle in exchange and compel then to labor or accept the alternative of starvation (Engs 1999).

In the first ten years of the Hampton Institute program, 31 of the 427 students died, and 111 were sent home gravely ill. Of those who survived, many did not see their homeland for many years and were virtual strangers when they returned (Engs 1999). Had this been a mainstream boarding school with those statistics, it is doubtful it would have remained open.

Fort Berthold had a mission school, where the children were boarded, but far more children were in need of education than this school could afford to house. The reservation also had a public school, but because it was a distance from most homes, the children had no time for breakfast and little resources to provide a lunch from home. In 1931, a Mrs. Case, wife of the Reverend Harold Case, wrote that she believed this lack of nourishment was detrimental to their ability to study and learn. She believed the mission school was better than the public school because the children would have adequate nutrition and the parents would be closer. She also stated that this proximity would aid the missionaries in their efforts to convert families because the parents would be stopping in to see their children, and the Christian life could be demonstrated at that time. She wrote:

> The Mission school on the Reservation is far better than the large government school far from home, where the contact between parent and child is completely broken. You know the children are sent off at 6 years of age and kept away sometimes 3 years at a time. When their education is finished, there is such a gulf between them

and their parents that they don't fit any longer. In the long run, I know our way is best. Here, the parents can visit their children often (Case and Case 1977).

Dawes Act

Henry Dawes believed the American Indian had to be forced to live as those Dawes believed to be civilized. In 1899, Dawes wrote:

> It was plain that if he were left alone, he must of necessity become a tramp and beggar with all the evil passions of a savage, a homeless and lawless poacher upon civilization and a terror to the peaceful citizen (Dawes 1899).

His solution was to partition the land given to the tribes under treaty and give it to those who were defined by blood quantum as American Indians. The allotments of 160 acres per married couple and 80 for single adults left much unallotted land, which was to be sold to homesteaders. The money given to the Tribes in exchange for that land was millions of dollars short of its value, and it was not until the second half of the twentieth century that the tribal members were reimbursed. The payments were based on what the land was worth in the 1880s, and no interest was paid (Deloria 1985).

The sectioning of the land put much terrain between the homes of each family. The split of the tribal community was effectively begun, and this split would eventually filter down to the individual family unit due to the influence of the boarding schools and the difficulty of maintaining close communication because extended family and clan no longer lived in villages. The historical sharing of communal foods during times of famine was now discouraged, and individualism was encouraged by the culture of the dominant society; however, the Native farmers and ranchers were able to continue the model of mutual aid and sharing (Meyer 1977).

Missionaries

Charles Lemon Hall arrived in North Dakota in 1876 and worked with the Fort Berthold Three Affiliated Tribes until 1922. He and his wife worked long hours and traveled over what were little more than ruts to take his message of Christianity to isolated family homes. Through his hard work, positive attitude, and good intentions, he was eventually accepted. He firmly believed that the ceremonial activities and beliefs of the Natives must be extinguished to give them a better life. In 1889, the government forbade the ceremonies of the Indigenous People. It is only in retrospect and by reviewing the current health statistics of the Native Peoples of the United States that we can see the damage done by the policy of extermination of the Native culture and religion.

Harold W. Case, missionary, who arrived to replace Reverend Hall in 1922, stated the goals of the missionary work quite clearly when he wrote:

> We will place considerable emphasis upon the social program for the young people who are outside of school. Further emphasis to be given to adult education. As Secretary Wilber says, 'in 25 years we will have the American with Indian descent' (Case and Case 1977).

The school at Elbowoods, North Dakota, was the first federal and public school in the country, and it sent more students to institutions of higher learning than did any other school of its size in the Nation. The devastation brought by the construction of the Garrison Dam in the 1950s mandated the beautiful town of Elbowoods be abandoned and eventually covered by the waters of Lake Sakakawea. This statement from the state and county officials in North Dakota in 1950 best illustrates the zeitgeist of public policy during that time:

> If you want to solve the Indian problem you can do it in one generation. You can take all of our children of school age and move them bodily out of the Indian country and transport them to some other part of the United States. If you take these kids away and educate them to make their own lives *they wouldn't come back here* (George 1997).

Impact of Public Policy on Family Systems

Although the Mandan and Hidatsa Nations were never at war with the colonizers, government policies almost exterminated them completely. These policies included land allotment, boarding schools, cultural and spiritual bans, extermination of languages, and the final blow: flooding the land where ancestors were buried and where the Mandan, Hidatsa, and Arikara tribal systems were finally supporting themselves.

Intergenerational family splits are the legacy of the good intentions of the missionaries who sought to instill dominant culture in the Native population but instead created a population among the Tribes who spent their lives trying to be like the white man while internalizing the underlying message that being Indian was somehow not good enough. Boarding schools taught the children much about various kinds of abuse when the employees incorporated abusive behavior into their treatment of the children. As adults these former students became abusive to their own spouses and children, modeling their parenting styles after the physical, emotional, and sexual abuse perpetrated in the boarding schools.

Tribal splits among the different Nations of Fort Berthold were exacerbated: The ability to meet and communicate easily declined as the physical distances separating people were increased through allotment and then because of the water that covered a large portion of the reservation. The tribes are now struggling to create a structure that will provide economically for the members who still reside on the reservation homelands. According to the Mandan, Hidatsa, and Arikara Nations website, unemployment is at 42 percent, but new businesses and industries are in place and increasing. It is doubtful, however, that a tribal and family system can be devised that comes close to providing the nurture, beauty, sustenance, and protection that our Native families of the Dakota Territory enjoyed before colonization.

Notes

Beauchamp, S. "Healing Alcoholism in Indigenous People," *Social Work Perspective* 8(1) (1998): 35–40.

Brave Heart, M. Y. H. "The Historical Trauma Response among Natives and Its Relationship with Substance Abuse: A Lakota Illustration," *Journal of Psychoactive Drugs* 35(1) (2003): 7–13.

Case, H., and E. Case. *100 Years at Fort Berthold*, Library of Congress Catalog Card Number 76–62987. Washington, D.C., 1977.

Catlin, G. *Letters and Notes on the Manners, Customs and Conditions of the North American Indians.* New York: Dover Publications, 1973.

Dawes, H. "Have We Failed with the Indian?" *Atlantic Monthly* (1899).

Deloria, V., Jr., ed. *American Indian Policy in the Twentieth Century.* Norman: University of Oklahoma Press, 1985.

Engs, R. *Educating the Disfranchised and Disinherited.* Knoxville: University of Tennessee Press, 1999.

George, L. "The Challenge of Permanency Planning in a Multicultural Society," *Journal of Multicultural Social Work* 5(3-4) (1997): 165–175.

Jaimes, M. A., ed. *The State of Native America—Genocide, Colonization, and Resistance.* Boston: South End Press, 1992.

Josephy, A., Jr. *The Indian Heritage of America.* Boston: Houghton Mifflin, 1991.

Letourneau, N. "Fostering Resiliency in Infants and Young Children through Parent-Infant Interaction," *Infants and Young Children* 9 (1997): 36–45.

Meyer, R. W. *The Village Indians of the Upper Missouri.* Lincoln: University of Nebraska Press, 1977.

Nebelkopf, E., and M. Phillips, eds. Introduction, "Morning Star Rising: Healing in Native American Communities." *Journal of Psychoactive Drugs* 35(1) (2003): 1–4.

U.S. Bureau of Indian Affairs, Indian Health Service. *The Indian Child Welfare Act of 1978: Summary.* Sacramento, Calif.: Author, 1997.

Wilson, Gilbert L. *Waheenee—An Indian Girl's Story Told by Herself.* Lincoln: University of Nebraska Press, 1983.

BUILDING HEALTHY COMMUNITIES   III

Taking a look at a community level we can't just say there is advanced healing, it's all healing. Indian healing is hope. There are so many that suffer in our community that are shamed, handcuffed, to be walking around with a black eye, and when they are mistreated, they have to walk through this. How do we get them to the next level? We need to think solution oriented to build a framework where we all contribute. The only way we are going to heal will have to come from within us, not from some outside source, not a curriculum manual from a shelf. The action and the attitude of the people in the community must change. Once it happens then we can go to work. You can't give away what you don't have.

People working for healthy communities go through the risks because of their passion. Creator blesses them in ways that let you appreciate the families that learn to parent children, you see how this affects their kids, they get their Indian name, you see them at powwows and go through ceremony, they grow up and prosper. I do this because that is the right thing to do.

—THEDA NEWBREAST (BLACKFEET)

THE COMMUNITY READINESS MODEL is an innovative, culturally specific methodology developed by Pamela Jumper Thurman and associates at the Tri-Ethnic Center for Prevention Research in Colorado. This model assesses the level of readiness of a community to develop and implement prevention efforts.

In order to move a community toward implementing effective and sustainable programs, community mobilization must be based on the involvement of multiple systems and utilization of the community's resources and strengths. Bernie Ellis describes community mobilization efforts for reducing substance abuse in New Mexico and Wyoming, and Mary Phillips and Sarah Nebelkopf organize lessons learned on incorporating managed information systems into a strategic plan for services for Native Americans.

Community Readiness

8

The Journey to Community Healing

PAMELA JUMPER-THURMAN, BARBARA A. PLESTED, RUTH W. EDWARDS, ROBERT FOLEY, AND MARTHA BURNSIDE

O N A SPRING DAY IN MARCH 2001, a Native woman from Alaska came to the Tri-Ethnic Center in Colorado looking for help. Her small village had suffered the loss of several of their youth in the six months prior to her visit. She described a community immobilized by grief yet motivated to find a way to stop the suicides. She had heard of a model developed at the Tri-Ethnic Center that gave her hope. She invited Center staff to her village to conduct a workshop using the model.

The training staff made the long trip expecting fifteen or twenty people from the village, if that many, to attend the workshop, given the short amount of time for preparation. They were overwhelmed to step into a community center and find almost 100 Native people, young and old. Six villages had gathered in unity to save their children. They were a grief-stricken audience who had spent a lot of time and money to gather in this one village. Despite the difficulty and cost of travel to remote Alaskan villages, these concerned people found a way to get there. The outer walls of the community center were lined with elders who had come in to support the effort—most couldn't hear what was going on and some were blind, yet they sat there from eight in the morning until eleven at night in order to offer their caring and their support. The benches were hard, yet their stamina came from the heart.

Initially the people spoke of their grief and losses and their inability to move forward because of the pain in their hearts. The concept of the model was presented, and then the people divided into village groups. Each group used the model to assess its village's stage of readiness and then to identify its strengths and resources. The participants later talked about how grateful they were to find those strengths because they had forgotten them or didn't recognize them as strengths.

Then each village, through its commitment and caring, developed a proactive plan to stop the suicides by using the resources in the village. The youth also attended the workshop and formed their own group to develop strategies to offer support to friends in school. Someone from the outside looking at one of these small villages might think the resources very sparse, given that the villages are small and have no shelters, counseling centers, or the other entities usually thought of as resources. However, the villages' resources came from the heart—their volunteerism, their culture, their creativity, and their readiness to change.

Each village stood and shared with the others the strategies that it had developed. The people were motivated, and although the grief was still there, hope was also present. The experience was very moving. All six villages then formed a larger circle and, again using the model, worked together to brainstorm their action plan to keep intervillage communication and support going.

These villages were ready for change and made changes in their communities that significantly reduced youth suicide. To this day, they continue their efforts. They created a vision and have kept it going.

We often hear that it takes a village to raise a child. While that is true, it is also imperative that the village be ready to assume its responsibility, or it just won't happen. The villages described above were ready. They knew that mobilizing and changing a community system would require vision, voices, and commitment. Addressing any community social problem is a multifaceted task with many potential pitfalls. Changing national policy rarely has immediate local effects and in fact may never have public support. Locally initiated efforts are not always successful either. They may lack community investment. Many good programs have met with failure for any number of reasons. Often, in these days of competitive, time-limited grant funding, there is no sustainability for a program when funding sources end. Programs generally have a beginning and an end. With vision, however, prevention efforts can be far reaching and sustainable. Daniel Quinn (1996) suggests:

> If the world is to be saved, it will be saved by people with changed minds, people with a new vision—yet if the time isn't right for a new idea, it will fail. If however, the time is right, an idea can sweep the world like wildfire. The measures of change are not the ease or difficulty with which it can be effected, but the readiness or unreadiness of the entity needing change.

Successful local prevention and intervention efforts must be conceived from models that are community specific, culturally relevant, and consistent with the level of readiness of the community to implement an intervention. Communities vary greatly one from another. Resources also vary from community to community, as do strengths, challenges, and political climates. It isn't really surprising, then, that what works well in one community may be minimally effective in another. Readiness is an important factor because differences in readiness indicate what needs to be done. Each community needs to use its own knowledge of its assets and limitations, its culture and characteristics, its values and beliefs, to build policies and programs that are congruent with the community's characteristics and that meet the community's needs. The Community Readiness Model helps communities create a vision and work toward achieving it in an orderly fashion.

Helping professionals tell many stories about outside consultants who have been called into a community to prescribe solutions for community problems but who have met with only minimal success. This lack of success in no way reflects on the expertise of the consultant but only proves that in a short period of time, it is rarely possible to acquire the understanding of the cultural nature and political climate of a community necessary to develop appropriate strategies and programs. When those "experts" leave, their "prescription" often falls by the wayside.

Communities have also shared stories about their frustrations related to implementing an intervention or curriculum that requires a great deal of resources, human or financial. Because they are unable to access those resources, the strategies fail. Finally, because so many different sectors of a community may be affected by a community problem, efforts for prevention or intervention are often fragmented. It is not unusual for one agency to know nothing about what another agency may be doing. In order to effectively mobilize a community and implement potentially sustainable community change, it is essential that a community pull together in the development of interventions appropriate to its unique situation and region. It is our contention that the real experts are those who reside within each community. All they may need are the proper tools. The Community Readiness Model (Oetting et al. 2001; Edwards et al. 2000; Plested et al. 1999, 1998; Donnermeyer et al. 1997; Oetting et al. 1995) is one such tool.

Community readiness is a research-based theory that provides a basic understanding of the intervention process in communities. Edwards and colleagues (2000) provide the most recent and comprehensive review of the development of the theory and include all the instruments needed to apply the model. The theory allows one to accurately describe the developmental level of a community relative to a specific issue or problem. It defines the developmental stages that have to be worked through in order to move the community toward implementing and maintaining efforts to reduce the problem, and it provides specific guidelines at each stage for the type and intensity level of strategies that may lead to movement to the next stage. Finally, it provides direction to the community on means to achieve the necessary community involvement to create a vision that can lead to change. These guidelines are stated broadly so as to allow specific cultural values and beliefs to be taken into account and to optimize use of local assets and resources. They include development of an understanding of local barriers and obstacles to progress; in fact, the guidelines embrace those barriers as part of the nature of the community. Although it is important to note that the model is a research-based tool, its real validation comes from the many communities who have discovered its utility and have claimed it as their own. Development of the model has been greatly enhanced by these communities' feedback for modifying the readiness tool to make it even more useful. It truly is a model that has successfully made the journey from research to practice.

The Community Readiness Model is an innovative and easy method for assessing the level of readiness of a community to develop and implement prevention and/or intervention. It was originally developed at the Tri-Ethnic Center for Prevention Research at Colorado State University to address alcohol- and drug-abuse prevention efforts. However, it was soon discovered that, as in the case study above, it encompassed the broader aim of assessing readiness in a variety of areas, ranging from health and nutritional issues (such as sexually transmitted diseases, heart disease, and diet) to environmental issues (such as water and air quality and litter and recycling) and social issues (such as poverty, homelessness, and violence). The model has already been successfully applied to prevention of intimate-partner violence, HIV/AIDS, methamphetamine abuse, environmental trauma, suicide, and head injury. The model identifies specific characteristics related to a community's history, resources, level of problem awareness, and readiness for change. In order to increase an intervention's chance of success, its introduction in a community must be consistent with the awareness of the problem and the level of readiness for change present among members of that community.

The model proposes that a community has six primary dimensions that need to be explored to order to view the community clearly. The six dimensions are community efforts (programs, activities, policies, etc.); community knowledge of the efforts; leadership (including appointed leaders and influential community members); community climate (the attitude of the community concerning the issue); community knowledge about the issue; and resources related to the issue (people, money, time, space, etc.). Specific questions relating to each of the dimensions assist in a community assessment and act as a diagnostic tool to provide information about the type of intervention that should be planned within each of the dimensions. Each dimension is scored using a nine-stage level-of-readiness scale.

The Community Readiness Model identifies nine stages of readiness. The first stage, no awareness, suggests that the behavior is normative and accepted. Denial, the second stage, involves the belief that the problem does not exist or that change is impossible. The vague awareness stage involves recognition of the problem but no motivation for action. The preplanning stage indicates recognition of a problem and agreement that something needs to be done. The preparation stage involves active planning, and the initiation stage involves implementation of a program. Stabilization indicates that one or two programs are operating and are stable. Confirmation/expansion involves recognition of limitations and attempts to improve existing programs. The final stage, professionalization, is marked by sophistication, training, effective evaluation, and application of readiness knowledge and skills to other problems in the community.

Assessment

The Community Readiness Model can be used in two phases, assessment and application/mobilization. During the assessment phase (the first step in the community readiness process), the goal is to determine the stage of readiness for addressing a particular problem. For example, a community may have a strong, stable program for drug abuse prevention, but community members may still be at the denial stage for utilizing the program or even accepting that they may need the program. The program is therefore underutilized, and without consumer recognition, utilization and support will likely fail. It is important that strategies be planned in collaboration with key people in the community so that the strategies will have a higher level of cultural integrity and the community residents will have a greater investment in enhancing the intervention. The result is an increased potential for mobilization of efforts. Because community members assist in identifying and owning the problem, identifying potential barriers in their own language and context and collaborating in the development of interventions that are culturally consistent with their populations, the investment in success is greater.

Because the consequences related to a specific problem often affect many segments in a community, it is very unlikely that any one organization or person will have the complete picture. The consequences of substance abuse, for example, may include one or more of the following: birth defects, child abuse or neglect, property damage, injuries and fatalities, criminal activity, lost productivity, on-the-job problems, and emotional distress. To assess a community's level of readiness to address its substance abuse problem, a key-informant survey is used to obtain fact-based information from several community people knowledgeable about the issue. The survey questions are designed to tap into specific areas of information and can be modified to be more compatible with the culture, language, and resources in a community.

The transcribed interviews are then scored on each of the model's six dimensions, which are anchored by descriptive statements that can be utilized for ranking the responses of each interviewee on each dimension. In order for a particular score to be assigned, the conditions set forth in all lower-ranking anchor statements must be satisfied as well. After reviewing the ratings on all six dimensions for all interviews in a given community, the interviewer can assign the community to the stage that best represents the aggregate ratings of the dimensions.

Application/Mobilization

Once a community readiness stage has been assessed, it is time to develop strategies for moving the community from its current level to the next higher one. The interventions suggested here comprise a very brief sampling of potential interventions for each stage. For communities in the first four stages (no awareness through preplanning), effective strategies are aimed at raising a community's awareness that a problem exists. For instance, activities at the stage of no awareness are focused on the singular goal of raising awareness of the issue. Intervention activities for communities at this stage should be restricted to one-on-one or small group activities. Home visits to discuss the issues and win people over, small activity groups, talking circles, and one-on-one phone calls have been used effectively at this stage by some communities, knowing that the problem is one the community accepts as a way of life.

At the denial stage, the goal is to focus on creating awareness that the problem exists on a local level. National and sometimes even local statistics are less important than descriptive incidents that have a direct, significant impact on community members. At this stage personalized case reports and critical incidents are likely to be more successful than general statistics or data. Media reports, presentations to small community groups, and similar awareness-raising interventions can focus on the general problem in similar communities; they must include local examples to create awareness that the problem is also local.

At the vague awareness stage, the singular goal is to raise awareness that the community can do something about the problem. At this stage, members of the community can go to existing small groups to garner support and use existing community events to present information to a larger group of people. Native communities have had success using pot lucks or potlatches. Media efforts should focus on creating local newspaper editorials or articles about local incidents. National or regional data will still make little impression on community residents; however, local survey data can help to make the case for community mobilization around the issue—that is, results of school surveys, phone surveys, focus groups, etc. It should be noted that at this stage of readiness, some people in the community, such as school officials and parents, may be resistant to initiating these types of activities. However, they can still be persuaded through visits and phone calls by those who know them or by someone who can appeal to their overall concern about the health of the community.

At the preplanning stage, the goal is to raise awareness with concrete ideas to combat the problem. At this stage, communities can begin to gather information related to existing prevention or treatment programming and why it does or doesn't work. They should begin to examine curricula and educational materials that are currently in use in schools, churches, and so on. Are they culturally relevant? What is their level of success? Communities should continue involving key people—leaders, formal and informal—in the planning process. This is the point at which the initiators can also conduct local focus groups or small public forums to discuss the issues and make suggestions for using local resources. Media exposure can be expanded to present local data and local stories and tie them to national incidents and statistics.

For communities in the stages of preparation and initiation, efforts are generally aimed at gathering and providing community-specific information to the general public. At the preparation stage, the goal is to continue to gather and then review existing information that can be used to help plan strategies. At this stage, the community may want to utilize a valid and reliable school drug-and-alcohol survey so that accurate local data are available. Community telephone surveys could be initiated to gain information about community attitudes and beliefs related to the problem, in-depth local statistics should be gathered, and more diverse and wider-reaching focus groups should be held to gain a broader representation of the community and develop practical prevention strategies and proposals for grants.

For communities at the initiation stage, the goal is to provide community-specific information to all members of the community. At this stage, it is recommended that efforts be made to get everyone educated and working "on the same page." This would include conducting training for professionals and paraprofessionals, conducting consumer interviews to gain information about improving services, identifying service gaps, and utilizing computer searches to identify potential funding sources that match community needs. Publicity efforts might focus on education programs currently in use in the community, with feature presentations on specific programs and resources and how to access them, and so forth.

For communities in the final three stages—stabilization, confirmation/expansion, and professionalization—strategies are more programmatic in nature. For communities in the stabilization stage, the goal is simply to stabilize efforts or programs. Stabilizing them might mean initiating evaluation techniques in an effort to modify and improve services, providing in-service training to increase the number and quality of trained community professionals, planning community events, offering community volunteer recognition events, and conducting community workshops.

At the confirmation/expansion stage, the goal is to expand and enhance existing services. The same types of activities can be utilized as in the stabilization stage, but at a higher level of sophistication. They might include utilization of external evaluation services to provide a more comprehensive community data base, initiation of activities that change local community policy/norms, and media outreach that focuses on presenting evaluation data and thus the trends, improvements, and areas of need that still exist. It is recommended that community focus groups or public forums still be used, but with a different focus, that is, to maintain grassroots involvement and continue to improve services based on consumer needs.

For the rare community that has achieved the final stage, professionalism, the goal is to maintain momentum and continue growth. Interventions at this stage consist of very high level data collection and analysis, sophisticated media tracking of trends, local business sponsorship of community events, and diversification of funding resources. At this stage, communities may also apply their knowledge of and experience with the Community Readiness process to another issue.

In summary, effective and sustainable community mobilization must be based on involvement of multiple systems and utilization of within-community resources and strengths. Efforts must consider historical issues, be culturally relevant, and be accepted as long term in nature. The Community Readiness Model takes these factors into account and provides a practical tool that communities can use to focus and direct their efforts toward a desired result, maximizing their resources and minimizing discouraging failures. Thus it creates a vision that is sustainable and motivating.

It is hoped that the communities that utilize this method will provide feedback to the authors on their experience with the model. In many ways, this model is community driven because of the feedback provided by those using it. Many communities have maintained contact with the Center, reporting on their experiences using the Community Readiness Model. Most have experienced few difficulties in moving through the stages. For those communities that have not moved forward, the reasons are varied, but consistent themes have been political or personnel changes within the communities or tribes or villages. For some, a community crisis has arisen that has forced the original problem into the background while the community deals with an even more immediate problem. The majority of communities who have utilized the model, however, have experienced success in developing and applying their strategies. Others have made plans for implementation and are seeking additional resources for start-up of the programs. Some communities have chosen not to utilize funding but rather to engage the community in volunteer action. In any case, many of the communities have indicated that they will continue to utilize the model to monitor their progress and assist in developing their future plans and creating their own vision. "Best practices" or "promising practices" in prevention are only best for a community when they are culturally appropriate and match the community's level of readiness to recognize the problem, to understand the importance of prevention, and to invest in and implement such practices.

Notes

"Community Readiness: The Journey to Community Healing" is an abridged version of "Community Readiness: The Journey to Community Healing," by Pamela Jumper-Thurman, Ph.D., Barbara A. Plested, Ph.D., Ruth W. Edwards, Ph.D., Robert Foley, B.A., and Martha Burnside, B.A., which appeared in the *Journal of Psychoactive Drugs* 35 (1). Reprinted by permission of Haight-Ashbury Publications, 612 Clayton Street, San Francisco, California.

Donnermeyer, J. F., E. R. Oetting, B. A. Plested, R. W. Edwards, P. Jumper-Thurman, and P. and L. Littlethunder. "Community Readiness and Prevention Programs," *Journal of Community Development* 28(1) (1997): 65–83.

Edwards, R. W., P. Jumper-Thurman, B. A. Plested, E. R. Oetting, and L. Swanson. "Community Readiness: Research to Practice," *Journal of Community Psychology* 28(3) (2000): 291–307.

Oetting, E. R., J. R. Donnermeyer, B. A. Plested, R. W. Edwards, K. Kelly, and F. Beauvais. "Assessing Community Readiness for Prevention," *International Journal of Addictions* 30(6) (1995): 659–683.

Oetting, E. R., P. Jumper-Thurman, B. Plested, and R. W. Edwards. "Community Readiness and Health Services," *Substance Use and Misuse* 36 (2001): 6 (7), 825–843.

Plested, B. A., P. Jumper-Thurman, R. Edwards, and E. R. Oetting. "Community Readiness: A Tool for Community Empowerment," *Prevention Researcher* 5(2) (1998).

Plested, B. A., D. M. Smitham, P. Jumper-Thurman, E. R. Oetting, and R. W. Edwards. "Readiness for Drug Use Prevention in Rural Minority Communities," *Journal of Substance Use and Misuse* 34(4,5) (1999): 521–544.

Quinn, D. *The Story of B.* New York: Bantam Books, 1996.

Mobilizing Communities to Reduce Substance Abuse in Indian Country

9

BERNARD H. ELLIS JR.

⊡

THE IMPACT OF SUBSTANCE ABUSE is notable on Indian reservations in the United States and in the border communities surrounding them. Beginning in 1989, one Indian country community, McKinley County, New Mexico, developed and implemented a series of alcohol policy and program reforms that have reduced the impact of substance abuse on this community. Learning from the McKinley County experience, Fremont County, Wyoming, home of the Wind River Indian Reservation, has implemented similar reforms. This chapter introduces the efforts to reduce substance abuse and delineates the specific innovations implemented in these communities. The influence that these two communities have had on substance abuse policy and programming in New Mexico and Wyoming is also reviewed.

Much has been written regarding substance abuse problems among American Indians. While a number of studies have shown that the proportion of Indians who drink is equal to or lower than that of the rest of the U.S. population, these studies have also shown that the prevalence of problem drinking among Indians who drink is two to three times higher than among the general U.S. population (Kunitz and Levy 1994; May 1989, 1982a; Whittaker 1982). Alcohol is a factor in five of the ten leading causes of mortality for American Indians (Becker et al. 1993; IHS 1993). In the criminal justice arena, substance abuse contributes to most police and court activities involving Indians (May 1982b).

Until the last decade, alcohol policy reform had seldom been utilized effectively for preventing substance abuse problems in Indian country. Since that time, researchers and government agencies have called on impacted communities to emphasize primary prevention using social policy initiatives, environmental change, and broadly based action (May 1992). In the late 1980s, a major challenge remained: to apply these ideas to Indian communities in real-life situations in which power, politics, economic interests, ideology, individual rights, and the democratic process all interacted (Saunders 1989; Morgan 1988; O'Gorman 1988; Robinson and Thether 1985). Developing a consensus regarding which policies to use to reduce substance abuse was expected to be difficult in border town areas, given their multicultural and multijurisdictional nature (May 1992).

Although the potential for community-wide policy and normative change in Indian country was viewed as immense, implementing such change was expected to be treacherous and slow. After all, going from science to social policy is always uncertain and is highly influenced by type of scientific evidence, cultural and social influences, timing, and many other factors. It needed, then, detailed examples of successful efforts to implement change in Indian country and border town communities so that the path could be made smoother for others. Two communities, McKinley County, New Mexico, and Fremont County, Wyoming, present successful examples of broadly based policy and programmatic changes that reduced substance abuse within Indian country.

McKinley County, New Mexico, is located in the northwest corner of the state, not far from the point where the corners of Arizona, New Mexico, Colorado, and Utah meet. McKinley County contains approximately 43,000 American Indians who are members of the Navajo Nation, the Pueblo of Zuni, and other tribes (Daw and Mosher 1994).

To a great extent, societies get the type of behavior that they allow (MacAndrew and Edgerton 1969). For many years, McKinley was the most notorious county in the United States for profiting from its proximity to several large "dry" reservations by placing few restrictions on the sale and use of alcohol. McKinley County's main border town (and the county seat), Gallup—widely known as "Drunk Town"—has been heavily impacted by alcohol abuse for decades. It has over sixty liquor outlets, exceeding New Mexico's quota system by fifty. The National Institute on Alcoholism and Alcohol Abuse (NIAAA) reported that McKinley County had the highest composite index of alcohol-related mortality of all United States counties for the 1975–1977 period (NIAAA 1981). In 1975, the mortality rate for cirrhosis of the liver in McKinley County was 2.3 times higher than the national average, the alcohol-induced mortality rate was 9.8 times higher, and mortality from all alcohol-related causes was 3.7 times higher.

The impetus for the transformation of "Drunk Town" (and the rest of McKinley County) was the considerable media attention that Gallup received in 1988 after the *Albuquerque Tribune* published a six-part exposé, "Gallup: A Town under the Influence" (Guthrie 1988). Broadcast media followed up on the story, and segments on Gallup's severe substance abuse problems were aired on NBC's *Today Show*, ABC's *20/20*, PBS's *McNeil-Lehrer News Hour*, and the syndicated *Inside Edition* (Gomez 1989; Sneddon 1990). The unflattering media attention that

McKinley County received demanded the attention of community and tribal leaders and a broad section of the citizenry and mobilized the entire community to action (Daw and Mosher 1994). Beginning in 1989, a number of initiatives were launched in McKinley County, including the following:

- The March of Hope: A 200-mile march from Gallup to the state capital (Santa Fe), involving over 2,000 participants, fostered the development of a community coalition to bridge the gap between what was historically perceived by state leaders as McKinley's local "Indian problem" and the more global concerns of regional and state lawmakers.
- The Robert Wood Johnson Foundation's Fighting Back program: In 1989, the Foundation selected northwest New Mexico as one of fourteen sites for the Fighting Back program. Northwest New Mexico Fighting Back received a seven-year, multi-million-dollar grant that it used to mobilize tribal and nontribal communities, to generate support for many new alcohol reform initiatives, to mold a new set of community leaders, and to keep track of the community's progress.
- End of liquor sales at drive-up windows: Despite vigorous opposition from the powerful state liquor lobby, the New Mexico legislature allowed a local referendum on closing drive-up alcohol sales windows. The referendum passed in McKinley County by a three-to-one vote of the electorate. The windows were closed in 1992.
- Local alcohol excise tax: A local-option referendum allowing McKinley County to impose a 5 percent wholesale alcohol excise tax was approved in 1989 by a four-to-one vote. This tax was enacted in 1990 and now generates $750,000 per year for local efforts to reduce substance abuse.
- Na'nizhoozhi Center (NCI): This 250-bed center for treatment of substance abuse has replaced the "drunk tank" of the Gallup jail. NCI provides detoxification, short-term treatment, and referral services, as well as a month-long program (Eagle Plume) incorporating Navajo and Zuni healing traditions.
- Alcohol server training: McKinley County organized the first Responsible Hospitality Council in New Mexico in 1989, and began a sixteen-hour training program for alcohol servers in 1991.
- Sunday alcohol sales ban: McKinley was the first New Mexico county to ban alcohol sales on Sundays, a decision that later became state law. When this state law was repealed in 1994, Gallup led the state in a successful petition for the return of its Sunday sales ban.
- DWI (driving while intoxicated) reform: McKinley became the first New Mexico county to lower the presumed intoxication level from 0.10 to 0.08

for arrests for driving while intoxicated and to institute mandatory jail
time for persons convicted of multiple DWIs.
- Closing troublesome bars: A number of Gallup bars have been closed for
  repeat code violations or have decided to relocate outside the city. The
  increased diligence of code enforcement, as well as the enforcement of
  other liquor laws, has reduced the frequency of inappropriate alcohol
  sales.

Since the initiation of McKinley's efforts to reduce substance abuse, community
leaders and others have been interested in measuring the effects of the innovations
in substance abuse policy and practice. The public release of a comprehensive report in late 1994, developed with support from the Fighting Back initiative,
sparked particular interest (Ellis 1994). *Taking the Long View: A Review of Substance
Abuse-Related Social Indicators in McKinley County, New Mexico* provided documentation
of McKinley's long-term improvement across a number of indicators, including
mortality and morbidity, crime, traffic accidents, adolescent substance use, alcohol sales, and admissions for treatment for substance abuse. A follow-up report, *A
Longer View*, found that these indicators had continued to improve through 1995
(Ellis 1997). This report showed that, between 1974 and 1995, McKinley's mortality rate for motor vehicle accidents declined by 60 percent and was matched by
similar declines in mortality from homicide (58 percent), suicide (59 percent), alcohol-induced causes (30 percent), and drug-induced causes (50 percent). It indicated that, between 1989 and 1995, alcohol-related arrests had declined 42
percent in Gallup, and protective custody detentions had been cut in half. Finally,
the report indicated that, between 1982 and 1995, traffic crashes declined 32 percent in McKinley County. All declines experienced in McKinley County exceeded
improvements in New Mexico and the nation.

As these reports circulated throughout Indian country, McKinley County
leaders received requests from other communities for advice on implementing similar policies and programs to reduce substance abuse. Among these communities
was Fremont County, Wyoming, which encompasses the Wind River Indian
Reservation. Fremont is in the north-central portion of Wyoming and has a population of around 36,000, approximately 7,000 of whom are American Indians.
The majority of Indian people are Eastern Shoshone or Northern Arapaho, the
two resident tribes.

Leaders from the Eastern Shoshone and Northern Arapaho tribes, as well as
other community leaders from throughout Fremont County, made a series of visits to McKinley County, beginning in the summer of 1997, to learn firsthand
about the successful strategies implemented there (Freese 1997a, b; Over 1997a,
b). Four separate visits to McKinley, involving forty-five key tribal and nontribal

leaders, occurred over the next year. In addition, McKinley County leaders visited Fremont County on three separate occasions to bring information on their positive experiences to larger audiences in Wyoming. Public meetings on and off the Wind River Indian Reservation drew hundreds of interested citizens (Ferguson 1997a, b, c; Newman 1997a, b).

Convinced that elements of the McKinley model would be worth repeating in Fremont County, the leaders who had visited McKinley organized themselves and a large group of interested citizens into five task forces to prioritize the elements needed in Fremont and to begin implementing them. Since the release of the task force recommendations in early 1998, Fremont County has implemented the following policies and programs, modeled on the McKinley example:

- Abate Substance Abuse Project (ASAP): This nonprofit organization is modeled on McKinley County's Fighting Back program and has spearheaded initiatives to reduce substance abuse in Fremont County.
- Jail-based treatment for substance abuse: In 1998, Fremont County taxpayers approved a capital facilities tax to build a new Fremont County detention center to replace the overcrowded jail. This facility was designed to accommodate a treatment pod for sixty adult inmates, a twenty-eight-bed juvenile wing, and substance abuse programs for all inmates.
- Fremont County Alcohol Crisis Center (FCACC): This is a twenty-eight-bed version of the Na'nizhoozhi Center. It provides both short- and long-term residential detoxification and treatment referral services, and to serve chronic substance abusers, it works closely with the Fremont County Detention Center and with tribal and nontribal providers of treatment for substance abuse. Since its inception, public intoxication arrests have declined 82 percent in Fremont County.
- Adolescent programs: Two new programs were developed to serve at-risk adolescents. Pathfinder is an alternative high school for students who have dropped out or been removed from other school settings, and the KICK-IT program is an intensive outpatient treatment program for substance-abusing youth. KICK-IT involves the first instance of joint case management, by tribal and nontribal treatment agencies, for juveniles in Fremont County.
- Alcohol server training: In 1999, over half of all alcohol servers in Wyoming who were trained in responsible hospitality techniques received their training in Fremont County.
- Fewer drive-up windows for alcohol sales: The city of Riverton has restricted the hours for drive-up alcohol sales, and some Fremont County alcohol sellers have voluntarily closed their drive-up windows.

- Special courts: Adult and juvenile substance abuse courts have been established to provide treatment in lieu of incarceration for substance-abusing offenders.
- Prevention of underage drinking: Despite Wyoming's widespread cultural and legal acceptance of underage drinking, Fremont County persuaded the state to apply for federal funds for preventing drinking by minors. As a result, many communities now have active programs for preventing drinking by minors and enforcing laws about the legal drinking age.
- Joint powers: In order to implement substance-abuse-reduction efforts in a cooperative manner, the ASAP board of directors is now appointed by both tribal and nontribal governments in Fremont County and is empowered to pursue resources collectively to serve all communities there. The ASAP board provides oversight for both the FCACC and the KICK-IT programs.
- Media support: Wyoming media have run numerous stories on Fremont County's innovations. The Fremont media have actively supported efforts to reduce substance abuse. From 1997 to 2002, over 400 articles have been written about the Fremont initiatives.

These two Indian communities in McKinley and Fremont counties mobilized their citizenry to address local substance abuse problems through coordinated and community-supported initiatives. They developed a long-term mentoring relationship to enhance their efforts. They have modeled the benefits of specific policies and programs and have helped lead successful efforts to extend these innovations statewide. Finally, these two communities have witnessed the challenges that often face community-based efforts as these efforts mature and draw more resistance from the alcohol industry and other vested interests.

These two efforts at reducing substance abuse of course have much in common since Fremont leaders studied the McKinley experience in depth and sought the long-term advice of McKinley leaders throughout the development of their own efforts. But these communities had other things in common that also contributed to their successes. Both communities developed a community-based coalition, led by well-informed tribal and nontribal leaders, to build consensus for reducing substance abuse. In both counties these early efforts involved, and were embraced by, tribal elders and recovering persons. In addition, both communities received considerable local and statewide media coverage of both the heavy toll of substance abuse in these communities and the efforts to reduce the problem.

Both communities also had access to local epidemiological evidence that not only informed decision makers and the public about the dimensions of the substance abuse problem in their areas but also helped monitor progress (Ellis, Glover, and

Heilman 1999a, b). Both communities faced (and continue to face) well-organized opposition from vested interests (e.g., the alcohol industry and its allied politicians). These two communities have become important models that have helped shape public policy within their own states and throughout Indian country. The experiences of McKinley County provided an excellent opportunity for Fremont County to learn from a community with a decade of experience with implementing a coordinated approach to reducing substance abuse. The elements of the McKinley experience that Fremont County believed necessary to replicate were as follows:

- A core group of leaders collectively developed a commitment to work cooperatively and accomplish set objectives.
- Research-based evidence was used to compare local conditions with the state and the nation across a host of indicators related to substance abuse.
- Substance abuse problems of all populations within the county (rather than those of Indian people only) were researched to reinforce the message that substance abuse affected, and involved, all people.
- The importance of harnessing the energies and ideas of community members on and off the reservation was acknowledged.
- The media were involved in a sustained effort to educate the general public and other decision makers in the county, the state, and the nation about the local problems related to substance abuse.
- Small, focused work groups were needed to identify, support, plan, and accomplish a definable set of targeted interventions.
- A coordinated and well-organized effort was made to obtain grants to enhance the local resource base.
- Local funds were raised to support elements of the effort to reduce substance abuse.

In addition to these overall components, Fremont leaders identified several specific interventions in McKinley County that they felt were important to replicate. These included therapeutic interventions instead of incarceration for public intoxication offenders, training program for alcohol servers, and a partnership with local media to inform audiences of the severity of the substance abuse problem and of the value of working collectively to reduce the problem.

Fremont County was fortunate to have the McKinley "road map" and could avoid some of the hurdles that took up much time and energy in McKinley County. But Fremont County faced some different hurdles, related in part to its much larger non-Indian population. As a result, it was necessary from the beginning to focus on the entire population of Fremont County and to discuss the impact of substance abuse on, and among, all ethnic groups in the county and state.

Fortunately, the Fremont initiative was launched at the same time a statewide needs assessment was under way to highlight the prevalence of substance abuse among all populations in the state (Ellis et al. 2001a, b). Fremont used information from this large-scale research project to help keep the focus on substance abuse in the county and state. Thus, Indian people were an important part of a much larger effort rather than the sole focus of the research and interventions.

One serious problem Fremont County faced that had not been addressed in depth in McKinley's innovations was substance abuse among adolescents. But the process used to identify interventions for adolescent populations in Fremont County benefited from the same methods used to arrive at consensus in the other task forces working in areas addressed in McKinley County.

Fremont faced several impediments that were somewhat different from McKinley's experience. The presence of two tribes (the Eastern Shoshone and the Northern Arapaho) on the same reservation, with their separate and combined tribal governments and elders, required appropriate attention to ensure support from and involvement of both tribes in the effort. In addition, Fremont had a number of cities, towns, and villages on and off the Wind River Indian Reservation to both engage and serve whereas McKinley had only Gallup.

In retrospect, another impediment faced by the Fremont effort was the very success that McKinley had modeled for them. When McKinley received approval from the New Mexico legislature to pursue some of its innovations, it was viewed as a unique situation, and legislators did not extend approval for other counties to pursue the same options. However, the successes that McKinley achieved and documented later influenced decisions to change policies statewide in New Mexico. When the Fremont group, in its own public education and planning process, focused on McKinley County as their mentor and model, they unintentionally alerted both the Wyoming alcohol industry and advocates of less government that similar statewide changes might be in the offing.

The Fremont group also faced a different regulatory and cultural environment in terms of involving alcohol sellers in the change process. The political influence of this group and the widespread cultural support for heavy alcohol consumption and underage drinking that existed in Wyoming in the late 1990s were powerful forces opposing progress. These impediments remain strong and well-funded in Wyoming, and their influence extends into using the political process to delay progress and muddy the focus of even the most well-intended community-based groups in Wyoming today.

Despite the differences between these two Indian country communities, the Fremont group was able to identify goals and objectives and to design and implement several significant initiatives that can be traced directly to the McKinley model. The FCACC is a small version of the Na'nizhoozhi Center in McKinley

County, but it is having a similar dramatic, positive effect on the chronic public intoxication problem. Using a local tax initiative to fund the Fremont County Detention Center, with its planned substance-abuse-treatment services, also was modeled on McKinley County's tax initiative. The alcohol-server training program, initiated in 1998 in Fremont County, even benefited directly by having the person who had developed the McKinley program conduct the first training sessions in Fremont. Finally, the considerable media attention that the Fremont County initiatives stimulated used the McKinley County mentoring relationship as a consistent story line.

But even those Fremont County initiatives that were not modeled directly on McKinley benefited from the models of cross-cultural cooperation and the heightened interest in addressing substance abuse problems that the Fremont-McKinley dialogue engendered. In producing the initiatives aimed at adolescents, particularly the KICK-IT program, a cooperative process was developed that brought tribal and nontribal treatment and social service providers to the same table. The drug courts for adults and juveniles in tribal and county courts are also being implemented in a coordinated fashion to allow these jurisdictions to share resources and better serve overlapping clients.

McKinley County's influence on the national movements to encourage community coalitions to reduce substance abuse has been far-reaching. More than two dozen delegations have visited McKinley County, including delegations from South Africa and India, to learn about the McKinley innovations and their impact. Elements of the McKinley model have been replicated in dozens of communities throughout the Navajo Nation, the Zuni Nation, and the Pueblos of Acoma and Laguna. Many other tribes and Indian country communities have been exposed to the McKinley model through involvement in the Robert Wood Johnson Foundation's Fighting Back and Healthy Nations programs, as well as the Center for Substance Abuse Treatment's Targeted Capacity Expansion program.

It would be worthwhile to chart the dissemination of the McKinley innovations throughout Indian country. But there is no more concrete evidence for the influence of good community models than the number of statewide changes in New Mexico that were influenced by McKinley County's experience. These include dedicating a larger share of state and local alcohol taxes to fund efforts to reduce substance abuse, mandating training for alcohol servers, more stringently enforcing DUI laws, and addressing public intoxication in a more therapeutic fashion. Perhaps the most visible impact of this influence was the use of data on McKinley's traffic crash trends to support the statewide closure of drive-up windows for alcohol sales, enacted in 1998 (Ellis and Tomada 1998).

Because Fremont County's initiatives are less than five years old, it is perhaps premature to speak about their statewide influence. However, the increased awareness of and concern about substance abuse in Wyoming since 1997 have been influenced by activities in Fremont County. Fremont County led the way in a statewide campaign for voluntary training for alcohol servers, and it helped bring federal funds to the state for prevention of underage drinking. Fremont tribal and nontribal leaders have been involved in the implementation of a statewide network of drug courts and the expansion of treatment services for incarcerated populations. Legislation has been introduced in Wyoming to create a protective custody alternative to arrest in order to address chronic public intoxication more therapeutically. More importantly, the Wyoming legislature increased more than twentyfold its expenditures for substance abuse prevention, intervention, and treatment services in 2001, using the Fremont County conditions and responses to substance abuse to help inform those decisions (State of Wyoming 2002, 2000).

McKinley and Fremont counties represent two successful examples of community efforts to reduce substance abuse in Indian country. They illustrate the power and effectiveness of a long-term, dedicated mentoring effort between two communities with similar populations and problems, and they demonstrate how well-researched local data documented the need for and the impact of their efforts. They also demonstrate the power of good example among communities of like-minded people, both for suggesting policy and programmatic innovations that provide measurable benefits and for modeling better ways of seeking collective solutions to serious social problems.

Notes

"Mobilizing Communities to Reduce Substance Abuse in Indian Country" is an abridged version of "Mobilizing Communities to Reduce Substance Abuse in Indian Country," by Bernard Ellis Jr., M.A., M.P.H., which appeared in the *Journal of Psychoactive Drugs* 35 (1). Reprinted by permission of Haight-Ashbury Publications, 612 Clayton Street, San Francisco, California.

Becker, T. M., C. L. Wiggins, R. S. Elliot, C. R. Key, and J. M. Samet, eds. *Racial and Ethnic Patterns of Mortality in New Mexico*. Albuquerque: University of New Mexico Press, 1993.

Daw, R. and H. Mosher. *The Bridges of McKinley County: Building Rural Recovery Coalitions*. Seattle, Wash.: Third Annual State Systems Development Program, CSAT, 1994.

Ellis, B. H. *A Longer View*. Gallup, N. Mex.: Northwest New Mexico Fighting Back, Inc., 1997.

———. *Taking the Long View: A Review of Substance Abuse-Related Social Indicators in McKinley County, New Mexico*. Gallup, N. Mex.: Northwest New Mexico Fighting Back, Inc., 1994.

Ellis, B. H., and G. Tomada. "Voters Deserve Say in Drive-Up Sales." *Albuquerque Tribune*, February 18, 1998, A9.

Ellis, B. H., W. A. Glover, and B. Heilman. *Fremont's Indicators of Substance Abuse: 1987–98.* Cheyenne, Wyo.: Substance Abuse Division, Wyoming Department of Health, 1999a.

———. *Fremont's Youth: Indicators of Substance Abuse: 1987–98.* Cheyenne, Wyo.: Substance Abuse Division, Wyoming Department of Health, 1999b.

Ellis, B. H., W. A. Glover, G. Price, B. Heilman, and J. Miner. *The Wyoming Substance Abuse Treatment Needs Assessment Project (1995–99): American Indian Studies.* Cheyenne, Wyo.: Substance Abuse Division, Wyoming: Department of Health, 2001a.

———. *The Wyoming Substance Abuse Treatment Needs Assessment Project (1995–99): Integrated Report.* Cheyenne, Wyo.: Substance Abuse Division, Wyoming Department of Health, 2001b.

Ferguson, N. "Big Crowd Hears Alcohol Discussion." *Riverton Ranger,* October 2, 1997a, 1.

———. "Stopping the Toll of Substance Abuse: Officials from McKinley County, New Mexico Are Coming to Fremont County This Weekend." *Riverton Ranger,* September 25, 1997b, 1.

———. "Liquor Dealers, Others Pledge Cooperation in Solving Alcohol Problem." *Riverton Ranger,* September 10, 1997c, 1.

Freese, B. "Gallup Shares Its Recovery from 'Drunk Town.'" *Gallup Independent,* June 13, 1997a, 1.

———. "Traditional Teaching vs. Alcohol: Gallup Teaches Wyoming Town." *Gallup Independent,* June 11, 1997b, 1.

Gomez, D. "Gallup Mayor Threatened after TV Show: Calls Follow '20/20' Segment on Alcoholism." *Albuquerque Tribune,* August 19, 1989, 1.

Guthrie, P. "Gallup: A Town under the Influence." *Albuquerque Tribune,* September 1988, 1.

Indian Health Service (IHS). *Trends in Indian Health.* Rockville, Md.: U.S. Department of Health and Human Services, 1993.

Kunitz, S. L., and J. E. Levy. *Drinking Careers: A Twenty-Five Year Study of Three Navajo Populations.* New Haven, Conn.: Yale University Press, 1994.

MacAndrew, C., and R. B. Edgerton. *Drunken Comportment: A Sociological Explanation.* Chicago: Aldine Press, 1969.

May, P. A. "Alcohol Policy Considerations for Indian Reservations and Border Town Communities," *American Indian and Alaska Native Mental Health Research* 4(3) (1992): 5–59.

———. "Alcohol Abuse and Alcoholism among American Indians: An Overview." In *Alcoholism in Minority Populations,* eds. T. D. Watts and R. Wright. Springfield, Ill.: Charles C. Thomas, 1989.

———. "Substance Abuse and American Indians: Prevalence and Susceptibility," *International Journal on the Addictions* 17 (1982a): 1185–1209.

———. "Contemporary Crime and the American Indian: A Survey and Analysis of the Literature," *Plains Anthropologist* 27 (1982b): 97, 225–238.

Morgan, P. "Power, Politics and Public Health: The Political Power of the Alcohol Beverage Industry," *Journal of Public Health Policy* 9 (1988): 2, 177–197.

National Institute on Alcoholism and Alcohol Abuse (NIAAA). *U.S. Alcohol 1981 Epidemiological Data Reference Manual 3: County Alcohol Problem Indicators: 1975–77.* Rockville, Md.: U.S. Department of Health and Human Services, 1981.

Newman, L. "Leaders Urge Large Crowd in Kinnear to Make It Happen . . . Now," *Wind River News*, October 2, 1997a: 1.

———. "Crowd at Wind River Life Center Agrees "It's Time,'" *Wyoming State Journal*, October 1, 1997b, 1.

O'Gorman, P. A. "The Conflict between Personal Ideology and Prevention Programs," *Alcohol Health and Research World* 12 (1988): 4, 298–303.

Over, E. "County Delegation Heading to Gallup," *Wyoming State Journal*, October 26, 1997a,: 1.

———. "Fremont County's Dirty Little and Not So Secret Problem," *Wyoming State Journal*, August 20, 1997b, 7.

Robinson, D., and P. Thether. "Prevention: Potential at the Local Level," *Alcohol and Alcoholism* 20 (1985): 1, 31–33.

Saunders, B. "Alcohol and Other Drugs: The Prevention Paradoxes," *Community Health Studies* 13 (1989): 2, 150–155.

Sneddon, M. "A Town under the Influence," *McNeil-Lehrer News Hour* (Public Broadcasting System), January 31, 1990.

State of Wyoming. *Reclaiming Wyoming: A Comprehensive Blueprint for Prevention, Early Intervention and Treatment of Substance Abuse.* Cheyenne, Wyo.: Substance Abuse Division, Wyoming Department of Health, 2002.

———. *Wyoming: The Image, the Reality and the Vision.* Cheyenne, Wyo.: Governor's Advisory Board on Substance Abuse and Violent Crime, 2000.

Whittaker, J. O. "Alcohol and the Standing Rock Sioux Tribe: A Twenty-Year Follow-Up Study," *Journal of Studies on Alcohol* 43 (1982): 3, 191–200.

Data Reconnaissance for Native Americans   10

MARY PHILLIPS AND SARAH NEBELKOPF

THE INTRODUCTION OF THE WORLD WIDE WEB has shifted the emphasis of mental health professionals from experiential and academic knowledge to the amount that can be processed at Internet speed. Synthesis of subjectivity and objectivity is the source of intellectual power and responsibility—and truth (Du Bois 1983). The New Freedom Commission on Mental Health has responded to the nation's total technology eventuality by supporting a national health information infrastructure that will transform unequipped health-care facilities into responsive Web-connected centers for the twenty-first century. According to the final report by the President's New Freedom Commission on Mental Health, "Achieving the Promise," in a transformed mental health system, technology is used to access mental health care and information. Recommendations include using health technology and "telehealth" (an integrated information technology and communications infrastructure electronically linked to multiple service systems) to improve access and coordination of mental health care, especially for Americans in remote areas or in underserved populations. The recommendations also include developing and implementing integrated electronic systems for health records and personal health information (DHHS 2003). In nonprofit management, the "accidental techie" has become a common nickname for employees who demonstrate interest or competency in computer language (Forrester 2003). Health-care service providers are closing the digital divide by enacting organizational technology policies and budgeting for computer training.

Managed information systems can promote program sustainability. The authors explore integrating, in a culturally appropriate way, managed information systems with substance abuse and mental health treatment for Native Americans. Creating a coordinated data collection system of care requires a distinct communication line between direct services and effective data collection and management.

The result will include high-quality treatment for clients and dissemination of appropriate data. Community-based participatory research is one approach that has yielded outcomes valuable to researchers and community members (Davis et al. 2002). Effective infrastructure development and deployment require more than purchasing up-to-date hardware and software. They also require an appreciation of how the nonprofit work process, integrating multiple funding criteria and programs, contributes to an organization's mission and mixes with its work flow (Osten, Smith, and Stuart 2003). Many times, nonprofit health organizations function according to the grant funds made available. Although each grant has specific reporting requirements, there is a great deal of commonality among the data sets each requires. At the same time, each funding organization imposes unique data and reporting requirements, and the schedules for reporting also vary. These funding organizations are, in turn, all responsible for reporting to the Department of Health and Human Services. Nonprofit organizations with limited research capacity but positive results find it hard to assemble and communicate their information. As a consequence, their excellent services may fall by the wayside from a lack of recognition, funding, sustainability, capacity expansion, and attention from decision makers.

The Bay Area Red Road (BARR) project provided an opportunity to design and plan a data system that would provide wireless intake and output of information. The project was funded by the Center for Substance Abuse Services of the Substance Abuse and Mental Health Services Administration (SAMHSA). The Family and Child Guidance Clinic (FCGC) of the Native American Health Center (NAHC) received a three-year grant to strengthen the system of treating substance abuse among Native Americans in the San Francisco Bay Area; Friendship House Association of American Indians (FH), in San Francisco, became a subcontractor. The project had multiple purposes: to develop a comprehensive, integrated, and culturally relevant managed information system for the treatment of substance abuse; to increase access to treatment for an underserved population; to increase coordination among service providers; to offer services "under one roof"; and to improve community partnerships. The overall objective was to improve services and reduce the inequities in Native Americans' access to health care. In particular, the project intended to develop an information system that would help non-profit organizations resolve gaps between funding and programming.

The task began with the collaboration of two agencies providing outpatient and residential care for Native Americans. This collaboration provoked a reconditioning of the current Managed Information Systems (MIS) shared between the collaborators, which is used as a depository for data information and trafficking its uses, then storing the data to later be manipulated into output for coordinated reporting. Such a system provides organizations with the armory to report the most vital and lucrative commodity of the outsource knowledge epoch, that is, data.

The mental health department of NAHC, FCGC, a 501(c)(3) agency, has provided outpatient mental health and substance abuse services for Native Americans in the five-county Bay Area for over thirteen years. It provides its services for clients at various levels of treatment. Located in the Fruitvale district of Oakland, an area alive with many cultures, FCGC uses an innovative model for health services within a comprehensive and integrated system of care for those suffering from substance abuse, mental illness, and HIV/AIDS. NAHC's mission is

> to assist American Indians and Alaska Natives to improve and maintain their physical, mental, emotional, social and spiritual well-being with respect for cultural traditions, and to advocate for the needs of all Indian people, especially the most vulnerable members of our community. (NAHC 2003)

Friendship House is a 501(c)(3), tax-exempt corporation. It incorporated in 1973 to serve American Indians relocated from their reservations to the San Francisco Bay Area. FH is state licensed, certified, and nationally accredited by the Commission on Accreditation of Rehabilitation Facilities (CARF). FH operates two culturally relevant residential facilities, a thirty-bed residential treatment facility in San Francisco and a five-bed residential substance abuse facility in Oakland for American Indian women and their children. Along with substance abuse treatment, FH offers aftercare, women's health care, job readiness support, youth services aimed at preventing substance abuse, outreach, and health education for American Indians. FH is dedicated to carrying out its mission:

> To promote healing and wellness in the American Indian community by providing a continuum of substance abuse prevention, treatment, and recovery services that integrate the traditional American Indian healing practices and state-of-the-art substance abuse treatment methodology. (FH 2003)

The BARR project supports a continuum of care consisting of best practices based on clinical research and successful outcomes demonstrated by local outcome data. FH and the FCGC integrate culturally appropriate American Indian traditional strategies with proven substance abuse treatment methods in a core system of care. A system of care is a child-centered, family-focused, coordinated, community-based, and culturally competent approach to provide children with access to a comprehensive array of services (Stroul and Friedman 1986). Several models created by and for Native American communities that have been successful for our patients in recovery are based on varied tribal teachings. These culturally relevant models reflect solutions used by clinicians, community organizers, and healers.

Systems Resource through Collaboration

The effort to strengthen the San Francisco Bay Area Indian community through linkages has been going on for years. Building a sound system of care with a technology interface achieves these goals: to build a centralized intake system between residential and outpatient care; to implement a shared, Web-based database system; to track clients for evaluation and coordination of client care; to streamline infrastructure to improve communication; and to create a stable infrastructure for internal and external data transmission. In order to keep our direct services human while also meeting an assortment of data and reporting needs, we decided to track individuals, not ethnic groups; to provide instant identification of current and past caregivers; to offer immediate consultation for critical care or long-term tracking; to track clients' episodic encounters with the system of care; to provide clinical assessment results quickly; to share assessment outcomes in order to reduce intake time; and to eliminate redundancy and consolidate obscure data systems into one for quality control. While bold efforts to improve service for culturally diverse populations are currently under way, significant barriers in access, quality, and outcomes of care still thwart minorities (DHHS, 2003).

The work group began its task by creating a blueprint for its in-house database. The team members collected and recorded the data operations of each agency. Each agency disseminates information to various stakeholders through a flow of information and files. Upon documenting and mapping specific patterns of this flow, we identified barriers within the internal and external data systems of each agency. This preplanning phase included input from all project members involved in timely, system-wide data collection, manual and electronic, required by funding agencies.

The collected information helped prepare for the adaptation process, to enable the system's work flow to absorb the impact of the transition from paper to data entry screens. The BARR transition factors included invasive client interaction while data entering; initializing new client process flow efficacy; the disruption of service; the import and export of data to multiple funder databases' encryption process; and securing the Information Technology (IT) environment by monitoring its capacity expansion needs. Next the planners produced a requirements document, which clearly pictured the strengths and weaknesses of our current data flow. The document also recommended the staff positions needed and their duties.

The workgroup next planned for the purchase of software applications and hardware components for building and expanding our database. Extensive time was devoted to researching the services and costs of various Internet Service Providers and servers. The group worked with information technology (IT) staff to avert problems associated with integrating new hardware and software components with existing ones.

Recommendations

Only recently have funders and nonprofits alike begun to view capacity building as a way for nonprofits to be more effective (McInerney 2003). Nonprofit organizations experience gross changes in funding priorities from the federal government, from month to month in some cases, or from new grants, which increase the organization's scope of work. Such changes place more and more demands on information systems. Responding effectively to growing demands typically requires organizations to evolve from a reactive stance into stable, planned operations. (McNamara 1999). Nonprofit organizations can focus on strengthening relationships with funders by consulting with them before building new databases. In addition, we advocate avoiding some of the problems created when databases are designed and implemented without recognizing the needs of direct service providers and the specific needs of culturally relevant mental health programs and substance abuse treatment. The mainstream service system reflects the needs of the funding agencies instead of the needs of the clients. Community-based programs are caught in the middle, but with far too little in the way of resources to do a good job (Nebelkopf, Phillips, and King 2001). Table 10.1 illustrates the BARR

Table 10.1.   BARR Correlation of Project Needs and Database Design

Identified Needs and Barriers	Corresponding Component of MIS/IT Action Plan
Expand MIS/IT capacity Increase MIS/IT staff positions Plan database Implement database Continue training and support	Chart data flow Design a requirements document to develop a web-based database Build and implement Web-based database with import/export data transfer to funders' databases Add MIS/IT line item to organizational budget
Anticipate shifts in governmental funding priorities	Network with funders Research potential technology
Obtain buy-in by key stakeholders	Communicate needs with key stakeholders Conduct database usability assessments Advocate cultural competency component
Maintain, expand, and harmonize hardware and software Fund purchase costs Fund upgrade costs Fund maintenance costs Fund sustainability costs	Increase collaboration and communication with referral agencies, funding organizations, and subcontractors. Conduct strategic technology needs assessment Research Health Insurance Portability and Accountability Act (HIPAA) requirements and include in organizational strategic planning and technology planning (including timeline) Provide technology cost analysis

project approach, which correlates the project needs and barriers with an Action Plan for a database in a mental health setting.

Nonprofit organizations that rely on multiple funding sources must comply with certain best practices that ultimately affect operations. Adhering to all legislative and regulatory standards imposed by local, state, and federal government bureaus creates dilemmas in reporting. In addition, incorporating the organization's accreditation standards and the requirements of the Health Insurance Portability and Accountability Act (HIPAA) to improve patient confidentiality place immense time demands on organizations. The load is not lightened when the policies imposed by regulatory agencies are inconsistent and occasionally contradict each other.

From the Data Community to the Native Community

Strengthening data collection in the Native American community has helped prioritize programmatic investments for a concentrated funding strategy. Organizational sustainability requires this type of collaboration that speaks to specific cultures.

The BARR project's primary reason for designing and implementing a culturally relevant database is to have full access to data that is collected internally and stored in house. Funder-required databases rarely allow full access to information once it is exported, sent to a collection of unmanaged subsets, and then archived, purged, or deleted. The cultural aspect of the BARR project is that data criteria are determined collectively by members of the community to effectively treat clients in an in-house data center. The MIS/IT teams work with the decision-making staff and the community on an ongoing basis to ensure that all relevant data on Native Americans are being collected and reported. "Change is usually best carried out as a team-wide effort. . . . To sustain change, the structures of the organization itself should be modified, including strategic plans, policies and procedures" (McNamara 1999).

Our Logic Model (fig. 10.1) represents a plan for implementing managed information systems using a community-sensitive applied research outcome. It includes imperative steps in planning segments of the route to create stable reporting systems, which in turn create viable options to use information for progress. The steps include *collaboration* among agencies that collect data on Native Americans to establish a *consensus building* process, bringing a focus to data collection efforts in the community; assessment of the *service delivery* tracking system utilized in the clinical care continuum; preparation for the *programmatic impact* technology will have on the relationship between caregiver and client; *MIS* outcomes from culturally perceptive data collection; *decision making* guided

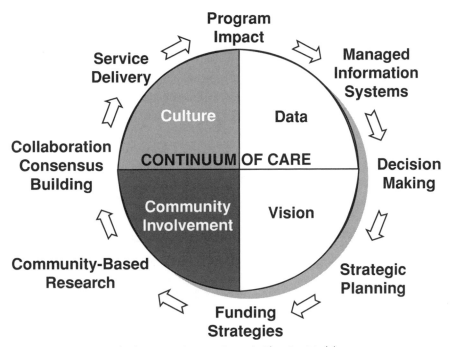

Figure 10.1.   Managed Information Systems Strategic Planning Model

by data results; *strategic planning* by the decision makers for sustainable programming; and *funding strategies* based on the direction of the strategic plan, which
provides a mode for *community-based research*. These segments revolve around aspects of a cultural community and community-based data that support a continuum of care.

   In the future, it will become increasingly important to leverage resources for
the growing technology needs of organizations. We anticipate that the transition
from the planning process to the implementation phase of our technology efforts
will require additional staff time and expertise. Having the capacity for dedicated
MIS/IT staff is becoming a crucial component of nonprofit organizations, especially in the fields of mental health and substance abuse treatment. Nonprofits
that have an MIS/IT team will be more organized and efficient, taking much of
the burden of data tracking and reporting away from the clinical staff. Clinical
teams can then focus more on treatment and spend more time working with the
clients. In organizations that are growing and building capacity, increased training
and increased data management staff are necessary to meet the increased demands
of funders and capacity expansion.

Notes

Davis, J. D., J. S. Erickson, S. R. Johnson, C. A. Marshall, P. Running Wolf, and R. L. Santiago, eds. *Work Group on American Indian Research and Program Evaluation Methodology; Lifespan Issues Related to American Indians/Alaska Natives with Disabilities.* Flagstaff: Northern Arizona University, American Indian Rehabilitation Research and Training Center, 2002, p. 12.

Department of Health and Human Services (DHHS). New Freedom Commission on Mental Health, Achieving the Promise: Transforming Mental Health Care in America. Final Report. Rockville, Md.: DHHS, 2003.

Du Bois, B. "Passionate Scholarship: Notes on Values, Knowing and Method in Feminist Social Science." In *Theories of Women's Studies,* ed. G. Bowles and R. D. Klein. Boston: Routledge and Kegan Paul, 1983, pp. 105–116.

Forrester, J. J. "Revolution or Evolution: A Longitudinal Study of Technology Use by Nonprofit Organizations." Bayer Center for Nonprofit Management: Robert Morris University, Pittsburgh, Pennsylvania, 2003, p. 23.

Friendship House Association of American Indians of San Francisco (FH). Mission statement. http://www.friendshiphouseSF.org (accessed July 1, 2003).

McInerney, Paul-Brian. *Nonprofits, NTAPs and Information Technology.* Nonprofit Technology Enterprise Network, San Francisco, California, 2003, p. 3.

McNamara, C. *Basic Context for Organizational Change.* 1999. http://www.mapnp.org/library/mgmnt/orgchnge.htm (accessed September 30, 2003).

Native American Health Center (NAHC). Mission Statement. http://www.native-health.org (accessed July 1, 2003).

Nebelkopf, E., M. Phillips, and J. King. *Strategic Plan: A Holistic Model for a System of Care for Native Americans in the San Francisco Bay Area.* Oakland, Calif.: Native American Health Center, 2001.

Osten, M. J., J. Smith, and R. Stuart. *From Obstacles to Opportunities: Six Interlocking Elements of Strategic Technology Grantmaking.* http://www.summitcollaborative.com (accessed August 8, 2003).

Stroul, B., and R. Friedman. *A System of Care for Children and Youth with Severe Emotional Disturbances.* Washington, D.C.: National Technical Assistance Center for Children's Mental Health, 1986.

TRADITIONAL CEREMONIES AND HEALING   IV

THE DOCUMENTATION OF traditional Native American healing practices is crucial in bridging the gap between Native culture and Western medicine. Larry Murillo, a member of the board of directors of the Native American Health Center, provides a balanced perspective on traditional healing and justifies the need for support of these practices. There is very little on the efficacy of traditional healing practices. J. Phillip Gossage, Ruthie Alexius, Pamela G. Monaghan-Geernaert, and Philip A. May provide both quantitative and qualitative data on the Peacemaking Ceremony, a traditional Navajo healing practice. Otis Parrish, a Kashaya Pomo elder, renders an in-depth description of the framework of his tribe's traditional healing practices. Fascinating is the Kashaya interweaving of dreams, herbs, emotions, and prayer in their healing ceremonies. Otis's mother, Essie Parrish, was an herbalist, sucking doctor, and the last Kashaya prophet. In 1972, she spoke about her healing journey (as recorded by George Quasha in *Somapoetics*) in a lecture at the New School for Social Research in New York City:

> It is a test you have to pass. Then you can learn to heal. 'Be careful on the journey,' they said, 'the journey to heaven.' They warned me. And I so I went thru [sic] the rolling hills. I walked and walked, through mountains and valleys, and rolling hills. I walked, and walked and walked. You hear many things there in those rolling hills and valleys. And I walked and walked and walked until I came to a footbridge. And on the right side were a whole lot of people. And they were naked and crying out 'How'd you get over there?'
>
> They said, 'We want to get over there too, but we're stuck here. Please come over here and help us cross, the water's too deep for us.' I didn't pay no attention, I just walked and walked and walked. And then I heard an animal, sounded like a huge dog and next to him a huge lady, wearing blue clothes. And I decided I had to walk right thru [sic] and I did. And the dog only snarled at me. Never go back. I walked

and walked and walked. And I came to only one tree, and I walked over to it and looked up at it and read the message, 'Go on, you're half way.'

From there I felt better, a little better. And I walked and walked and walked and walked. And I saw water, huge water. How to get thru [sic]? I fear it's deep. Very blue water.

But I have to go. Put out the first foot, then the left. Never use the left hand. And I passed thru [sic]. Went on and on and on, and I had to enter a place and there I had to look down.

It was hot and there were people there. And they looked tiny down there in that furnace, running around crying. I had to enter.

You see, these tests are to teach my people how to live. Fire didn't burn me. And I walked and walked and walked. On the way you're going to suffer. And I came to a four-way road, like a cross. Which is the right way? I already knew.

—Essie Parrish, Kashaya Pomo

Perspectives on Traditional Health Practices   11

LARRY MURILLO

T HE PROFESSIONAL LITERATURE related to American Indian/Alaska Native (AI/AN) traditional health practices (THP) is growing. This article uses a broader perspective on THP that includes the practice of medicine people, community ceremonies, and any other socio-cultural practices, beliefs, attitudes, and behaviors related to health from an AI/AN perspective. This perspective will broaden the discussion beyond access to sociocultural resources, such as a medicine person or specific practices such as sweat lodges and talking circles, which are noted in professional journals. This broadened perspective will more accurately portray the complexity of health issues in AI/AN communities.

Four issues are presented to illuminate the need for employing and researching THP for AI/AN communities. The first issue identifies support for and barriers to THP in public health research. The second issue describes competing cultural values that have implications for the definition and treatment of illness. The third issue is a brief discussion of broadening community support for THP through building resource capacity using a healthy-community concept. The fourth and last issue will address implications for research and the potential benefits for AI/AN communities.

THP are cited in various professional journals, and their use has been the focus of several studies. Buchwald et al. (2000) report that 70 percent of urban AI/AN patients in primary care used traditional health practices. The results of this study suggest that health care providers should anticipate use of THP among urban AI/AN clients. Kim and Kwok (1998) found that 62 percent of Navajo patients had used Native healers, and 39 percent used Native healers on a regular basis. Their study summarized the most common reasons for visits to a medical provider and the frequency of concomitant use of Native healers. Use of Native healers was highest for arthritis, abdominal pain, depression/anxiety, and chest pain. Gurley et al. (2001) studied service use among AI/AN veterans, comparing use patterns of biomedical care with those of traditional healing options and testing whether utilization varied as a function of need or of availability. Results indicate that traditional options were used more where such options were more readily available. The current service ecology on the Northern Plains and Southwest reservations incorporates both traditional and biomedical forms and has been described aptly as a pluralistic system.

Several researchers have studied such specific traditional practices as the talking circle, storytelling, and sweat lodges. The talking circle produced consistent and significant improvement in levels of knowledge about cancer. Storytelling was combined with the talking circle in one study, and the researchers found that storytelling and talking circles are valuable tools for improving the health of AI/AN people. The sweat lodge ceremony (SLC) has been an integral part of Navajo (and many other tribes') culture for hundreds of years. The role of the SLC has examined in jail-based treatment of alcohol abuse and is a start in providing empirical insight into the traditional ways of Native Americans.

Talking circles, storytelling, and sweat lodge ceremonies comprise a small sample of THP used for individual and community health interventions. Studies are needed of THP utilizing Native healers, herbal medicines, cultural diets, philosophy, traditional ceremonial grounds, healing ceremonies, and traditional forms of living such as hunting, fishing, and shepherding. "Healthy" THP, such as learning an AI/AN language, running, participating in cultural games or powwows or arts and crafts, and recognizing "life passage" events (e.g., birth, death, and marriage), also play a role in the broad sense of healing.

Many indications point to the effectiveness of THP. Native and nonnative professionals alike are beginning to see the benefit of THP use in AI/AN health agencies. The first landmark support for THP came in 1978, when the American Indian Religious Freedoms Act was passed, signaling the United States government's recognition of traditional medicines and religious ceremonies in health-related matters among AI/AN people. In spite of the repression of Native religions, the ancient art of indigenous healing has survived intact and is still practiced today. Within their communities, indigenous healers continue to provide holistic healing using ancient methods and techniques that have been passed down.

Prior to this recognition by the government, THP had been pushed underground. People in California, for example, remember when their relatives were practicing healing ceremonies but could not even tell their own family of their cultural practices. They could not discuss their beliefs because of the fear of retribution from the Christian church and police. Native practices were generally considered evil and synonymous with witchcraft, devil worshipping, and pagan religion. Even after the Religious Freedoms Act became reality, many Native healers were hesitant to bring their beliefs and practices into the open. This reluctance is beginning to change.

Today a network of indigenous healers acts as a support system for the AI/AN professionals and community members who are reviving THP in their personal and professional lives. This informal network exists in both rural and urban settings. Many times a healer from a specific tribe will visit urban settings with a significant population of AI/AN people of the same tribe. Other healers travel to various geographical areas within and between states.

A physician who works in an AI/AN health agency may be aware of this informal network but usually does not have direct access to it. Usually a Native employee, such as an administrator, a clinician, a clerical support worker, or a maintenance or janitorial employee, has contact with individuals or networks of indigenous healers. Each health agency is different in the ways it uses THP activities. The medical, dental, health promotion, and administrative departments of health agencies tend to work less directly with indigenous healers and more with other types of educational activities related to THP. Alcohol and drug abuse programs use sweats and work with Native healers more directly than the medical services do.

Navajo patients in a study (Kim and Kwok 1998) in Crownpoint, New Mexico, commonly sought help from traditional healers for arthritis, abdominal pain, and chest pain. Pain is often difficult to treat and may lead sufferers to explore numerous interventions in hopes of relief. In this situation, AI/AN patients may be more likely to turn to the culturally salient options embodied in their healing traditions than to more recently popularized alternatives (e.g., acupuncture and massage). Traditional health practices often focus on underlying causes, conceptualized as spiritual in nature, rather than on the relief of acute symptoms.

Traditional healing practices are often a significant element of family, community, and spiritual life. In AI/AN communities, traditional healing ceremonies long predate biomedical care. Traditional healing is used to address both the physical and the spiritual needs of AI/AN people. Many people choose alternative or complementary services in keeping with their social networks and belief systems. Increased understanding of this deeply rooted system can improve communication between providers and patients and therefore can help medical providers improve the quality of care provided.

Barriers to Traditional Health Practices

Research gives some examples of tribal-specific and general ideas concerning barriers. In their research with the Navajo tribe, Kim and Kwok (1998) found that cost was cited by 36 percent of the patients in their study as the reason for not seeking Native healer care and was the most common barrier to Native healer care.

The cost of visiting a Navajo healer includes such customary expenses as transportation, food for all those who participate in a ceremony, and costs of materials needed, such as buckskin or herbs.

It is a common practice for Native healers not to "charge" a fee for their work. A Native healer in modern times must hold a regular job to support a family. In addition to their full time employment, Native healers are expected to serve the community on a twenty-four-hour basis. Native healers are required to travel long distances when they are requested to work with Native patients. The burden of time and travel expense is on the healer. Native people who are aware of this situation typically will help out with healers' travel expenses by finding a place for them to stay, feeding them, and pooling money to pay for gas and for a healer's time. This is done without the healer's requesting a payment. This burden on the Native healer is a major reason so few people will commit to a healer's lifestyle of voluntary community service.

Kim and Kwok found that a lack of trust in Native healers (25 percent), the patient's own religion (23 percent), unsupportive families (12 percent), lack of belief in traditional Navajo medicine (11 percent), lack of knowledge about traditional Navajo medicine (7 percent), good health (4 percent), and lack of local Native healers (3 percent) also acted as deterrents to Native healer care. An important issue surfaced when many patients reported that they did not trust certain individuals claiming to be Native healers. While these patients still believed in traditional Navajo medicine, they could not find a trustworthy practitioner. One patient stated, "There are a lot of quacks out there," applying the term *quacks* to those masquerading as Native healers. In addition, Gurley et al. (2001) include personal time as a barrier: Some ceremonies require a week to perform, and consultations may take hours.

The Indian Health Service (IHS) has a policy that supports access to AI/AN medicine people in order to protect the right of AI/AN people to their traditional beliefs and health practices. However, the IHS does not directly cover payment for traditional health services, and any cost is typically paid "out of pocket" by the patient. There are exceptions, such as when an IHS or tribal program will invite and pay a stipend to a Native healer. Typically the clinic will schedule the healer to work throughout the day and to see a variety of patients.

One final barrier is the unfair expectations of patients who seek treatment from a Native healer. Duran and Duran (1995) state, "our (Native) people place [a] tremendous burden on 'true' spiritual leaders as they pressure them for miracles and quick magical fixes for the pain and suffering that never seems to end."

In pluralistic systems, people pursue hierarchies of resort in selecting particular providers. If the first resort does not produce improvement, other systems will be tried until satisfaction is achieved. Those who are not familiar with traditional Native medicine usually seek it as a last resort. More study is needed in the area of THP and health outcomes.

Competing Cultural Values

Traditional health practices are steeped in the philosophy, language, culture, and ceremonies of AI/AN communities. This "system" of health care was systematically replaced by a medical system provided by the United States government and administered by the IHS. One basic distinction between the AI/AN system and the medical system is the way they each perceive health. The medical approach focuses on physical symptoms, etiology, and interventions. Native medicine uses a holistic approach that includes individual health dimensions: the physical, mental, spiritual, and environmental context of the person.

Waldram (1996) notes there is no concrete evidence concerning whether and how traditional medicine actually works. This is a complex statement mainly because what "works" is based on the medical gold standard of the randomized, double-blind, controlled study. THP are not standardized because there are as many "ways" to practice as there are Native healers. In addition, it does not make sense for Native healers to "treat" everyone the same way when it is perceived that each patient's body chemistry and presenting life situation are different. Research methodology that takes AI/AN epistemology into account must be developed so that THP can be valued within the context of its original culture.

Successful clinical interventions are not possible in an AI/AN setting unless the provider or agency is cognizant of the sociohistorical factors that have had devastating effects on the AI/AN family. This axiom applies not only to those conditions that are in the realm of mental health but also to medical conditions. Diabetes, heart disease, depression, cancer, domestic violence, intentional and unintentional injury, and all public health issues must be understood in the context of individual and community response to historical trauma (Duran and Duran 1995; Brave Heart et al. 1998).

During the process of collecting data for a dissertation project, I have had the opportunity to observe how several AI/AN health agencies are using and developing THP along with providing medical health services. Several sociocultural movements are increasing exposure and access to THP for local AI/AN communities.

Some medicine people and elders have maintained their cultural practices, ceremonies, language, and philosophy. They did so in the face of enormous pressure to assimilate from (a) the mainstream culture, (b) the legal and education systems, (c) Christian religions, and (d) government policy. Mainstream media support a consumer culture whose major value is money and which follows a scientific mantra of the "survival of the fittest." These factors have led to further separation from AI/AN cultural values.

Many AI/AN people attend cultural activities, but the majority of THP are more social and do not provide culturally based health care to Native people. Powwows and sweats can contribute to the well-being of people. A Native healer with knowledge and experience of healing people is the most direct form of Native health care. One elder recently commented to me that if you have a broken bone, it doesn't matter how many times you go in the sweat; it will not heal the bone. However, there is a need to increase access to a Native healer and to healing-specific ceremonies. There are many AI/AN people who have never been to a healing ceremony or had contact with a Native healer. Many have heard of these things but do not have direct experience.

In California, for example, there are local communities that are restoring songs, ceremonies, and healing practices. This process requires time, patience, and the ability to deal with people who are angry over having lost this knowledge in their family and community. Yosemite National Park, Grinding Rock State Park, and Patrick's Point State Park, all in California, are examples of communities that have rebuilt villages with traditional ceremony structures. This work is usually undertaken by a handful of committed individuals who want to restore (not discover) THP for their community. Many local communities are coming back to a cultural understanding of life.

Native professionals now take advantage of culturally based training from a variety of programs and agencies. The University of Oklahoma sponsors Native Wellness conferences for men and women. The Gathering of Nations (GONA) and Red Road approach have contributed culture-based interventions and curriculum for alcohol and drug abuse programs. No cultural training or support existed when I first began my career in 1984 as an Indian Child Welfare (ICW) worker in Fort Hall, Idaho. The first training I encountered was by Terry Cross in Portland, Oregon. He received funding to create a training program for ICW workers, and it had a cultural component. The use of THP has grown exponentially since the early 1980s. Efforts to include THP need to be documented and studied to understand its impact on AI/AN communities.

Implications for Research

Documenting THP and its use for health intervention can potentially increase funding from foundations and local, state, and federal agencies. The holistic, cultural approach to health care is very appealing to public health and criminal justice officials everywhere who seek ways to effectively provide treatment, to lower recidivism, and to control costs. The Native American Health Center (NAHC) has implemented a holistic system of care in the San Francisco Bay Area based on a strategic plan that links prevention with treatment in a continuum of care and stresses collaboration with a variety of AI/AN and public agencies. Proof of a THP approach is supported by the NAHC plan, and this plan has resulted in bringing significant resources to the community.

Using a cultural model of health may also open doors to go beyond current thought regarding health of minorities and determinants of health. The determinants-of-health approach can refocus analytical explanations for health outcomes from the immediate biomedical context of health problems to the wider living conditions that interact with individual physiological, psychological, and sociocultural dispositions that give rise to those health problems. This broad approach can eventually lead researchers to explain how THP can be used to improve the health of AI/AN communities. Native researchers will be needed to guide appropriate questions based on culture and to interpret the findings.

Notes

Brave Heart, M. Yellow Horse, and L. M. DeBruyn. "The American Indian Holocaust: Healing Historical Unresolved Grief," *American Indian and Alaska Native Mental Health Research Journal* 2 (1998): 56–78.

Buchwald, Dedra, Janette Beals, and Spero M. Manson. "Use of Traditional Health Practices among Native Americans in a Primary Care Setting," *Medical Care* 38(12) (2000): 1191–99.

Duran, E., and B. Duran. *Native American Postcolonial Psychology*. Albany: State University of New York Press, 1995.

Gurley, Diana, Douglas K. Novins, Monica C. Jones, Janette Beals, James H. Shore, and Spero M. Manson. "Comparative Use of Biomedical Services and Traditional Healing Options by American Indian Veterans," *Psychiatric Services* 52(1) (2001): 68–74.

Kim, Catherine, and Yeong S. Kwok. "Navajo Use of Native Healers," *Archives of Internal Medicine* 158 (1998): 2245–2249.

Waldram, J. B. "Aboriginal Spirituality in Corrections." In *Native Americans, Crime and Justice*, ed. R. A. Silverman and M. O. Neilson. Boulder, Colo.: Westview Press, 1996.

Healing the Kashaya Way

12

OTIS PARRISH

FROM ANCIENT TIMES the Pomo people lived in a continuous area in the northern California Coast Ranges covering over 3,000 square miles. The Kashaya at Stewart's Point Rancheria are one of twenty federally recognized Pomo tribes in northern California. Kashaya traditional territory ranges from the Gualala River's confluence with the Pacific Ocean on the border of Mendocino and Sonoma counties southward to Duncan's Point, about five miles south of where the Russian River meets the sea (Peri 1976; Klasky and Nelson 2002).

Our land once spanned over 300 square miles but has been reduced to just seven usable acres. Although it is a beautiful, lush redwood forest, the current reservation cannot sustain the 500 Kashaya tribal members. Only about 100 people live on the reservation. The rest live in the surrounding areas and in the town of Santa Rosa. The Kashaya are a very traditional tribe and maintain close family ties. The fact that many tribal members have to live far from their homeland has challenged this deep sense of place and community (Parrish 2002).

The first name the Kashaya gave to themselves at creation was People from on Top of the Land. The land takes care to embrace us with its nourishment, speak to us in our language, give us stories to educate us, and listen to the songs of beauty we sing in its honor. We need to sing to the land and tell the stories of the land so the spirits of the land will remember us. For the Kashaya, stories are a type of "soul-speech," a way of communicating and sharing life. Stories are guides to morality, to understanding the past and the way things are. Some stories are for all of the tribe, but others are for only the dreamers, the spiritual leaders. But there are many other stories and songs, dance songs, love-medicine songs, hunting songs, and social songs.

In the creation history of the tribe, the relationship between the Kashaya and their land began with the appearance of the tribe's ancestors at the place of creation on the northwestern Sonoma coast, or Place Where People First Walked onto Land, a piece of land that juts out into the ocean. Tribal elders have always maintained that it is a special and sacred place. During my childhood, elders told about the reason the Creator gave sacredness to this place where the land and the ocean come together: to create a place of special resource abundance found nowhere else in the region for the survival of the people. This abundance is a special indication that this place should forever be considered sacred. Since that time of creation, the Kashaya have considered this special place the most sacred of all sacred places.

Dances, songs, and stories are intimately tied to the land. Our stories tell us how we are all related. They teach us how Coyote is our Creator, the Redwood tree is a grandfather, and Whale is one of our daughters. Whale helps young girls in their transition to womanhood. Stories map out our sacred places, gathering areas and historical sites important to the tribe's collective identity. Traditional dances, songs, and stories help establish aboriginal territorial rights and educate landowners and state and federal agencies about a tribe's ancestral connection with a place.

Although we need to share our unique culture within our own community and with the outside world, so that it can better understand and respect our ways, there are limits and guidelines on what can and cannot be shared with outsiders. There are even limitations on families' sharing their stories and songs with tribal members outside the specific family group. And within a family, certain members are trained to be the keepers of certain songs and stories and to recite them at special ceremonial times.

The Before World

The connection between the people and the land, as the old people told, began in the Before World, and that relationship was based on the sacred and ancient tradition of reciprocity. The one spiritual law that continues to this day is the concept of balanced integration, or a "steady balanced state," which means that if we keep the spiritual laws that we agreed to in the Before World, we will have a continuation of the balance between the natural world and ourselves. This can be achieved only through the use of the sacred act of reciprocity (Parrish 2002).

To understand the full flavor of what transpired in the Before World between humans and those entities that are scattered over the Kashaya aboriginal territory, we must first view the spiritual landscape of the Before World. In the Before World, as perceived by the Kashaya, agreements were made between the land and all those entities that are harbored within the ancient geographical landscape.

Every living being that exists in our present reality is descended from those ancestors. Before the Kashaya people were created on Earth, all of those entities that inhabit our aboriginal territory were believed to be of one family with us. The Kashaya language was spoken, and communication was possible with everything that exists today over our lands. Each being, in the final act of creation, met for the last time in the Before World to make agreements that would have a dramatic impact on how humans would behave in this world to carry out the creation plan. Those agreements were so important that without them there would be no structure or framework to act as our guide. The final act of creation was to create the social and ceremonial behavior that would be exhibited by the Kashaya people since that time.

Those agreements dictated how the Kashaya people would carry out their relationships and contribute to the rest of the creation plan. In our tribal definition, reciprocity is the act of coming together in the agreement process of "give to be given." Today, that sacred act is the founding strategy that is carried out each time the elders need anything from the environment. The act of reciprocity is the key to keeping the balance with the land, to keeping it happy and healthy.

The belief is that this world is a living organism and that the continuation of Earth's life is dependent on the continuation of the Before World agreements. This core belief ensures the continued practice of "give to be given."

The Dreamer

My mother, Essie Parrish, was the last Kashaya prophet, healer, and dreamer. She influenced my world view through her great strength of character, the wonder of her intellect, the beauty of her wisdom, the truths of her prophecies, and the wisdom of her beauty. She was comfortable to be around. If you met my mother as a stranger, you would feel the comfort as if you were an old friend. You could count on getting a feeling of the warmth, compassion, and love she had for her family, her people, and all the peoples of the world. One of the things that was so inspiring about my mother was that she would give you her friendship without questioning your motives or station in life. She gave you the responsibility to take her friendship and hold it in peace.

The old people say that when a person is born to be a shaman, that person is born with the gifts of healing, dreaming, and having visions. Everything my mother taught me was for a specific purpose. I've always wondered why it was so difficult to learn all of the formulas, songs, and ceremonies. I remember my mother telling me, "If this was easy, it wouldn't mean that much to you. Because you are interested in this work, the difficulty is like a test. We know you won't give up and walk away from the teachings; that's why we keep teaching you and correct you when you make mistakes."

When she was teaching me the songs and ceremonies, it was as if we were one. The closeness, I later found out, was a necessary ingredient in the teaching process. I remember as a baby lying on my mother's shoulder and listening to her heart beating. At times her heartbeat felt like a light jolt of electricity. It would wake me up, and it made me feel good. I felt alive.

Essie Parrish worked with social scientists, anthropologists, and scholars as a key informant on Kashaya ways. In 1972, she spoke at the New School of Social Research in New York about her dream visions. She helped compile a dictionary of the Kashaya Pomo language, published by the University of California Press, and a book about Kashaya herbal medicine (Oswalt 1964; Kroeber 1976; Gifford 1966; Quasha 1972; Barrett 1972; Goodrich et al. 1980).

Essie performed curing ceremonies, combining dream visions with singing, dancing, herbs, and removal of disease by sucking. In her curing ceremonies, she entered a trance in order to "see" the sickness, locate it, and suck it out of the patient's body. In the Kashaya belief, sucking doctors or shamans continue from the distant past within a family line, but not by chance; rather, as the old people say, "It meant to have been that way."

Born in 1902, Essie was six years old when her family recognized her gifts. One day she saw a man wearing a feather cloak sitting beside the trail as she was on her way home through the woods. This was a magic garment, and to see such a person could produce sickness or even death. She was badly frightened, ran home, and went straight to bed. Almost immediately she lost consciousness, and despite all efforts she could not be aroused during that day or the following night. Finally, a man who was thought to possess one of these magic garments was called in. He restored her to normal health. Very soon after this experience, Essie Parrish began to dream and have the revelations so important for the Kashaya people.

Essie dreamed the dances that her helpers performed in ceremonies. In addition to dreaming the movements and details of the dance, she dreamt the designs of the costumes and the decorated cloths or hoops the dancers would hold while they were dancing. Essie Parrish said the life of a dream doctor is not an easy one, because "Your dreams keep you awake."

My mother made the experiences of her life like a storybook for me to enjoy. Mother's stories about the old ways were the window through which I could travel in time. I could pierce the time between the present and the past. The past became the now in my child's mind and filled me with beautiful pictures of her life. She told stories for hours on end. Mother was an excellent speaker of the Kashaya language. When she told those stories in our language, it was like going to the movies. I could hear and picture each of the characters as she gave them life. My three favorite stories were "The Yellow Jackets and the Fleas"; "The Rabbit and the Elk"; and "Crane, Bear, and His Wife the Cricket Woman."

Herbal Medicine

One of the areas of knowledge that my mother passed on to me was the use of plants and their healing powers. Research for *Kashaya Pomo Herbs,* published by the American Indian Studies Center at UCLA, began in 1974, with a preliminary survey of ethnographic, linguistic, and botanical references coordinated by Dr. Robert Oswalt, who arrived at correct translations of the herbs by taking Essie to the California Native Plants section of the University of California, Berkeley, Botanical Garden. Field trips were made to places around the Kashaya reservation to collect plant specimens (Goodrich et al. 1980; Peri et al. 1982).

When I was seven years old, my mother took me out into the wilderness to teach me about healing plants. She gathered some dry twigs from her burden basket to make a fire. We cleared the area of any dry grass, piled the twigs on the ground, and were ready to start the fire. She said, "We gonna do special ceremony for you to learn what this is and why our people do this. These herbs repr'sent very sacred thing."

She had this ground tea, pine pitch, and a grass that in our language is called sibu.ta'. It's a grass that our people eat and which tastes somewhat like parsley, but milder. She reached into another small basket and picked out the tea. She said, "This tea has special flavor and smell. There's 'nother kind tea too, but this one is used for this ceremony.

"It is also because it go inside of you," she said as she put the tea branch next to the firewood. Next she took out the sibu.ta,' the grass, and said, "This is hard to find now. Long ago before white people come into the mountains, there use to be lots of this grass; now it is hard to find. . . . Because this grass go inside of you it repr'sent all the wild plants that you eat or the things it grows that you eat. Like nuts and things."

Then she takes out the pine pitch and puts it on the firewood. "This pitch is the one I have in my doctoring basket. That's the one will let the plants know that this is dedicated to you, and they will recognize you when you make prayer to them when you get ready to use them for healing. You got to be good to all plants and animals. That's the rule."

After she finished her explanations, she said a prayer: "This old-time prayer. This goes with the song I'm gonna sing over you." She said the sacred prayer as I sat there on the ground, and when she finished, she sang one of her doctoring songs. She sang it four times over me, and when she finished, she lit the fire. I was surprised; there was not a wisp of smoke from the fire. She picked up the tea vine and held it over the fire, and I could smell the aroma of the tea waft over the world as I watched the vine wither from the heat. As soon as this happened, she took off a leaf and gave it to me and instructed me to swallow it without chewing it, and that's what I did. Then she laid the vine upon the fire, and it burned to ashes and disappeared into the air over the fire. Next she took the grass and did the same thing. I could see the pine pitch melt into the heat of the fire and disappear into the ashes of the fire.

Fire is very important in the process of learning about the use of plants for healing. Fire is what unlocks the healing power of the plants. The old people say that without the fire, plants are only part alive. The fire unlocks the energy and healing powers. As the fire died, my mother began to sing a song I had never heard before, a beautiful song with a haunting, melodic rhythm. She sang this song until only ashes were left.

We believe that without the ceremonials, you become the wanderer. The trance takes you out into the universe and lets you experience things that may seem real but are without meaning to anyone except yourself. I believe it is that way because the Spirit World will not recognize you that way. When you work with plants in ceremony, the trance takes you to a place before creation, and you are given the opportunity to see the world when we were all together. Like a mirror. In trance you have the ability to see the natural world, reality, like stretching a rubber band over the whole of the universe.

Plants have a smell of their own, and each smell is unique to its plant. In the Before World, all the plants smelled the same. The Creator admonished those plants who were destined to cohabitate this earth with the humans, because the plants didn't want to smell different from each other. So the Creator gave each plant a different smell. And that's how the plants have different smells now. The most sacred smell of all the plants is Angelica (*Angelica tomentosa*). This is the mother of all plants in Kashaya beliefs. It is burnt like cedar, like sage. Angelica is the sacred medicine. It is the sacred food. This plant is imbued with being the caretaker of every living thing there is.

Huckleberry and Bear

The Huckleberry bush has a number of uses. The way our people tell of the Huckleberry bush and its healing properties is to tell the story about its song.

When the Creator, the great Coyote, made people and plants and animals, some of the plants and animals were paired off with one another. The Huckleberry was given the right to be made for food, and the Bear was given the taste for huckleberries. The Creator gave Bear a great and beautiful song. When the Creator was singing the song to give it to the Bear, the Huckleberry heard it and fell in love with the song. And when the Creator gave the berries to the Huckleberry bush, the Creator made the Bear taste them, and the Bear fell in love with the taste.

So they each liked what the other had, but they were each stingy. So they made a deal. First the Huckleberry bush said, "If you want to have my beautiful, tasty berries, you have to sing your most beautiful song for me every time you want my beautiful, tasty berries."

Bear had a beautiful voice at first, but the Bear was stingy and didn't want to sing his song. Huckleberry said to the Bear, "The longer you wait, the worse your voice will sound."

Still the Bear didn't want to sing his song. That went on for a long time. Finally the Bear couldn't stand it any more, and he said, "OK. I will sing my song."

When he went to sing with his beautiful voice, only grunts came out of his mouth—like the Bear sounds today. The Huckleberry said, "Oh, that sounds ugly. I warned you, Bear, but you didn't listen."

The Bear started crying, big tears running down his face, and he rolled around on the ground, kicking up dust all over the place. Then the Huckleberry felt sorry for him and gave him the right to eat the berries, but the Bear still had to sing anyway, but with his ugly voice.

Along came the Humans, who also liked the berries. The Bear didn't like that and warned the Humans, "If you eat my berries, I'm going to kill you. If you want to eat the berries, you have to sing my song to the Huckleberry."

And the Huckleberry bush said to the Humans, "You have to sing the Bear's song before you pick any berries off my limbs, and if you don't, old lady Bear will drag you into the deep woods, and you'll never come back."

And so from that point on, the Humans said to the bush, "We'll sing the Bear's song to you for your berries and not make Bear mad, but you have to do something for us, too."

And so the Huckleberry bush said, "OK." The Humans said, "We'll sing Bear's song if we can use your medicine and food." And Huckleberry said OK to that deal. So from that time on, Humans had to sing the Bear's song every time they went to use the Huckleberry bush.

Dream Vision

I was the first one in my family to leave the reservation and go to college. I was studying archaeology and had all these questions why I had gone into that field in the first place. As I sat reading in my front room by myself, one part of my mind was dealing with reality, and the other half was in the spirit world. In my vision I was talking with my parents, grandparents, great-grandparents, backwards into the world of my ancestors. We were in a huge glass dome in the entrance to the spirit world, where one could look back out at the real world in which I existed in the present. The surrealism of it all was the fact, and the ancestors showed how it worked. They made the eyes of vision disappear, and I could not see to the spirit world.

"This is what people who don't have what you kids have see," said my ancestors. "When they come this far, they think they are having a vision, but it's all what they think they need to see. That's not real vision. It's not vision at all. But you kids of ours have our gift to see to the spirit world if you know how to do it."

Suddenly my whole being was there in the spirit world with my mother and all of my grandmothers as far as my genealogy goes back. All these grandmothers and my mother speak to me with different voices and words, and I hear all as I listen to each. "What are your questions about?" they asked me.

"I am looking for the knowledge of my ancestors," I said sadly.

They each give me a hug, and I lay my head on their shoulders. I said "I don't think I'm going to have enough time to finish my task. I've looked all my life to find this knowledge. I've looked under rocks, under water, beneath old tree stumps, beneath a fallen leaf. I've even looked between cracks in a large boulder, between old rotted tree bark; I've looked between the forests and grasslands of the mountains. I've tried to find the knowledge of and about you here in the stars at night, in the dense fog and the beautiful bellowing clouds, even at the end of the lightning bolt. But I can find you nowhere."

My grandmother said to me, "Here is the place where you can feel those feelings. This is the place where you get rid of those kinds of feelings. When we take you to the real spirit world, that's where you will feel only happiness."

The glass dome disappeared, and I was happy. The language was so beautiful that it sounded like a song. The grandfathers come up to me and asked me to go with them now. My dad was with me, and we were at this place where things lay over the earth. Everything the ancestors made, did, and used was scattered over the earth layer upon layer, pregnant with meaning. I saw skeletons of human beings and animals, black rocks, and green rocks. I saw shells of all different species from the sea and fresh water.

"This is what you are looking for. This is where you must look," my father and grandfathers said. I felt good. I heard beautiful music, a fast dance song. Everyone is singing and dancing. The song carries me back to reality, my ancestors' words in my ears.

Healing Song

I was sitting on top of a large rock by the beach at Big Sur, enjoying my solitude, the wind whistling in my ears. The wind is blowing from the northwest, a good sign in our tradition. This is the wind that carries songs, healing songs. Suddenly I heard a voice singing in the distance behind the noise of the wind as it flowed past my ears. The sound of the wind disappeared, and I heard a beautiful song, a healing song for the soul. My soul danced to the rhythm of the words of the song. The beat vibrated through my body from within.

> I come to you from beyond, on the winds that flow,
> And caress the world with my touch.
> I leave the spiritual imprint for you of the healing powers.
> The wind blows to awaken the spiritual center of your humanness,
> To feel the flow of its touch.
> Listening for the wind's voice,
> Coming to sing its voice of beauty into my ears, I hear the beauty of its voice.
> The songs that have come across the vast distances of Time and Space.
> The wind whose voice comes back to us from the future.
> The spiritual Songs that it brings, to fulfill a purpose for me.
> For the voices of the wind whose songs caress human awareness, bring the voice of healing to my ears.
> The wind rides the waves of the ocean and gently flows through the branches of the healing tree, bringing with it the gentle fluttering of the leaves with the spiritual essences of the healing trees.
> There is a spiritual awareness that one must come to.
> It's a place where one has the right to hear the sacred voice of the wind.
> The wind must be felt as it flows through our body.
> One must know which wind you are listening to.
> Each wind has a personality of its own.
> Each wind has a physical being separated from all others.
> To recognize that is only the first step in this spiritual dance.
> I and the wind continue to dance our spiritual dance.
> Into the universe our spirits flow.
> It brings me back to the rock to listen, at another time.
> So it shall be as the old people are.

Notes

Barrett, S. A. "The Stewarts Point Maru of 1958." In *The Maru Cult of the Pomo Indians: A California Ghost Dance Survival*, ed. C. Meighan and F. Riddle. Los Angeles: Southwest Museum Press, 1972.

Gifford, E. W. *Ethnographic Notes on the Southwestern Pomo*. Berkeley: University of California Publications, Anthropological Records, 25, 1966.

Goodrich, J., C. Lawson, and V. P. Lawson. *Kashaya Pomo Herbs*. Los Angeles: American Indian Studies Center, 1980.

Klasky, P., and M. Nelson. "Storyscapes: Living Songs in Native Lands," *ReVision* 25 (2) (2002): 17–18.

Kroeber, A. L. *Handbook of the Indians of California*. New York: Dover Publications, 1976.

Oswalt, R. L. *Kashaya Texts*. Berkeley: University of California Press, 1964.

Parrish, O. "The People from on Top of the Land: A Kashaya Pomo Elder's Journey," *ReVision* 25 (2) (2002): 34–38.

Peri, D. "Pomoan Plant Resource Mangagement," *Ridge Review* 4 (1976): 14–18.

Peri, D., S. Patterson, and J. Goodrich. *Ethnobotanical Mitigation: Warm Springs Dam, Lake Sonoma California*. Penngrove, Calif.: Environmental Analysis and Planning Office, 1982.

Quasha, George. "Essie Parrish in New York," *Somapoetics* Fremont, Mich.: Sumac Press, 1972.

Peacemaking Ceremonies for Substance Abuse Treatment

13

J. PHILLIP GOSSAGE, RUTHIE ALEXIUS,
PAMELA G. MONAGHAN-GEERNAERT, AND PHILIP A. MAY

IN THE SPRING AND SUMMER OF 1993, a mystery illness cast a pall over the Four Corners region of the Navajo Nation. The mystery illness came to be known as the hantavirus; it led to the death of twenty-seven people. Two explanations were given for the outbreak: scientists determined biomedically that the virus was carried by deer mice and that it was spread either through direct contact with mouse urine or saliva or through inhalation of dust infected with the virus. Dine' medicine people of the Navajo nation equated the disease to mythical monsters; the real cause was claimed by some to be disharmony within the Navajo Nation (Schwarz 2001; Schwarz 1997).

In the summer of 2003, as this article is being written, the Navajo Nation was bracing for a possible visit by another monster, an outbreak of the West Nile Virus (National Native News 2003). While there is a biomedical certainty that the vectors of the West Nile virus are mosquitoes, we hypothesize that Navajo medicine people may attribute the real cause to a continuing disharmony within contemporary Dine' culture.

Alcohol and American Indians

Many works have documented the struggle of Native peoples with "crazy water" (Longclaws et al. 1980; Maracle 1994; May 1982; 1996; May and Gossage 2001; Whittaker 1962, 1982). Others have written works specifically about the Dine' and their struggle with alcohol (Levy and Kunitz 1974; Topper 1995; May and Smith 1988; May and Del Vecchio, 1993; Kunitz and Levy 1994, 2000; Gossage et al. 2003). Alcohol use and abuse among the Dine' have been characterized as a rather unique pattern of binge drinking. As few as 64 percent of the men and 40 percent of the women drink at all, which is below the prevalence of drinking in the general U.S. population. However, among those who do drink, a pattern of sporadic and severe binge drinking causes many problems for a number of individuals, families, and communities. Morbidity and mortality, child neglect and abuse, family disruption, and criminal behavior are all caused by binge drinking in a not insignificant proportion of the sub-population of Navajo drinkers. In other words, most Navajo drink infrequently, but among those who do drink, severe consequences and problems can result from some of the drinking episodes.

Alcohol abuse, alcoholism, and use of illicit substances are manifestations of disease in Dine' culture. Illness occurs when there is an imbalance. Western behavioral, psychoanalytic, or cognitive behavioral therapy methods are used widely throughout Indian Country but are frequently ineffective for Indians (Stewart, May, and Muneta 1980). Symbolic healing is the answer (Sandner 1979); however, as noted by Zion (2002), there is no single traditional healing ceremony within Dine' culture to address alcohol and substance abuse.

The Navajo Nation began a demonstration substance abuse treatment program in October 1993 entitled the Dine' Center for Substance Abuse Treatment (DCSAT). The DCSAT was one of six Rural, Remote, and Culturally Distinct population projects funded by the Center for Substance Abuse Treatment (CSAT). The DCSAT's focus was to provide culturally competent counseling to its clients. DCSAT traditional counselors used twelve traditional healing ceremonies to treat clients with alcohol and substance abuse problems and to return the clients to balance. The twelve ceremonies were (1) diagnostic ceremonies (including Hand Trembling, Star Gazing, and Charcoal Gazing or Expurgation Way), (2) Ajile or "Excessive Way" ceremonies (including Coyote Way, Deer Way, Moth Way, and Feather Way), (3) Blessing Way, (4) Life Way, (5) Shooting Way or Lightning Way, (6) Evil Way, (7) Enemy Way, (8) Wind Way, (9) Night Way, (10) traditional ceremonial use of peyote via the Native American Church, (11) Lodge Ceremony (commonly known as the sweat lodge), and (12) Peacemaking.

The Peacemaking Ceremony focuses on the whole sphere with which the individual is intimately connected, including but not limited to the personal, social, and cosmic dimensions. As Schwarz (1997) notes,

> A fundamental aspect of every Navajo healing ceremony is a cleansing of the mind and body to facilitate the ritual return to the beginning of the world. Through this process a state of balance or harmony is restored.

This study examines the role of Peacemaking in traditional counseling. (For a history and overview of Peacemaking, see Adam et al. 1993; Bearcub-Stiffarm 1993; Bluehouse and Zion 1993; Gross 1998, 2001; LeResche 1993; Mansfield 1993; McCray et al. 1993; Thomas and Kihoi 1993; Vicenti 1993; Young 1978; Zion 1983, 1998, 2002; Zion and McCabe 1982.)

The Process of Peacemaking

A Peacemaking ceremony is recommended in the following situations: (1) a problem or dispute between individuals or groups of individuals that may affect the whole chapter's residents (a chapter is the smallest tribal government unit); (2) conduct that would be a crime that hurts public peace; or (3) conduct that affects chapter government (Zion and McCabe 1982).

In the DCSAT program, the Peacemaker was sought typically in situations of alcohol or drug abuse or when a child's safety was involved. Of the fifty-two patients who received Peacekeeping ceremonies, all but one case involved issues of alcohol consumption or alcohol-related behavior. Additionally, the majority of cases reflected child neglect or abuse as a result of drinking behavior.

The Peacemaker's job is to mediate people's problems and disputes by bringing people together and encouraging them to agree on (1) the definition of the problem and (2) what needs to be done to resolve it (Bluehouse and Zion 1993). The Peacemaker's role in the ceremony is to guide parties to harmony. Everyone is given an opportunity to speak on the matters in dispute, and those in attendance are patient in arriving at solutions. The Peacemaker's authority is persuasive, not coercive (Bearcub-Stiffarm 1993). The Peacemaker helps parties identify how they have come to a state of disharmony (anahoti'); Peacemakers are mostly concerned with the cause of the disharmony rather than any individual act or dispute.

The Peacemaker does not judge the parties involved but rather encourages them to work together. The Peacemaker may use traditional Navajo teachings and beliefs as a guideline for future behavior of the patient and the patient's family (Austin 1993).

Peacemaking sessions are concluded when a group decision has been reached that is acceptable to *everyone* involved. Peacemaking implies that all parties accept the decision without ill feelings, discontent, or dissatisfaction. Because of this condition, the decisions reached through Peacemaking are honored and respected by all. An apology is usually given by the party involved as a first step to repair relationships with family and community. This apology reinforces harmony and makes a place for continuing relationships through atonement (Tso and Austin 1993).

Methodology

A comprehensive model was developed by the DCSAT staff for screening, assessing, matching, referring, and treating patients. [The research protocol was reviewed and approved by the Navajo Nation Health Research Review Board (NNR-96–04) and the University of New Mexico Institutional Review Board (01–96–50–9804R).] A total of 302 intensive outpatient program (IOP) clients received services between January 1994 and March 1998. Entry into the program occurred in one of four ways: under court order, as a referral from treatment centers, on a walk-in basis, and as a referral from family and friends. Fifty-two patients received Peacemaking ceremonies (17 percent of the overall sample of the IOP).

Extensive notes were taken by the Peacemaker (coauthor Ruthie Alexius) during the fifty-two Peacemaking ceremonies. A content analysis uncovered common themes and meanings within those notes. Key sentences, phrases, and words were selected as being denotative of the relationships between patients and other attendees of the Peacemaking ceremonies. These quotations were then given short code names that identified the prevalent theme. As each case was read, new codes were created when necessary to reflect new ideas. At the completion of the analysis of the ceremony notes, thirty-five broad codes were identified.

The quotations attached to each of the thirty-five codes were reviewed. Further coding and recoding then took place to break apart large codes into more meaningful subcomponents. Seven large codes were reanalyzed, and their quotations were refined into more significant categories. This recoding procedure resulted in fifty-one codes. After the fifty-one codes were defined, they were subjected to a meta-analysis in which they were organized into thematic categories. Grouping codes together based on similarities in meaning yielded eleven broad themes.

It is appropriate here to speak to some of the limitations of the research as those limitations concerned sample sizes and collection of data. The DCSAT experienced substantial staff turnover and instability in the first two years. The evaluation team did not join the project until eighteen months after it had started. Clients were not randomly assigned to treatment modalities, nor was there a pure control group. Some data collection instruments were not available or used at the start of the project, and others were added incrementally. Some patients were still in treatment when the project ended, and discharge and treatment outcome data for those individuals were not available.

Quantitative Analysis

Selected demographic and cultural data, collected at intake, reveal that the percentage of men and women receiving Peacemaking ceremonies were almost identical to the sample of other patients (OPs); both samples were 72 percent men. Peacemaking Ceremony clients averaged a year older than the OPs (thirty-eight years versus thirty-seven years). Educational achievement was almost identical (eleven years versus ten years). More Peacemaking Ceremony clients were married (36 percent versus 25 percent). Self-assessments of their attachment to Dine' culture as measured by level of traditionality revealed both groups of clients were "medium" to "very traditional."

The data reveal that both groups first tried alcohol at sixteen years of age. The DCSAT traditional counselors sensed modest differences in the two groups when rating the severity of the patients' substance abuse problems; the Peacemaking Ceremony clients were more "dependent" but lower in the "episodic" and "dysfunctional" categories. None of these minor differences were statistically significant.

The actual Peacemaking Ceremony can take various forms. For example, in a few cases only the client, the client's spouse, and the Peacemaker may be present. In other instances the entire family, relatives, and friends may attend the session. Occasionally, the family attends, and the client becomes uncooperative and leaves; in this instance the session would continue with only the family present. Although these scenarios occur infrequently, they are viable configurations of the Peacemaking Ceremony. In the DCSAT program, the typical Peacemaking Ceremony consisted of seven people, most of whom were family members. The average ceremony lasted nearly three hours.

Peacemaking Themes

Certain themes contained a larger number of quotations than other themes. In this study, the themes of positive steps, psychosocial stressors, traditional teachings, and family support contained the largest numbers of quotations. Overcoming addiction had a large number of quotations within the "positive steps" theme. Notes revealed the numerous struggles clients face in admitting they have a problem and trying to overcome the powerful effects of alcohol and drugs. Personal responsibility also was a popular theme; clients, family, and traditional counselors emphasized that the individual was responsible for his or her own recovery and that only through his or her willpower could the addiction be overcome. The thematic category of psychosocial stressors was the second-largest classification of the codes. Anger appeared to be a prevalent issue that had to be dealt with by clients in the Peacemaking ceremonies. Anger affects the way in which the patient deals with his or her spouse, children, and other people. In addition to anger, notes for Peacemaking ceremonies revealed that some clients spent some time during the Peacemaking ceremonies blaming others for their behavior and addiction. The third-largest theme that emerged from the analysis was that of traditionalism. Ke' is a Navajo word that encompasses peace, harmony, and balance. Ke' is the desired outcome of every peacekeeping ceremony (Bluehouse and Zion 1993). It is assumed that people have forgotten the premise of Ke' if they have become addicted to alcohol or other substances. Teachings were also mentioned frequently in the Peacemaking Ceremony notes. Often participants in the Peacemaking ceremonies would ask the client to remember traditional teachings. Notes from the Peacemaking ceremonies provided a rich base of information for use in planning culturally based treatment.

Treatment can help clients make improvements in many areas, including their personal lives, their families, their jobs, and their medical and legal affairs as well as their mental health in general and substance abuse in particular. We conclude this section with analysis of some selected intake and discharge data that suggest improvement via traditional healing and Peacemaking ceremonies.

More Peacemaking Ceremony patients completed treatment than did other IOP clients (31 percent versus 15 percent), a result that approached statistical significance. Encouragingly, DCSAT traditional counselors noted improvement in the majority of clients' substance-abuse-related dysfunction at discharge, with modestly more improvement in the Peacemaking Ceremony sample (77 percent versus 73 percent). DCSAT traditional counselors utilized the Global Assessment of Functioning (GAF) Scale (Luborsky, 1962) at the assessment and interim-treatment-outcome milestones. At intake both groups of clients displayed "moderate symptoms," such as flat affect and circumstantial speech, occasional panic attacks, or moderate difficulty in social, occupational, or school functioning (e.g., few friends, conflicts with peers and coworkers). Peacemaking Ceremony patients scored 3.5 points higher at intake. Both groups displayed better GAF scores at discharge, with IOP clients improving to the "some mild symptoms" category, yet the differences were not statistically significant. Peacemaking Ceremony clients remained in the "moderate symptoms" category.

Case Studies

Three Peacemaking Ceremony patients were also interviewed for inclusion in the evaluation team's ethnographic case studies (McCloskey 1998). Brief extracts from those case studies help convey the value of the Peacemaking ceremonies. The first case, Relative 3, was in the tribal jail for domestic violence and was referred to the Peacemaking Court. During the Peacemaking session, his wife and children expressed their frustration with and dislike for his drinking. In the session, Relative 3 asked for help with his drinking and other problems. Relative 3 said of the Peacemaking Ceremony, "I had no hope. I was thinking if there was anybody to help me. At that Peacemaking Court, I asked if there was any help. [My wife] said, 'Yes, if you really mean it.' I really needed help. I had nobody to go to that time. So that's where I went. They really helped me."

The next case was a problem drinker referred by the spouse. About ten years before, Relative 8's husband would binge drink about every three months. Five years later, his drinking increased in frequency and severity and began to affect the family. His drinking upset his daughter and gave his spouse a lot of heartache.

When he was drinking, he became angry and was verbally abusive to his spouse and the children. She suggested that his anger may have originated during the time he spent in the army. However, he resisted having any ceremony, such as an Enemy Way to counteract the effects of being in the service. When the binges began coming closer and closer, Relative 8 requested a Peacemaking session. It was the first time she was able to confront her husband about his drinking. They had an opportunity to talk to one another. Now her husband is more aware of his actions. Before the Peacemaking session, Relative 8's daughter would sit and cry when her father drank. Now she can talk to her father more. She feels better about him and tells him that she is going to pray for him. Relative 8 believes that the Peacemaking was effective for her. She wants to have the same thing done for her son because she knows it works.

The final case example was self-referred. Relative 9 attributed the escalation of his drinking to the problems he had with his wife. His wife grew suspicious when he was out of town all week working as a carpenter. Relative 9 was a binge drinker who might drink for as long as three weeks at a time. He had had four citations for driving while intoxicated (DWI), had not paid the fines, and no longer had a driver's license. He had also lost jobs because of his drinking. When Relative 9 had stopped drinking in the past, overwhelming thoughts about his losses led to relapses. He felt unable to change the course of his life. Relative 9 had a Peacemaking session with his family. The purpose was not to bring about a reconciliation with his wife and family but to establish better communication, make amends, and promote peace and harmony with his natal family and his family of procreation. He felt that the Peacemaking session was helpful.

Discussion

The DCSAT selected twelve traditional healing ceremonies to use in its therapy for men and women seeking help for alcohol and substance abuse. Fifty-two (17 percent) of 302 clients assigned to intensive outpatient therapy received a Peacemaking Ceremony during their treatment by DCSAT traditional counselors. Qualitative data from case records revealed several common themes: (1) the variety of psychosocial stressors that influence an individual's behavior and that may account for substance abuse problems, (2) the value of traditionalism and traditional teachings to therapeutic outcomes, and (3) the positive steps the patients were taking to overcome addiction and bring their lives back into balance. A thematic review of case notes suggests the Peacemaking Ceremony was a valuable way for clients to interact with family and friends to discuss and resolve substance abuse problems with the ultimate goal of reestablishing tranquility and harmony and maintaining Navajo traditional ways.

In 1993, the Navajo Nation joined five other Rural, Remote, and Culturally Distinct population projects funded by the Center for Substance Abuse Treatment. Traditional teachings were incorporated into alcohol and drug treatment to improve treatment outcomes. Data pertaining to Peacemaking ceremonies suggest that these patients did achieve greater "balance" than is usually achieved in programs that emphasize only Western methods. Given that the qualitative and subjective measures revealed more positive sentiments and outcomes from the Peacemaking Ceremony, one might question whether the quantitative scales were sensitive enough to measure as dependent variables. For future studies of Peacemaking ceremonies, Dine' traditional counselors should construct and validate specific assessment instruments based on the Dine'-specific cultural and personal themes identified by the qualitative analyses in this study. Such are the challenges of evaluating the effectiveness of traditional therapies and ceremonies.

Notes

The authors are especially appreciative of the close collaboration they had with two CSAT staff, Clifton Mitchell, branch chief, and Captain Cheryl LaPointe, rural program project officer. We thank Philmer Bluehouse, coordinator of the Peacemaker Division of the Judicial Branch of the Navajo Nation and member of the DCSAT Policy Steering Committee, for sharing his expertise. Carol Leonard was the longest-serving project director for the DCSAT, and we thank her for her leadership and valuable collaboration. Patricia Gunn assisted with data management.

Adam, J., T. Porter, and M. Thompson. "Canadian Akwesansne Community Peacemaker Process." Paper presented at the National Conference on Traditional Peacemaking: *Remaking Justice*, Arizona State University, Tempe, Arizona, September 20–22, 1993.

Austin, R. "Incorporating Tribal Customs and Traditions into Tribal Court Decisions." Paper presented at the National Conference on Traditional Peacemaking: *Remaking Justice*, Arizona State University, Tempe, Arizona, September 20–22, 1993.

Bearcub-Stiffarm, J. "Cultural Rights and Responsibilities." Paper presented at the National Conference on Traditional Peacemaking: *Remaking Justice*, Arizona State University, Tempe, Arizona, September 20–22, 1993.

Bluehouse, P., and J. W. Zion. "Hozhooji Naat'aanii: The Navajo Justice and Harmony Ceremony," *Mediation Quarterly* 10(4) (1993).

Gossage, J. Phillip, Louie Barton, Lenny Foster, Larry Etsitty, Clayton LoneTree, Carol Leonard, and Philip A. May. "Sweat Lodge Ceremonies for Jail-Based Treatment," *Journal of Psychoactive Drugs* 35(1) (2003): 33–42.

Gross, E. K. "Traditional and Navajo Peacemaking: An Analysis of the Relationship between Self-Reported Traditionalism and Justice Outcomes on the Navajo Reservation, Chinle District." Paper presented at the Crime and Justice Research in Indian Country: Strategic Planning Meeting, Arizona State University, Tempe, October 14–15, 1998.

————. "Evaluation/Assessment of Navajo Peacemaking," *The NIJ Research Review* 2(3) (2001): 1–2.

Kunitz, S. J., and J. E. Levy. *Drinking Careers: A Twenty-Five Year Study of Three Navajo Populations.* New Haven, Conn.: Yale University Press, 1994.

————. *Drinking, Conduct Disorder, and Social Change: Navajo Experiences.* New York: Oxford University Press, 2000.

LeResche, D. "Native American Perspectives on Peacemaking," *Mediation Quarterly* 10(4) (1993).

Levy, J. E., and S. J. Kunitz. *Indian Drinking.* New York: John Wiley and Sons, 1974.

Longclaws, L., G. Barnes, L. Grieve, and R. Dumoff. "Alcohol and Drug Use among the Brokenhead Ojibwa," *Journal of Studies on Alcohol* 41(1980): 1, 21–36.

Luborsky, L. "Clinicians' Judgments of Mental Health," *Archives of General Psychiatry* 7 (1962): 407–417.

Mansfield, E. "Balance and Harmony: Peacemaking in Coast Salish Tribes of the Pacific Northwest," *Mediation Quarterly* 10(4) (1993).

Maracle, Brian. *Crazywater.* Toronto: Penguin Books, 1994.

May, Philip A. "Substance Abuse and American Indians: Prevalence and Susceptibility," *International Journal of the Addictions* 17 (1982): 1185–1209.

————. "Overview of Alcohol Abuse Epidemiology for American Indian Populations." In *Changing Numbers, Changing Needs: American Indian Demography and Public Health,* ed. G. D. Sandefur, R. R. Rundfuss, and B. Cohen. Washington, D.C.: National Academy Press, 1996.

May, Philip A., and A. Del Vecchio. *Navajo Townsite Alcohol and Drug Abuse Prevalence, Survey Results.* Albuquerque, N.Mex.: Center on Alcoholism, Substance Abuse, and Addictions, 1993.

May, Philip A., and J. Phillip Gossage. "New Data on the Epidemiology of Adult Drinking and Substance Use among American Indians of the Northern States: Male and Female Data on Prevalence, Patterns, and Consequences," *American Indian and Alaska Native Mental Health Research* 10(2) (2001): 1–26. Available at http://www.uchsc.edu/ai/ncaianmhr/journal/10(2).pdf (accessed August 16, 2002).

May, Philip A., and M. B. Smith. "Some Navajo Indian Opinions about Alcohol Abuse and Prohibition: A Survey and Recommendations for Policy," *Journal of Studies on Alcohol* 49 (1988): 324–334.

McCloskey, J. E. "Traditional Components of Treatment for Navajo Alcohol Abusers: Ethnographic Case Studies June 1997–April 1998." Unpublished report. Albuquerque, N.Mex.: Center on Alcoholism, Substance Abuse, and Addictions, 1998.

McCray, M., E. Green, L. Moore, and D. Pierre. "Gitksan and Wet'suwet'en Society." Paper presented at the National Conference on Traditional Peacemaking: *Remaking Justice,* Arizona State University, Tempe, Arizona, September 20–22, 1993.

National Native News. *Today's Headlines.* www.nativenews.net (accessed August 6, 2003).

Sandner, Donald. *Navajo Symbols of Healing.* Rochester, Vt.: Healing Arts Press, 1979.

Schwarz, Maureen Trudelle. *Molded in the Image of Changing Woman.* Tucson: University of Arizona Press, 1997.

————. *Navajo Lifeways: Contemporary Issues, Ancient Knowledge.* Norman: University of Oklahoma Press, 2001.

Stewart, T., P. A. May, and A. Muneta. "A Navajo Health Consumer Survey," *Medical Care* 18 (1980): 1183–1195.

Thomas, L., and L. Kihoi. "Ho'oponopono Hawaiian Peacemaking." Paper presented at the National Conference on Traditional Peacemaking: *Remaking Justice*, Arizona State University, Tempe, Arizona, September 20–22, 1993.

Topper, M. D. "Navajo 'Alcoholism': Drinking, Alcohol Abuse, and Treatment in a Changing Cultural Environment." In *The American Experience with Alcohol: Contrasting Cultural Perspectives*, ed. L. A. Bennett and G. M. Ames. New York: Plenum Press, 1995, 227–251.

Tso, T., and R. Austin. "Visionary Process." Paper presented at the National Conference on Traditional Peacemaking: *Remaking Justice*, Arizona State University, Tempe, Arizona, September 20–22, 1993.

Vicenti, C. "Traditional Peacemaking and the Remaking of Justice." Paper presented at the National Conference on Traditional Peacemaking: *Remaking Justice*, Arizona State University, Tempe, Arizona, September 20–22, 1993.

Whittaker, J. O. "Alcohol and the Standing Rock Sioux Tribe," *Quarterly Journal of Studies on Alcohol* 23 (1962): 269–287.

———. "Alcohol and the Standing Rock Sioux Tribe: A Twenty-Year Follow-Up Study," *Journal of Studies on Alcohol* 43 (1982): 191–200.

Young, R. W. *A Political History of the Navajo Tribe.* Tsaile, Ariz.: Navajo Community College Press, 1978.

Zion, James W. "The Navajo Peacemaker Court: Deference to the Old and Accommodation to the New," *American Indian Law Review* 11 (1983): 89–109.

———. "The Dynamics of Navajo Peacemaking," *Journal of Contemporary Criminal Justice* 14 (1998): 1, 58–74. http://www.realjustice.org/Pages/mn98papers/nacc_zio.html (accessed August 16, 2002).

———. "Navajo Therapeutic Jurisprudence," *Touro Law Review* 18(563) (2002).

Zion, James W., and N. J. McCabe. *Navajo Peacemaker Court Manual: A Guide to the Use of the Navajo Peacemaker Court for Judges, Community Leaders and Court Personnel.* Window Rock: Navajo Nation, 1982.

NATIVE AMERICANS AND HIV/AIDS   V

Through my participation with Native Circle program, I have established a positive direction and a solid foundation for my spiritual wellness. Native Circle program has given me support that has improved my life in all areas: mental, emotional, physical, spiritual. The support empowers me to have a healthier relationship with myself. Today, I am healthy, and have the strength to participate in and support my community.

—NATHANIEL COSTELLO

HIV/AIDS IS AN URGENT PROBLEM in Native American communities, especially in urban areas like San Francisco and Los Angeles. The AIDS epidemic among Native Americans is underreported, and it is linked with other sexually transmitted infections, substance abuse, and mental illness. In this section, Nelson Jim, clinical director of the Family and Child Guidance Clinic in San Francisco, writes about the Native Circle, a federal Center for Mental Health Services–funded program to provide mental health services for American Indians with HIV/AIDS. Rose Clark and Antony Stately describe the issues facing American Indians and Alaska Natives with HIV/AIDS in Los Angeles. David Barney, Betty Duran, and Caitlin Rosenthal describe several innovative programs funded under the Ryan White CARE Act. These research and demonstration projects of the Human Resources and Services Administration are designated as Special Projects of National Significance.

The Morning God Comes Dancing   14
Culturally Competent Mental Health and HIV Services

NELSON JIM

T HE DINEH COSMOLOGY speaks to the prophecy foreseen in the future of the Dineh people by the ancient ones. The prophecy illustrates that there will be a time of world destruction, mass death of the people of Mother Earth, a time of deadly disharmony (plague), and many other signs the people shall see. During these times, the Morning God of the East shall return.

As we come into the third decade of the AIDS epidemic, it is more evident from the many lessons learned that there has to be a strategic plan of treatment to address this new epidemic that is described by many authors as "the new small pox" (Vernon 2001) and, most certainly, no longer the "gay white man's disease" (Sing 1996). The AIDS epidemic has not only presented the indigenous people and cultures of the world with a need for conscious and direct intervention and prevention; it has challenged the very foundation of Western medical practices, philosophy, and understanding of wellness and health. Never until the AIDS epidemic have modern medicine and systems of health care been forced to reevaluate and modify their approach so completely. AIDS has completely changed our relationships with the world around us, impacted our sociopolitical realities, and, most fundamentally, shifted the relationship with our health, our bodies, and ourselves.

HIV/AIDS mental health treatment has a very short history in Native American community clinics or health centers; thus information and data are very limited or unavailable at this time. However, as in every other racial and ethnic minority community in the United States, the impact of AIDS is genocidal and lethal. The author, although very tempted, will refrain from repeating the testimonies, data, and outcry of the ways many health disparities afflict Native Americans disproportionately as they are mentioned throughout this book.

This chapter will highlight the Native Circle, a community-based, holistic HIV mental health program developed by the Family and Child Guidance Clinic (FCGC) of the Native American Health Center (NAHC) in San Francisco. Specifically, this chapter will focus on the NAHC's strategic plan of treatment, which integrates the multidisciplinary team, community collaborations, and clinical treatment to improve the psychological and medical well-being of Native Americans living with HIV or AIDS. The latter part of the chapter will provide an overview of clinical characteristics of the target population.

The Native Circle program is a five-year demonstration project funded by the Center for Mental Health Services (CMHS), Substance Abuse and Mental Health Services Administration (SAMHSA). The program was funded in October 2001, and is entering its third year at the time of this writing. NAHC's medical department in San Francisco began providing HIV primary medical care in 1987 and nurse case management in 1993. In 2002, NAHC secured and established funding for Special Projects of National Significance (SPNS), an American Indian/Alaska Native Initiative from the Health Resources and Services Administration (HRSA), HIV/AIDS Bureau, which provided the resources for NAHC to establish an HIV services department in order to develop comprehensive, multidisciplinary, holistic HIV/AIDS services by integrating medical, mental health, dental, and cultural/spiritual wellness services.

In 2001, FCGC established and submitted ten grant applications for county, state, and federal funding initiatives, of which nine were awarded, including Native Circle. Thus, NAHC-FCGC was faced with the monumental challenge of establishing, developing, implementing, and integrating these grants. The Native Circle program is the only American Indian/Alaska Native–specific program funded for this CMHS HIV mental health initiative. Native Circle has established itself, uniquely, as one of the most culturally competent community-based HIV mental health services in the nation and has implemented innovative mental/emotional/spiritual wellness interventions to meet the needs of one of the most disenfranchised and oppressed communities in America and Native America: Gay, Bisexual, Transgender, Native men who have sex with men (MSM) and other individuals living with HIV/AIDS.

For the funding agency, CMHS, the primary objective of this Native Circle is the development of "a culturally competent HIV mental health program." The staff of Native Circle met this objective by (1) integrating and linking mental health services with primary medical care, nurse case management, HIV support services, outpatient substance abuse services, and culturally based healing systems; (2) developing comprehensive coordination of care with other HIV/AIDS programs in San Francisco, which includes provision of cultural competency training; and (3) developing culturally competent clinical treatment.

Integration of Services

Many of the current Native Circle clients are referred from the NAHC medical department, which has established rapport, trust, and advocacy through receiving primary medical care, HIV testing and counseling, nurse case management, peer advocacy, and treatment advocacy. Other clients are referred from the NAHC dental department, which offers an HIV dental program. NAHC staff (medical, mental health, and dental) working with HIV clients established a weekly case conference to develop coordinated care planning to increase treatment adherence and follow-up. The case conference has provided the space, place, and time for the HIV staff to coordinate client care and may involve making referrals for intake into any of the three departments, presenting cases for grand round discussion, making referrals for outreach home visits by the HIV mental health outreach worker, planning community HIV-awareness gatherings or events, following up referrals, and receiving clinical in-service training.

The mental health clinical staff took the initiative of providing education and consultation. It also recommended establishing boundaries and a format for the HIV case conference in order to protect client confidentiality and provide clinical containment and structure for intervention plans. Throughout the collaboration process, establishing clear confidentiality protocols and treatment and service domains has always remained primary. As a result, potential HIV clients who did not seek "therapy" previously have become more engaged in mental health services.

Community Collaborations

The primary objective of developing a culturally competent HIV mental health program cannot be achieved independent of collaborations with other programs treating HIV/AIDS, substance abuse, and mental health in the Bay Area and across the United States. From its inception, Native Circle has collaborated with numerous programs that have provided much-needed support. These programs include Friendship House Association of American Indians (residential treatment program for substance abuse), Walden House Planetree Program (residential program treating substance abuse for individuals living with HIV/AIDS), Continuum (HIV/AIDS day-treatment services), Project Inform and Asian Pacifica Islander Wellness Center (training programs for HIV/AIDS treatment for the California Statewide Treatment Education Program (CSTEP), Native American AIDS Project (HIV/AIDS case management program with support counseling services), Bay Area American Indian Two Spirit (BAAITS), and the University of California, San Francisco, Department of Neurology and Psychiatry and AIDS Health Project (HIV/AIDS research and psychiatric service program).

One of the most valuable rewards of collaborations with other community services providers is our increased visibility to other providers and consumers. Some of the most common challenges many Native American programs face when they attempt to collaborate are the lack of services specifically for Native Americans, few culturally competent services sensitive to Native persons, and beliefs and misperceptions that Native Americans are extinct. The reality is very much the contrary. Native American peoples today are a rainbow of colors and are multi-tribal, multicultural, multiracial, multilingual, multiethnic, and represented across all social classes, professions, and geographical divisions. Native Circle staff has provided myriad training to community services to increase and enhance overall community awareness of Native American peoples, culture, and history.

Culturally Competent HIV and Mental Health Treatment

Central to the process of establishing and developing a culturally competent treatment program for HIV and mental health are theoretical orientation and clinical infrastructure, which must complement and be compatible with traditional Native American healing systems. Thus, the clinical staff of Native Circle incorporated family systems theory and principles as the primary clinical approach.

Systemic clinicians work from the premise that treating individuals means working with systems because individuals do not exist apart from the various communities, such as family, clan, or tribe, they function in. This premise usually translates into working with families and communities, not individuals. Dr. Jonathan Rosenfeld, Ph.D., a consulting family systems psychotherapist, often emphasized that a therapeutic approach and interventions that integrate culture, history, the geographic significance of communities, and a host of other systems was essential. This approach is particularly crucial in working with Native Americans, who often define *family* as a large community not limited to blood relatives and much broader than the Western dominant-culture model of the nuclear family. Consequently, our treatment strategy looks at treating our community members as relations and not simply as discrete individuals. To accomplish this strategy, the clinical staff draws on both clinical psychology and traditional Native American healing principles and practices.

The strong systems perspective does not mean that the clinical staff ignores issues of individual psychopathology or trauma. To dismiss individual pathology and trauma history would invariably lead to compromised treatment plans and poor outcomes. However, while not disregarding these presenting issues, the clinicians are more attuned to mobilizing resources that engage the context in which individual psychopathology is understood and experienced. With the strategic integration of traditional Native American healing principles and practices, this author believes that it is neither helpful nor respectful to idealize traditional culture and the role of traditional practitioners in particular. All cultures have certain elements of the sublime and the prosaic. However, it is very important to recognize the inherent strengths and resources of any cultural tradition and to encourage them. For many Native Americans, regardless of tribe, this primarily involves community and the relationships with relatives, nature, and spiritual deities.

Treatment Orientation

There are two main mental health clinicians who work with Native Circle clients, and one HIV mental health outreach worker. Melanie Bien, M.A., A.T.R., is trained in art therapy and Bowen Family Systems theory. She is presently the primary mental health clinician for the Native Circle program and provides a wide array of therapies, including individual, couple, family, and group therapy. Two of the most innovative treatment approaches that she has contributed to culturally competent service delivery have been art therapy and in-home therapy.

Art therapy, though a relatively new organized philosophy of healing, has root in ancient thought. The use of art making and ritual is universal. Art can be transformational and meditative for its makers. In this nonverbal medium, information for assessment, diagnosis, and treatments of clients is gathered in a nonintrusive manner that is especially useful to minimize feelings of exposure. This can be especially useful for clients who are unaccustomed to or suspicious of talk therapy. This has been a valuable medium with the Native Circle clients, many of whom face ongoing issues of intergenerational and historical trauma, which leads to PTSD, substance abuse, poverty, isolation, homelessness, invisibility, anxiety and mood disorders, and a very complicated medical picture, which affect their capacity to access health care and respond to prevention efforts.

In-home therapy is a strategic treatment approach to better meet the needs of those community members who are not accessing health care due to any of the presenting issues just mentioned above. Invisibility and isolation are two key obstacles threatening and further compromising the lives of Native Circle clients. Many times the lack of resources to address the wide array of psychosocial conditions these individuals must overcome on a daily basis greatly limits their efforts for mental, emotional, and spiritual support. The in-home therapy component of Native Circle has been able to increase service utilization by 30 percent in the last year. Culturally, this parallels how, in many indigenous communities, healing (treatment) is facilitated in the most fundamental space and place in the individual's life, their homes.

The author is the mental health treatment director of the Native Circle program. He is professionally trained as both a body-centered and family systems psychotherapist. The late Maryanna Eckberg, a mentor and advisor of the author, describes body-centered psychotherapy as "a branch of psychotherapy based on distinct and explicit theory of mind-body functioning and on the relationship between the various levels of experience—cognitive, emotional, physical, and energetic. It is a way of understanding personality, or character structure, through one's experience and energetic processes. This is an integrative and holistic orientation, making no distinction between the mind and the body" (Eckberg et al. 2000).

Body-centered psychotherapy has a long tradition, dating back to the work of Wilhelm Reich, M.D., psychoanalyst and a student of Sigmund Freud. The author has always treated and supported HIV infection as trauma to the psyche, body, and person, very much as Eckberg treated survivors of shock trauma, an experience that she describes as "traumatized bodies being out of control." Interestingly enough, one of the most consistent responses or somatic reports from Native Circle clients is that they feel as if they "are going out of control": "I feel like I am going to go crazy." The primary difference between shock trauma victims and individuals with HIV/AIDS is that individuals with HIV/AIDS are constantly dealing with their trauma; thus a major area of the "work" is in the integrative process. The fact that the traumatic process is never finished invariably results in significant mind, body, spiritual, and social distortions and limits somatic presence. The pain of "being in the body" is often too great for those living with HIV/ AIDS.

Additional roles of the author are establishing and integrating traditional Native American healing systems by providing traditional Native American counseling, which may include rituals, prayer, consultation on traditional Dineh medicinal herbs, and talking circles; and coordinating consultation with traditional Native American healing practitioners from several different tribes or nations. Some of the traditional practitioners who support Native Circle are

- Hanson Ashley, M.A., Dineh Traditional Practitioner from Shonto, Arizona, located on the northwestern Navajo reservation.
- Lonnie Emhoolah, Kiowa/Comanche traditional consultant from Lawton, Oklahoma.
- Richard Moves Camp, Lakota Sioux traditional consultant of Pine Ridge. South Dakota.
- The late Lannie Pinola, Pomo traditional practitioner from Northern California.

Traditional Native American counseling, like Western therapy models, is composed in a structured system of thoughts, principles, and philosophies that incorporate indigenous cosmology and medicine ways. Unlike the Western perspective and approach to health, the traditional Native American wellness approach emphasizes and facilitates a process of "rebalancing," treating the spiritual, emotional, mental, and the physical capacities of community members. The concept of healing in this ancient wellness practice is that we are always "rebalancing." Thus, to cure someone (a Western concept) of an illness or disease is, if anything, a separation from nature and the natural cycle of life. Furthermore, Native Circle consciously integrates traditional Native American healing principles and practices as it strives to bring balance to the entire family or clan, and it supports and complements the internal resources of the individual, family, clan and community. With traditional Native American practitioners, FCGC can offer community members an opportunity for ritual and ceremonial healing (including prayer) that is not otherwise readily available due to the separation from traditional homelands and cultural traditions. One of the most important differences from Western health care is that traditional Native American healing practices not only provide support for returning from disharmony (illness or disease) to balance, but they also provide Native American community members the rituals and spiritual meanings with which to celebrate, honor, and acknowledge all of life (wellness as well as illness). Central to this ability is the establishment or reestablishment of patients' relations with "family," relatives, community, nature, gods, and most importantly, themselves.

Finally, the most frequent misunderstanding of traditional Native American healing is the mystification of spirituality. Essentially, the author would like to warn that just because something (a ritual, object, or person) is considered sacred or possessing spiritual essence, it is not necessarily "good" or "healing." On the contrary, Native American cosmologies and healing traditions teach that there are practices, objects, and people possessing spiritual capacity to inflict great harm.

Eduardo Duran and Bonnie Duran (1995) make the following culturally relevant observation:

> The models of treatment that are the most effective are those in which traditional Native American thinking and practice are utilized in conjunction with Western practice. In order to accomplish this integration, the therapist must understand and validate traditional Native American cosmology. In essence, the therapist cannot simply learn to apply cross-cultural techniques in the hope that these will help the client. The therapist must believe and practice these beliefs in his/her personal life if the intervention is to benefit the client. There is nothing more offensive to a Native American client than a therapist who is pretending to understand and provide therapy within a traditional perspective if that therapist is mimicking a value system through the production of therapeutic techniques.

The author wholeheartedly agrees with the Durans and is also an advocate for the protection of traditional Native American healing practices from exploitation and misconceptions.

Community Integration

The HIV mental health outreach worker primarily facilitates community integration activities, which include outreach (street, agencies/organizations, and powwows), nature and community outings, and community cultural gatherings at the NAHC. The basic idea behind "community integration" came when Native Circle staff became more attuned to the needs of its clients. Many of the clients challenged by HIV- or AIDS-related conditions are isolated, have very limited resources, and thus make themselves invisible to the mainstream. This intervention was established to provide a gradual reintegration into mainstream society through monthly outings, seasonal gatherings, and nature outings to reestablish connection with natural places and things and connection with the larger Native American community.

Generally, the HIV mental health outreach workers conduct weekly street outreach and visit community agencies, HIV/AIDS programs, HIV/AIDS local community advisory board meetings, and state prisons. They attend cultural events such as powwows, community gatherings, community health fairs, multicultural events, and art and craft shows. Overall, the HIV mental health outreach worker is an essential component of services linkage and integration with the Native American Health Center's medical, dental and nutrition programs, thus improving treatment and supportive services.

In summary, treatment interventions are provided in the form of conventional mental health treatment and traditional Native practices. However, both strands of treatment are interwoven in that clinical treatment is organized around an awareness of cultural identity issues and may incorporate traditional practices, and traditional practice is incorporated into overall treatment in a way that supports clinical interventions.

Native Circle Clients

The majority (90 percent) of the Native Circle clients are gay and bisexual men, MSM, and injection drug users (IDU). Most of the clients who utilized our mental health services also presented other issues, such as substance abuse, homelessness, history of trauma, poverty, and cultural displacement.

Trauma is endemic to the community we serve, and the roots of trauma are found in both cultural and familial experience. For many, if not most, Native Circle clients, their identity is organized around the trauma they have experienced as well as the specific ways they have either overcome or adapted to such trauma. As the HIV/AIDS disease progresses, so do fear, weariness, and hopelessness. One Native Circle client summarized the situation this way: "A simple common cold or the threat of a mosquito bite (West Nile virus) can cause a nightmare." Socially, the shame and stigma associated with AIDS, substance abuse, mental illness, or being gay or bisexual can manifest themselves in very complex and compromised wellness. Clients come from multiracial, multicultural, and multiethnic backgrounds and are disconnected literally and figuratively from tribal and traditional communities. Thus, issues of racism and homophobia and the illnesses of internalized racism and internalized homophobia suffered by many Native Circle clients further undermine out clients' integrity and their place in the circle of the Native community. The Native Circle staff believes that these mixed backgrounds and this physical and cultural disconnection often lead to gross distortions in identity formation and organization. Furthermore, such distortions are often compounded by growing up in chaotic family environments where physical, sexual, and psychological abuse are chronic problems and severely impact clients who are either witnesses or direct victims of abuse.

Many of our clients' identities are based on containing trauma and reenacting traumatic experiences. Such identity organization may activate a range of risk factors leading to many maladaptive behaviors, including substance abuse; unsafe sexual practices; domestic violence as perpetrator, victim, or both; and homelessness.

Psychiatric management has long been minimized or overlooked in the HIV disease process. However, research studies show us that HIV passes through the blood-brain barrier, lives in the brain, severely affects the central nervous system, and results in many complications (Cournos and Forstein 2000; Wallace et al. 2001; Levy 1989; and Forstien 2003). Some of the obvious complications exhibited by many of the Native Circle clients are HIV-associated dementia, HIV-associated minor cognitive motor disorder, viral meningitis, toxoplasma, Kaposi's sarcoma, and various types of neuropathy. Dr. Marshall Forstein, M.D., a consulting psychiatrist to CMHS, recently provided excellent neuropsychiatry training on "The impact of HIV on the brain and behavior" to Native Circle staff and other CMHS grantees, quite simply demonstrating how HIV is a silent killer in the deep darkness of the brain. Dr. Forstein emphasized that most HIV tests for viral load count do not determine the viral load in the central nervous system, specifically in cerebrospinal fluid. He further illustrated that most highly active antiretroviral treatment (HAART) medication does not enter into the central nervous system, so the virus can and will mutate undetectably to lethal capacity. Because of the overwhelming social, medical, and clinical challenges of Native Circle clients, along with their vulnerability to high-risk factors, the treatment staff coordinates psychiatric referrals with the NAHC director of HIV services, who facilitates referrals to Dr. George Harrison, M.D., of University of California, San Francisco, AIDS Health Project.

NAHC, located in an urban and alien world with no established cultural center, is home to many Native Americans who have been displaced from their homelands and communities. The health center is by default their cultural center; thus it strives to offer the most comprehensive services available to its community while preserving Native American traditions, practices, and other cultural mores—the very foundation of the Native Circle program.

Notes

This work was supported by Center for Mental Health Services grant SM 53893, Native Circle, of the HIV Mental Health Services Collaborative Program. The chapter's contents are solely the responsibility of the author.

Cournos, F., and M. Forstein, eds. *What Mental Health Practitioners Need to Know about HIV and AIDS.* New Directions for Mental Health Services 87. San Francisco: Jossey-Bass, Fall 2000.

Duran, E., and B. Duran. *Native American Postcolonial Psychology.* Albany: State University of New York Press, 1995.

Eckberg, M., P. Levine. *Victims of Cruelty: Somatic Psychotherapy in the Treatment of Post-Traumatic Stress Disorder.* Berkeley, Calif.: North Atlantic Books, 2000.

Forstein, M. "Neuropsychiatry and AIDS." Presentation on Native Circle and Center for Mental Health Centers at *The Impact on the Brain and Behavior*, San Francisco, Calif., August 15, 2003.

Levy, R. M., and D. E. Bredesen. "Controversies in HIV-Related Central Nervous System Disease: Neuropsychological Aspects of HIV-1 Infection." In *AIDS Clinical Review*, ed. Paul Volberding and M. Jacobsen. New York: Michael Dekker, 1989.

Sing, K. *Gay and Homosexually Active Aboriginal Men in Sydney.* Sidney, Australia: HIV, AIDS and Society Publications, 1996.

Vernon, I. S. *Killing Us Quietly: Native Americans and HIV/AIDS.* Lincoln: University of Nebraska Press, 2001.

Wallace, M. R., J. A. Nelson, J. A., McCutchan, T. Wolfson, and I. Grant. "Symptomatic HIV Seroconverting Illness Is Associated with More Rapid Neurological Impairment," *Sexually Transmitted Infections* 77 (2001): 199–200.

HIV/AIDS Care Programs for American Indians and Alaska Natives

15

DAVID D. BARNEY, BETTY E. S. DURAN, AND CAITLIN ROSENTHAL

H IV AND AIDS ARE IMPORTANT HEALTH CONCERNS for American Indian and Alaska Native (AI/AN) tribes and individuals. AIDS incidence has been steadily increasing among American Indians and Alaska Natives (Centers for Disease Control and Prevention 2002; Sileo and Gooden 2003; Metler, Conway, and Stehr-Green 1991). As of December 31, 2001, American Indians and Alaska Natives had the third-highest AIDS rate of all races at 11.7 per 100,000 and a total of 2,527 AIDS diagnoses plus an additional 962 HIV-infected individuals (Centers for Disease Control and Prevention 2002). Demographic characteristics of AIDS cases indicate that approximately 23 percent are women and 77 percent are men. In the year 2001, there were 194 newly diagnosed adult or adolescent AI/AN AIDS cases and no pediatric AI/AN AIDS cases (cases in people less than thirteen years of age) (Centers for Disease Control and Prevention 2002).

An earlier report found that the risk-of-HIV-exposure group characteristics of AI/ANs were similar to those of all persons with AIDS in the United States. The most frequently reported mode of HIV exposure was men who have sex with men (MSM), accounting for 49 percent of AI/ANs with AIDS (Centers for Disease Control and Prevention 1998). However, a larger percentage of AIDS cases in AI/ANs were associated with MSM who were also injection drug users (MSM/IDUs) than in people with AIDS in all races and ethnicities (14 percent versus 6 percent).

To date, most HIV/AIDS-related funding for AI/AN has come through two federal sources. HIV primary prevention has been funded by the Centers for Disease Control and Prevention (CDCP). The CDCP has funded nationwide prevention efforts through the National Native American AIDS Prevention Center (NNAAPC) (www.nnaapc.org) and has also provided funding directly to tribal groups. In mid-2003, the CDCP has also initiated HIV prevention efforts at the secondary and tertiary levels by funding prevention programs that target individuals who are already infected with HIV (Centers for Disease Control and Prevention 2003).

For AI/ANs who are living with HIV, programs have been established under funding provided by the Ryan White CARE Act of 1990 (CARE Act) [Pub. L. 101–381]. It is especially important to note that the Ryan White CARE Act is named for Ryan White and the battle that he fought against AIDS. Ryan White CARE Act programs are a continuing legacy of Ryan's struggle to help those infected with HIV/AIDS to fight the deadly effects of this disease. As a result of his own experiences with discrimination, Ryan was particularly concerned about the effects of discrimination and how discrimination disadvantaged individuals with HIV/AIDS—including American Indians—even further (White-Ginder 2003).

Under the CARE Act, funds for HIV/AIDS treatment are provided to areas highly inpacted by HIV/AIDS (Title I), to states for statewide distribution (Title II), to medical clinics specializing in treatment of HIV/AIDS (Title III), and to special populations: women, infants, children, and youth (Title IV). Overall, programs funded by the CARE Act have improved accessibility, quality, and outcomes for various populations living with HIV disease (McKinney and Marconi 2002).

AI/ANs are eligible for services and medical care under all CARE Act titles and are also eligible for HIV/AIDS treatment through Indian Health Service (IHS) programs or IHS/tribal medical clinics. Most important, however, AI/ANs have been specifically named under programs called Special Projects of National Significance (SPNS), established under Part F of the CARE Act (hab.hrsa.gov/programs/factsheets/spnsfact.htm). SPNS-funded interventions are research and demonstration projects using innovative service delivery models. They may ensure the ongoing ability of American Indian and Alaska Native communities to care for AI/ANs with HIV disease. SPNS may also include the delivery of HIV health care and support services to traditionally underserved populations, including AI/AN individuals and families with HIV disease (U.S. Congress 1990).

It is important to note that, on occasion, SPNS HIV/AIDS funding has also been extended to Native Hawaiians (NH) as an indigenous group of the United States. Native Hawaiians have become identified as indigenous people due to their cultural ties to traditional healing and ancestral ties to the lands of the Hawaiian Islands. Notably, Native Hawaiians also comprise a high-risk population in need of culturally responsive HIV/AIDS prevention and care services (Aiu and Reinhardt 1998; Aiu 1996). High rates of poverty, homelessness, substance abuse, teen pregnancy, domestic violence, and sexually transmitted infections (STIs) contribute to increased risk of HIV transmission and a need for HIV/AIDS prevention and treatment (Aiu and Reinhardt 1998).

Special Projects of National Significance

Four AI/AN initiatives have been funded under the CARE Act, Part F—SPNS, by the Department of Health and Human Services, Public Health Service, Health Resources and Services Administration. The first AI/AN initiative began in 1991 and lasted for three years; the second initiative began in 1994 and lasted for two years; the third initiative began in 1996 and lasted for five years; and the fourth, or most recent, initiative began in 2002 and will end in 2007.

In 1991, the NNAAPC, based in Oakland, California, became the first AI/AN organization to be awarded a SPNS grant. NNAAPC's core HIV/AIDS-care demonstration project was established in Oklahoma City and Tulsa, Oklahoma. The project was named Ahalaya, a Choctaw word that means "to care for deeply." A unique case management model was developed specifically for replication in American Indian tribal, Alaska Native village, and Native Hawaiian community health programs, as well as in CARE Act–funded programs. This HIV–case management model is entitled the Ahalaya model. It is a holistic approach that includes traditional healing and traditional world views for specifically serving AI/AN/NHs (Barney and Duran 1997; Barney and Burhansstipanov 1998; Kropf 1995).

In 1992, NNAAPC was awarded supplemental funding by HRSA SPNS to fund additional AI/AN/NH sites that would replicate the Ahalaya model. The ten additional HIV–case management projects were Native American HIV/AIDS Coalition (Kansas), Minnesota American Indian AIDS Task Force, Milwaukee Indian Health Board, the Southwestern AIDS Network, Indian Community Health Service (Arizona), a southeastern tribe, Seattle Indian Health Board, American Indian Community House (New York), a regional Alaska Native corporation, and Papa Ola Lōkahi (Hawai'i) (Burhansstipanov 1998). Two non-case-management projects were also funded: Positively Native, a national newsletter and support group for AI/AN/NH HIV-positive people, and the Indian Health Council in Pauma Valley, California, a project to coordinate traditional healing conferences and training for HIV-positive clients.

During the second SPNS AI/AN/NH initiative, a national multisite database was established to consolidate common variables from the eleven case management sites. The *National Database for HIV-Infected American Indians, Alaska Natives, and Native Hawaiians* had a sample size of 408 individuals and was the first multisite aggregation of data across multiple projects conducted under HRSA SPNS (Barney 1996).

The third SPNS initiative was awarded in the fall of 1996 for a five-year grant cycle ending in the fall of 2001. Under this initiative, HRSA SPNS funded four AI/AN projects. Each of these four projects proposed to develop a unique model of care for AI/AN/NH. The projects included the NNAAPC coalition of existing projects, the Navajo Nation, the Santa Barbara Indian Justice Center, and a regional Alaska Native corporation. These AI/AN projects were also required to participate in a national multisite evaluation, conducted this time, however, under the auspices of Columbia University.

In October 2002, the fourth SPNS American Indian/Alaska Native (AI/AN) initiative began funding projects to coordinate HIV care with substance abuse and mental health services. The initiative acknowledges and addresses continuing high rates of substance and alcohol abuse among American Indians and Alaska Natives. It aims to facilitate testing and entry into care. Other goals include increasing adherence to medical therapies and providing culturally sensitive counseling for prevention and care.

Six projects and a technical assistance center receive funding. Each project is developing and testing a model of care that may be incorporated into future Ryan White CARE projects, and each project is also charged with facilitating an important dissemination effort. These projects' encounters with the unique barriers related to service delivery in AI/AN communities will eventually inform future intervention efforts. Their experiences have already begun to fill a significant gap in our knowledge of the specific needs of AI/AN communities dealing with HIV/AIDS.

The National American Indian/Alaska Native HIV/AIDS Technical Assistance Center (TA Center), located at the University of Oklahoma, serves as the technical assistance center for the initiative with the primary goal of assisting the local projects in the development of rigorous and culturally appropriate care models (www.ou.edu/hiv). The TA Center also assists HRSA SPNS in evaluating the efforts and capabilities of each local project and helps to disseminate the findings of the HIV care models.

The six individual demonstration projects in this initiative are distributed across the United States. Two are located in Alaska, one in the San Francisco Bay area, one in New Mexico, another in southeastern North Carolina, and one in Washington state. The two programs in Alaska cover diverse and distinct populations. The Healthy Transitions Project in Anchorage is conducted by the Alaska Native Tribal Health Consortium (ANTHC). It targets the disproportionately high number of at-risk, incarcerated Alaska Natives. At the end of 2000, 36 percent of individuals in its custody were reportedly Alaska Natives, yet Alaska Natives comprise only 15.6 percent of the state's total population. Most of those in custody eventually return to the community, but, unfortunately, they receive few transitional services. The project facilitates their reentry by promoting HIV testing and encouraging HIV-infected and high-risk individuals to enroll in appropriate services. The Healthy Transitions Project is also improving HIV care for all Alaska Natives by assessing services currently available at ANTHC.

The Alaska Native Wrap-Around HIV/AIDS Project, administered by the Yukon-Kuskokwim Health Corporation, located in Bethel, Alaska, provides truly comprehensive "wrap-around" care for infected Alaska Natives. It works with local village elders and health care providers to increase awareness about HIV/AIDS issues. While it is suspected that the Yukon-Kuskokwim delta area may have increasing numbers of HIV-infected individuals, many individuals living in the region do not know their HIV status. Alaska Natives are infected at a higher rate than Alaskans statewide and have many HIV co-morbidities, such as STIs, substance abuse, and mental illness. Increasing awareness by heightening community education, training health care workers, and providing HIV testing opportunities, the project simultaneously improves the well-being of already infected individuals and helps uninfected individuals preserve their HIV-negative status.

In the San Francisco Bay Area, the Native American Health Center Holistic Native Network is identifying HIV-infected individuals and increasing the benefits of HIV interventions through a holistic system of care and case management (Nebelkopf and King 2003). By providing comprehensive and integrated case management, the agency is assisting clients who may be experiencing substance abuse or mental health issues in addition to HIV/AIDS. The Holistic Native Network is also conducting outreach with clients of Friendship House. Clients of this residential, program for treating drug abuse are referred to HIV testing and services at the Native American Health Center. Increasing access to confidential HIV testing and counseling for high-risk urban American Indian clients helps to slow the spread of HIV among AI/AN in the Bay Area.

The Four Corners American Indian Circle of Services Collaborative (4CC) is a network of seven collaborating organizations and departments in the Navajo Nation and the University of New Mexico. Na'Nizhoozhi Center, Inc. (NCI), in Gallup, New Mexico, coordinates and integrates services and project evaluation through this network of organizations. HIV rates in the Navajo Nation have steadily increased since 1987, but only in 2002 were cases discovered in which initial infection occurred within the reservation itself (Navajo Area Indian Health Service 2003). NCI is subcontracting to the Navajo AIDS Network to provide comprehensive case management services. It is also working to provide culturally appropriate outreach for substance abusers who are at high risk of HIV infection. Other activities include counseling, education, and HIV testing for persons at risk, training for health-care providers, and prevention education and traditional counseling for HIV-infected and high-risk clients.

More American Indians live in Robeson County, North Carolina, than in any other county east of the Mississippi River. Thirty-eight percent of the population is American Indian, and many communities have been historically isolated from the rest of the county. The Southeastern NC American Indian HIV/AIDS Project, which is administrated by the Native American Interfaith Ministries' Healing Lodge, extends and enhances culturally appropriate HIV/AIDS services throughout Robeson County and six surrounding counties. One unique component of the program is its use of ministers and lay leaders as access points for community intervention and outreach. By providing HIV/AIDS education to respected community leaders, the project recruits individuals into HIV testing and services. It is also improving the broader capacity of the community to focus on HIV/AIDS. Other goals include more flexible HIV testing and more culturally competent care for American Indian clients.

Finally, the South Puget Intertribal Planning Agency is providing HIV/AIDS services for three of its member tribes in southwestern Washington state. Expanding the Circle of Care responds to high rates of substance abuse and mental illness among the tribes. Not many HIV/AIDS cases have been reported, but these communities may be at risk, and very few individuals know their HIV status. Facilitating HIV testing and risk-factor awareness are the project's primary goals. It also encourages entry into care for any HIV-infected community members. These efforts are coordinated with ongoing prevention and awareness campaigns.

Contemporary HIV/AIDS Issues

The effect and impact of HIV/AIDS on tribal and village communities represents complexity in that health issues are tied not only to biology but to social and cultural elements as well (Pasick 1997). Health outcomes, disease susceptibility, and general well-being involve individual perceptions and behaviors, social structures, and community capacity. For AI/ANs, some of the unique and important issues, but not all, involve reservation-urban circular migration, limited health resources, a low priority for HIV issues among tribal governments, underreporting of HIV and AIDS, limited confidentiality, and a need to incorporate cultural values in interventions.

Circular migration from rural or reservation areas to urban places and back again is a risk factor for HIV/AIDS transmission as new entry into urban cities may lead to loneliness and isolation, increased socializing in American Indian bars, and sexual contact with people who are not very well known to the newly arrived individual (Brassard, Smeja, and Valverde 1996). The pattern of circular migration may be common among many American Indians and Alaska Natives as tribal members seek employment and education opportunities in more affluent urban communities. Tribal members residing in urban areas migrate back to reservation communities to participate in ceremonies, community events, and family gatherings (Weaver 1999). This pattern poses a challenge for many reservation communities as they have limited resources and expertise to address health outcomes that are influenced by mobility-related issues. For example, migrating AI/ANs may be receiving health care through multiple medical providers, such as IHS on the reservation and community health centers in urban areas. Lack of consistent medical care may limit the effectiveness of diagnosis and treatment of health-related problems.

Resources for HIV testing, prevention, and HIV/AIDS care are limited in rural or reservation areas. Ryan White CARE Act programs are scarce on reservations and in village communities. Thus, the majority of HIV/AIDS outreach, HIV testing, and medical care are provided by IHS clinics or hospitals (operated either by the tribe or by IHS). This is problematic, however. First, the IHS is underfunded and is the medical care provider of last resort. Second, the IHS provides medical care in only thirty-three reservation states. Third, IHS underestimates the importance of HIV/AIDS as service need estimates are based on the numbers of American Indians who have utilized IHS facilities within the last two years, yet many American Indians use health care services other than IHS (Office of Technology Assessment 1986). Fourth, comprehensive HIV primary care by IHS to tribal members residing in rural communities is problematic as medical workers are not likely to be trained in HIV primary care. Additionally, due to low HIV-positive patient loads, medical staff may lack expertise in treatment protocols. This may be further compounded if medical staff is not be interested in receiving HIV training due to the limited number of HIV cases in the clinic or their personal issues regarding homosexuality and HIV.

Lack of funding tends to place HIV/AIDS at a lower priority than health problems that affect greater numbers of tribal members (diabetes, cancer, heart disease, etc.). In a survey of 147 tribal health directors, AIDS ranks seventh of eight health problems. AIDS was estimated to receive the least amount of financial support (Michalek et al. 1996).

Underreporting of HIV/AIDS is a serious concern for AI/AN populations (Smyser and Helgerson 1992; Conway 1992). This underreporting results from racial misclassification in HIV testing programs and state epidemiological reporting as AI/ANs are sometimes unwilling to identify their race accurately because of discrimination or unwanted referral to Indian-specific health services (Lieb et al. 1992). This reluctance results in underrepresentation of the prevalence of HIV and AIDS among AI/AN peoples and ultimately reduces funding for HIV/AIDS care services, reduces resources for targeting AI/AN communities for HIV prevention, and minimizes the seriousness of the problem within AI/AN populations (Rowell 1998).

HIV testing and HIV care services are affected by concerns about a lack of confidentiality in tribal settings. Rural reservation and village communities consist of close-knit families many of whose members work in the facilities that provide health care for tribal members. In many situations, the high-risk or HIV-infected individual may prefer to seek HIV testing and services somewhere that does not employ tribal members. Individuals may commute great distances for HIV testing and support services to maintain confidentiality of their HIV status and avoid potential negative family and community perceptions of their sexual orientation.

On the other hand, accessing services outside the tribal community is affected by multiple barriers, such as poverty, lack of transportation, inability to identify with non-Indian service agencies, a lack of shared cultural beliefs and values, and a historic distrust of non-Indian programs (Lockart 1981).

For most AI/ANs living in an urban setting, programs funded by the Ryan White CARE Act become the primary vehicle for HIV testing and HIV/AIDS medical and social services. Often, AI/AN interests have been addressed by Ryan White CARE Act Planning Councils, and funding has been made available to non-Indian AIDS service organizations (ASOs) and urban Indian health centers. When HIV testing and services are provided by non-Indian or non-Native organizations, there is an increased need for cultural sensitivity awareness in interventions and staff training to enhance cultural competence. Unfortunately, not all CARE Act providers have included traditional (non-Western) healing ceremonies, talking circles, specific interventions for two-spirit gay men, alternative medications, or other culturally specific services for AI/AN populations (Duran 1995; Rendon 1993). Interventions need to be designed and implemented to include development of positive American Indian or Alaska Native self-esteem and self-identity (Nebelkopf and King 2003).

Notes

Aiu, Pua 'ala 'oklani. "The Native Hawaiian Case Management Project," *Innovations: Issues in HIV Service Delivery* (summer 1996): 20.

Aiu, Pua 'ala 'oklani, and Tyrone Reinhardt. "Papa Ola Lokahi, Hawai'i." In *Native Americans and HIV: A Summary of On-Going Special Projects of National Significance*, ed. L. Burhansstipanov. Rockville, Md.: Special Projects of National Significance, Health Resources and Services Administration, 1998.

Barney, David D. "The National Database for HIV-Infected American Indians, Alaska Natives, and Native Hawaiians," *Innovations: Issues in HIV Service Delivery* (summer 1996): 4–5.

Barney, David D., and Linda Burhansstipanov. "The Ahalaya Project, Oklahoma." In *Native Americans and HIV: A Summary of On-going Special Projects of National Significance*, ed. L. Burhansstipanov. Rockville, Md.: Special Projects of National Significance, Health Resources and Services Administration, 1998.

Barney, David D., and Betty E. S. Duran. "Case Management: Coordination of Service Delivery for HIV-Infected Individuals." In *HIV Mental Health for the 21st Century*, ed. M. G. Winiarski. New York: New York University Press, 1997.

Brassard, Paul, Christina Smeja, and Clara Valverde. "Needs Assessment for an Urban Native HIV and AIDS Prevention Program," *AIDS Education and Prevention* 8(4) (1996): 343–351.

Burhansstipanov, Linda, ed. *Native Americans and HIV: A Summary of On-Going Special Projects of National Significance*. Rockville, Md.: Special Projects of National Significance, Health Resources and Services Administration, 1998.

Centers for Disease Control and Prevention (CDCP). "HIV/AIDS among American Indians and Alaskan Natives—United States, 1981–1997," *MMWR: Mortality and Morbidity Weekly Review* 47(8) (1998): 154–60.

———. "U.S. HIV and AIDS Cases Reported through December 2001," *HIV/AIDS Surveillance Report* 13(2) (2002): 1–44.

———. "Incorporating HIV Prevention into the Medical Care of Persons Living with HIV," *MMWR: Mortality and Morbidity Weekly Review* 52(12) (2003): 1–32.

Conway, George A. "Racial Misclassification of AI/AN Patients with Class IV HIV infection," *HIS Primary Care Provider* 17(5) (1992): 72.

Duran, Betty. "Traditional Healing for American Indians Infected with HIV," *AIDSLink: NCIH HIV/AIDS Network Newsletter* (1995): 36, 4–5.

Kropf, Aleisha. "The Ahalaya Project: Redesigning HIV Services for Native Americans, Alaskan Natives, and Hawaiian Natives," *Innovations: Issues in HIV Service Delivery* (fall 1995): 2–5.

Lieb, Loren, George A. Conway, Michael Hedderman, John Yao, and Peter R. Kerndt. "Racial Misclassification of American Indians with AIDS in Los Angeles County," *Journal of Acquired Immune Deficiency Syndromes* 5(11) (1992): 1137–1141.

Lockart, Barbara. "Historic Distrust and the Counseling of American Indians and Alaska Natives," *White Cloud Journal of AI/AN Mental Health* 2(3) (1981): 31–34.

McKinney, Martha M., and Katherine M. Marconi. "Delivering HIV Services to Vulnerable Populations: A Review of CARE Act-Funded Research," *Public Health Reports* 117 (2002): 99–113.

Metler, Russ, George A. Conway, and Jeanette Stehr-Green. "AIDS Surveillance among American Indians and Alaska Natives," *American Journal of Public Health* 81(11) (1991): 1469–1471.

Michalek, A., M. Mahoney, D. Tome, L. Burhansstipanov, and M. Tenney. "Tribal-Based Cancer Control Activities: Services and Perceptions," *Alaska Medicine* 38(2) (1996): 60–65.

Navajo Area Indian Health Service. *Public Health Emergency! HIV and Syphilis Epidemiology: 2001–2003: A Report to the Navajo Nation Health and Social Services Committee*. Gallup, N.Mex.: US DHHS Public Health Service, Indian Health Service, 2003.

Nebelkopf, E., and J. King. "A Holistic System of Care for Native Americans in an Urban Environment," *Journal of Psychoactive Drugs* 35(1) (2003): 43–52.

Office of Technology Assessment. *Indian Health Care*. Vol. OTA-H-290. Washington, D.C.: U.S. Government Printing Office, 1986.

Pasick, Rena J. "Socioeconomic and Cultural Factors in the Development and Use of Theory." In *Health Behavior and Health Education: Theory, Research, and Practice*, ed. K. Glanz, F. M. Lewis, and B. K. Rimer. San Francisco: Jossey-Bass, 1997.

Rendon, Marcie R. "A Journey to Life: Native People with HIV Disease and Traditional Healing," *Season* (1993): 3–9.

Rowell, Ronald. "Overview of the AIDS Epidemic among Native Americans." In *Native Americans and HIV: A Summary of On-Going Special Projects of National Significance*, ed. L. Burhansstipanov. Rockville, Md.: Special Projects of National Significance, Health Resources and Services Administration, 1998.

Sileo, Thomas W., and Myrna A. Gooden. "HIV/AIDS Prevention in American Indian and Alaska Native Communities," *Tribal College Journal of American Indian Higher Education* 14(4) (2003): 44–48.

Smyser, Michael, and Steven D. Helgerson. "Racial Misclassification among AI/AN Reported with Class IV HIV Infection in Washington State," *IHS Primary Care Provider* 17(5) (1992): 74–75.

U.S. Congress, The Ryan White CARE Act: Public Law 101–381. Washington, D.C.: U.S. Government Printing Office, 1990.

Weaver, Hilary N. "Through Indigenous Eyes: Native Americans and the HIV Epidemic," *Health and Social Work* 24(1) (1999): 27–34.

White-Ginder, Jeanne. Personal communication, July 29, 2003.

American Indians and HIV/AIDS 16

ROSE L. CLARK AND ANTONY STATELY

MERICAN INDIANS/ALASKA NATIVES (AI/ANs) are unique compared to any other racial/ethnic group in the United States due to being members of sovereign nations. It is the social and political history of AI/AN people and their government-to-government relationship to the U.S. government that define their distinctive place in American life. AI/ANs have been intimately connected to the influence of European settlers and to the policies of the U.S. government, which have been primarily focused on genocide, assimilation, and termination of the tribes' sovereign status.

Duran and Duran (1995) discuss the phenomena of cumulative and community level trauma and the pain that AI/AN communities suffer as a direct result of the genocidal effects of colonization. They describe the notion of a "soul wound" that is at the core of much of contemporary suffering of AI/AN people, which they contend must be acknowledged and understood within a historical context. Brave Heart and De Bruyn (1998) proposed the phenomenon of chronic trauma and unresolved grief across generations and labeled it "historical unresolved grief." Such historical unresolved grief, originating from the loss of lives, land, and vital aspects of Native culture that resulted directly from colonization, contributes, they suggest, to American Indians' current pathology. Like the transfer of trauma from Holocaust survivors to their descendents, the effects of physical and cultural genocide directed at American Indians are transferred across generations. The current generations of American Indians face layers of repetitive traumatic losses that are physical, cultural, and spiritual in nature. These multiple layers of repetitive loss, in addition to the major traumas of the past, contribute to the pain, psychological numbing, and destructive coping that can best be described as a chronic stress disorder at a community level.

Similar to other ethnic minorities, AI/ANs have been disproportionately impacted by HIV/AIDS. More than half of AI/ANs diagnosed with AIDS reside in five states, with California accounting for one quarter of the diagnosed cases. Despite advances in highly active antiretroviral treatments that have led to dramatic declines in deaths since 1996, AIDS-related deaths dropped only 41 percent among AI/ANs compared to 53 percent for whites. Of the 2,337 cumulative toll of people with AIDS among AI/ANs, more than half have died (CDC 1998). In Los Angeles, site of one of the highest concentrations of urban AI/ANs in the country, AI/ANs comprise approximately 1.5 percent of the county's population and number approximately 138,000 (Census 2001). The AI/AN seropositivity rate (5.4 percent for AI/AN men and 1.3 percent for AI/AN women) was three times that of whites in Los Angeles County—particularly disturbing given that substantially lower numbers of AI/AN people tested in the county. Between 30 and 50 times more Latinos, African Americans, Asian Americans, and whites received HIV testing at county-funded test sites than did AI/ANs (LACDHS 1999). More disturbing is the trend reflected in the data on posttest return rates. While the county's posttest return rate for all racial categories (positives and negatives combined) is 75.4 percent, the AI/AN return rate is 77.8 percent. However, less than half (47.6 percent) of AI/ANs who tested positive returned for their results—compared with the overall posttest return rate of 80.3 percent of all racial categories for the county. Only 52.9 percent of AI/AN men and 33.3 percent of AI/AN women who tested positive returned for their results—by far the lowest return rates among all racial categories in the county (LACDHS 1999).

Although AIDS surveillance data suggest that total AI/AN AIDS cases are relatively low, these rates are likely greatly underestimated. Primary evidence for this assertion is the high rates of other sexually transmitted diseases (STDs) found among AI/ANs. During the period from 1992 to 1997, while the rate of gonorrhea decreased for every other racial group, it increased for AI/ANs. AI/ANs are second to African Americans in gonorrhea rates for the nation. Further support for this argument stems from the significant racial misclassification of AI/ANs in the public health system (Lieb et al. 1992).

HIV surveillance data may more accurately depict the epidemic among AI/ANs. For example, the Indian Health Service (IHS) reported that in three western states, HIV rates among third trimester AI/AN patients were four to eight times higher than among childbearing women of all other races (Conway et al. 1992). However, these data are problematic. Some states, such as California, home to the largest numbers of AI/ANs in the country, have only recently begun to report HIV cases to the Centers for Disease Control and Prevention, so it would be extremely difficult, if not nearly impossible, to truly estimate the prevalence of HIV in many AI/AN communities.

HIV Risk Factors among AI/ANs

The relatively low number of reported AIDS cases among AI/ANs belies the multiple factors contributing to increased vulnerability to HIV infection. AI/ANs are overwhelmingly disproportionately affected by negative social, economic, and health conditions that are used as surrogate markers for increased HIV risk. For example, 31.6 percent of AI/ANs live at or below the federal poverty level, compared to 13.1 percent for all races. Further, 16.2 percent of AI/AN men and 13.4 percent of AI/AN women are unemployed, compared to 6.4 percent of men and 6.2 percent of women in the total US population. High levels of STDs place AI/ANs at risk for exposure to HIV infection (Blum et al. 1992). Between 1984 and 1988, gonorrhea and syphilis was reported among AI/ANs at a rate twice the national average (MMWR 1998). Further, studies in Canada and the United States indicate that AI/ANs engage in unprotected sexual behavior and inconsistent condom use (Conway et al. 1992; Fenaughty et al. 1994; Metler et al. 1991; Myers et al. 1997; Rekart et al. 1991) and that HIV prevalence is increasing in this group. However, the majority of research on HIV/AIDS among AI/ANs to date has examined primarily the homeless (Rekart 1993) or AI/ANs in prison (Rothon 1993) and drug or alcohol treatment programs (Martin 1993), with very few published studies conducted on community-based samples (Myers et al. 1997).

Compared to the national average, AI/ANs with AIDS tend to be younger: 23 percent are between 20 and 29 years old. Further, among all racial and ethnic categories, HIV/AIDS continues to disproportionately impact MSM, with many of these men likely having become HIV infected as adolescents. This trend is particularly disturbing and threatening to AI/ANs because as a group they are relatively young. The median age for AI/ANs is 24.2 years, compared to the U.S. population median of 32.9 years (MMWR 1998). Further, in a recent study of risk behaviors among AI/AN youth (grades 9–12), 63 percent reported having sexual intercourse at least once in their lifetime; 25 percent had four or more sexual partners in their lifetime; 48 percent did not use condoms during those sexual encounters; and 38 percent reported alcohol or drug use just prior to engaging in sexual activity (BIA 1997).

Sexual Orientation and Sexual Risk

Studies on sexuality, sexual behaviors, and sexual orientation among youth in general indicate a disproportionate number of pregnancies among Euro-American lesbian and bisexual youth compared to their heterosexual peers. Further, recent studies indicate that lesbian/gay/bisexual and transgender (LGBT) youth are at increased risk for HIV and other STDs due to elevated numbers of sexual partners and encounters, early age of initiating sex, inconsistent condom use, and use of sex to barter for goods, history of STDs, older first sexual partners, and a sexual partner at risk for HIV (Rotheram-Borus et al. 1994; Rosario et al. 1999).

Relationship of Trauma and HIV/AIDS

Little is known about the relationship between trauma and risk for HIV among AI/ANs or for the general population. However, experiences of acculturative stress directly and indirectly related to the historical trauma inflicted upon AI/ANs have resulted in poor mental health outcomes such as posttraumatic stress disorder, alienation, depression, anxiety, and alcohol abuse (Duran and Duran 1995; Grandbois and Schadt 1994; Johnson 1994; Walker et al. 1996). Furthermore, daily stressors such as racism, social discrimination, and poverty exact a tremendous psychological cost from AI/ANs, further placing them at increased vulnerability. Perceived discrimination has been related to a number of negative health outcomes. Further, AI/ANs may experience more traumatic life events directly related to violence and trauma, which may place them at greater risk for HIV. AI/ANs are the victims of violent crimes at a rate more than 2.5 times the national average (BJS 1999). The violent crime rate was highest for urban AIs (207 per 1000) and lowest for AIs residing in rural areas (89 per 1000). AI women in particular appear to be at increased risk of physical and sexual assault (Bachman 1992; Chester et al. 1994; Norton and Manson 1995, 1997; Old Dog Cross 1982) and child abuse (NIJC 1990).

There is limited empirical evidence that suggests AI/AN LGBT persons are at higher risk for trauma than their heterosexual counterparts. Prejudice toward LGBT people can take many forms, ranging from avoidance and disregard to outright murder. In one study, LGBT people of color experienced higher levels of violent victimization and were more likely to be victimized in gay-identified settings than their white counterparts. It is has been shown that AI/AN LGBT people confront discrimination and racism within non-AI/AN lesbian and gay male communities (Walters 1999) as well as pervasive homophobia within AI communities (Myers et al. 1993). Because the documentation of antigay hate crimes is relatively new, the actual rates are unknown, particularly among AI/ANs.

Implications for Research and Policy

The evidence presented in this article suggests that AI/ANs are at increased vulnerability to HIV and AIDS. Such evidence further suggests that successful approaches to confront HIV/AIDS in AI/AN communities are those that coordinate prevention, education, and treatment models for AI/AN youth, their families, and their communities and those that include a variety of systems to address the multiple issues facing the community. Treatment programs that integrate a system-of-care approach are most effective when leaders, including tribal council members, elders, and spiritual leaders, are involved and supportive. Support must be generated from all aspects of the community to create community ownership and investment in improving the quality of life in their communities.

Walters and Simoni (2002) suggest that poverty, geography, racism, and discrimination undermine physical health and mental health outcomes and that historical and current traumas impact health. Within indigenous communities, these stressors are viewed as key factors related to health. This "indigenist" stress-coping model represents a preliminary attempt to articulate the stress and coping processes among indigenous people. It highlights protective and buffering factors, in contrast to the focus on pathology that characterizes much of the research on Native peoples.

The most successful prevention and treatment programs build upon local values and traditions (OCJP 2000). They utilize the cultural knowledge, methods, and resources in the urban community to make programs culturally appropriate and relevant. It is important to use culture as a resource to strengthen protective factors and to build on a tribe's cultural strengths. Community healing, along with individual and family healing, is necessary to thoroughly address historical unresolved grief and its manifestations and includes cathartic experiences and a reattachment to traditional Native values.

The use of cultural values, philosophies, and practices can enhance the credibility of programs and the success of client treatment. For interventions to be culturally relevant, they must be based on holistic philosophy, or principles that combine the biological, psychological, social, and spiritual aspects of a person's life. Traditional values of AI/ANs promote physical and emotional well-being among all Indian people. Interventions must also acknowledge that multiple factors contribute to poor health outcomes.

Notes

Bachman, R. *Death and Violence on the Reservation: Homicide, Family Violence, and Suicide in American Indian Populations.* Westport, Conn.: Auburn House, 1992.

Blum, R. W., B. Harmon, L. Harris, et al. "American Indian–Alaska Native Youth Health," *Journal of the American Medical Association* 267 (1992): 1627–1644.

Brave Heart, M. Yellow Horse, and L. M. DeBruyn. "The American Indian Holocaust: Healing Historical Unresolved Grief," *AI/AN Mental Health Research Journal* 8 (2) (1998): 56–78.

Bureau of Indian Affairs (BIA). *Youth Risk Behaviors Survey.* Washington, D.C.: 1997.

Bureau of Justice Statistics (BJS). *American Indians and Crime.* Washington, D.C.: U.S. Department of Justice, NCJ 173306, 1999.

Centers for Disease Control and Prevention. "HIV/AIDS among American Indians and Alaska Natives—United States, 1981–1997," *Morbidity and Mortality Weekly Report* 47(8) (1998): 154.

Chester, B., R. W. Robin, M. P. Koss, and J. Lopez. "Grandmother Dishonored: Violence against Women by Male Partners in American Indian Communities," *Violence and Victims* 9 (1994): 249–258.

Conway, G. A., T. J. Ambrose, E. Chase, E. Y. Hooper, S. D. Helgerson, P. Johannes, et al. "HIV infection in American Indians and Alaska Natives: Surveys in the Indian Health Service," *Journal of Acquired Immune Deficiency Syndromes* 5 (1992): 803–809.

Duran, E., and B. Duran. *Native American Postcolonial Psychology.* Albany: State University of New York, 1995.

Fenaughty, A. M., D. G. Fisher, D. P. MacKinnon, P. I. Wilson, and H. H. Cagle. "Predictors of Condom Use among Alaska Natives, White and Black Drug Users in Alaska," *Arctic Medicine Research* 53 (1994).

Grandbois, G. H., and D. Schadt. "Indian Identification and Alienation in an Urban Community," *Psychology Report* 74 (1994): 211–216.

Johnson, D. "Stress, Depression, Substance Abuse, and Racism," *American Indian and Alaska Native Mental Health Research Journal* 6 (1994): 29–33.

Lieb, L. E., G. A. Conway, M. Hedderman, J. Yao, and P. R. Kerndt. "Racial Misclassification of American Indians with AIDS in Los Angeles County," *Journal of Acquired Immune Deficiency Syndromes* 5 (1992): 1137–1141.

Los Angeles County Department of Health Services (LACDHS). *State of an Epidemic: HIV/AIDS in Los Angeles County, Trends and Future Directions.* Los Angeles: Office of AIDS Programs and Policy, 1999.

Martin, D. "Aboriginal HIV Seroprevalence in British Columbia." Paper presented at the seventh annual B.C. Conference, Conference Syllabus, 215–216, Vancouver, Canada, October 24–26, 1993.

Metler, R., G. A. Conway, and J. Stehr-Green. "AIDS Surveillance among American Indians and Alaska Natives," *American Journal of Public Health* 81 (1991): 1469–1471.

Myers, T., S. L. Bullock, L. M. Calzavara, R. Cockerill, and V. W. Marshall. "Differences in Sexual Risk-Taking Behavior with State of Inebriation in an Aboriginal Population in Ontario, Canada," *Journal of Studies on Alcohol* 58 (3) (1997): 312–322.

National Indian Justice Center (NIJC). "Child Abuse and Neglect in American Indian and Alaska Native Communities and the Role of the Indian Health Service." Unpublished final report, U.S. Department of Health and Human Services, 1990.

Norton, I. M., and S. M. Manson. "A Silent Minority: Battered American Indian Women," *Journal of Family Violence* 10 (1995): 307–318.

———. "Domestic Violence in an Urban Indian Health Center," *Community Mental Health Journal* 33 (1997): 331–337.

Office of Criminal Justice Programs (OCJP). *Promising Practices and Strategies to Reduce Alcohol and Substance Abuse among American Indians and Alaska Natives.* Washington, D.C.: U.S. Department of Justice, 2000.

Old Dog Cross, P. "Sexual Abuse: A New Threat to the Native American Woman: An Overview," *Listening Post* 6 (2) (1982): 18.

Rekart, M. "Trends in HIV Seroprevalence among Street-Involved Persons in Vancouver, Canada (1988–1992)." Paper presented at the ninth International Conference on AIDS, Abstract PO-C21–3105, Berlin, Germany, June 6–11, 1993.

Rekart, M. L., J. Barnett, C. Lawrence, and L. Manzon. "HIV and North American Aboriginal Peoples." Paper presented at the seventh International Conference on AIDS, Abstract M. C. 3237, Florence, Italy, June 16–21, 1991.

Rosario, M., H. F. L. Meyer-Bahlburg, J. Hunter, and M. Gwadz. "Sexual Risk Behaviors of Gay, Lesbian, and Bisexual Youths in New York City: Prevalence and Correlates," *AIDS Education and Prevention* 11 (6) (1999): 476–496.

Rotheram-Borus, M. J., M. Rosario, H. F. L. Meyer-Bahlburg, C. Koopman, S. C. Dopkins, and M. Davies. "Sexual and Substance Use Acts of Gay and Bisexual Male Adolescents in New York City," *The Journal of Sex Research* 31 (1994): 45–57.

Rothon, D. "Results from the HIV Prevalence Study of Inmates in British Columbia Prisons," Paper presented at the seventh annual B.C. Conference, Conference Syllabus, Vancouver, Canada, October 24–26, 1993: 229–236.

U.S. Census Bureau. "Overview of ACE and Hispanic Origin," Census 2000 Brief No. C2KBR/01-1 Washington, D.C.: 2001.

Walker, R. D., D. M. Lambert, P. S. Walker, D. R. Kivlahan, D. M. Donovan, and M. Howard. "Alcohol Abuse in Urban Indian Women: A Longitudinal Study for Assessment and Risk Evaluation," *AI/AN Mental Health Research Journal* 7 (1) (1996): 1–47.

Walters, K. L. "Urban American Indian Identity Attitudes and Acculturation Styles," *Journal of Human Behavior and the Social Environment* 2 (1, 2) (1999): 163–178.

Walters, K. L., and J. M. Simoni. "Reconceptualizing Native Women's Health: An "Indigenist" Stress-Coping Model," *American Journal of Public Health* 92 (4) (2002): 520–524.

WORKING WITH
SPECIAL POPULATIONS

VI

You do not feel your spirituality when you are loaded. Indian women on the road to recovery have common factors, which tie faith and growth as human beings to carry our mothers and daughters onward in recovery. Spirituality brings our culture, strong and everlasting, to our wounded women. As substance abuse healers we acknowledge every aspect of a Native women's being in order to give guidance with culture. We choose to not forget our memories that teach us and have been passed down historically through oral history. Most importantly our spiritual ceremonies passed down to us by grandparents and other family members. These we cannot lose through our generations to never forget what knowledge they give us. We shall not forget our most sacred medicine carried in our women, until we awaken from the hold of the poison brought by explorers.

Native women who enter treatment regain their awesome strength by understanding the nexus of substance abuse, will, and life force. People of indigenous nations practice sweat lodge ceremonies, honor eagle feathers, sing the forgotten songs of the land, and talk with truth and respect in talking circles.

We use the beat of the drum to reawaken the spirit heart, which never stopped beating through the abuse and self-destruction. We honor our women; the givers of life; the principal keepers of life, as we learn what virtue and respect are. This is our expression of spirit through song, dance and ceremony—strong medicine.

A young mother enters treatment. As she notices the sweat lodge she goes to it. She feels like singing. She offers the Bird song; she does this in a good way; she says a prayer and gives thanks to the person who gave her this song. She puts her head back and sings. She smiles afterwards; she remembers. A-ho, all my relations.

—VEDA GAMEZ, UMPQUA/ CHINOOK

HOMELESS PEOPLE, youth, women, and those entrapped in the criminal justice system are populations with tremendous problems. These special populations are difficult to work with because of multiple issues on many levels that demand specific programs tailored to meet specific needs. Christine Duclos and Margaret Severson report of the relationship of Indian offender status to past service use and provide some insight into how a jail or detention facility functions within a community service system. Susan Lobo and Margaret Mortensen Vaughan discuss the issues of homeless Native Americans. Karen Saylors and Nalini Daliparthy analyze the success of the Women's Circle, an exemplary program of the Family and Child Guidance Clinic. Ben Chavis, principal of the American Indian Public Charter School in Oakland, California, writes about the successes of a sensitive, disciplined approach with Native American adolescents in an educational setting. Many of these chapters depict ways of healing past wounds and embracing the future. The testimonies reflect this healing, for ourselves, for each other, for our youth. If the youth are our future, women are the backbone of our community.

Aiming to Balance
Native Women Healing in an Urban Behavioral Health Care Clinic

17

KAREN SAYLORS AND NALINI DALIPARTHY

T HE NAVAJO CONCEPT of *hózhó* connotes beauty, balance, and harmony. It is said that when one of the holy people, Changing Woman, first emerged in the body of an adult woman from a piece of turquoise after four days of ceremony, she said to her sister, White Shell Woman, "Why should we remain here saying nothing and doing nothing, seeing no one and waiting? Let us go higher and stand where we can see plainly what lies around us, both above and below" (Zolbrod 1984). In a symbolic interpretation of this statement, one might hear a call to action, prompting change and movement, at once externally in a sociocultural, interactive sense and internally in terms of delving into the psychological, spiritual self. As providers of mental health services and substance abuse treatment, our goal is to help alleviate psychological distress associated with the isolation, trauma, and abuse that many of our Native clients experience; likewise, in a culturally-based understanding of how a person thrives, our goal is to help people attain *hózhó* as well as happiness, cultural connectedness, and community.

The Women's Circle project of the Native American Health Center was initiated in 1996 to enhance women's HIV prevention through the promotion of healthier sexual and reproductive relationships. The California Department of Health Services, Office of AIDS, and the University of California, San Francisco, Center for AIDS Prevention Studies funded the project with support from the National Institute of Mental Health. Two hundred women participated in the program. Household poverty, single motherhood, family disruptions, and domestic violence were themes that often arose during the project. Cultural elements in the program design included the importance of linking physical and spiritual wellness and linking the individual's health with that of the community and the natural world (Klein, Williams and Witbrodt 1999; Klein, et al. 1997).

In 1999, the Center for Substance Abuse Treatment (CSAT) funded the Native American Women's Circle to expand the substance abuse treatment component of the program and provide HIV and mental health services for high-risk women in the San Francisco Bay Area (CSAT 1999). The NAHC served as lead agency in collaboration with Friendship House, a thirty-bed residential program treating American Indians for substance abuse, and Friendship House American Indian Lodge, a residential women's and children's facility in Oakland. The Women's Circle has allowed us to develop a holistic treatment model that focuses on the individual's developing self-awareness and clarity while also weaving in family, community involvement, and cultural practice as a way to deal with the struggles of mental health and substance abuse.

The Challenges

Substance abuse is a predominant health problem for American Indian women in what has been described as a triad that also includes violence and depression. Alcohol-related mortality rates are significantly higher for American Indian women than for other women (Moran and May 1995). In a study of lifetime exposure to trauma for Native women, over half the sample experienced physical or sexual assault (Walters and Simoni 1999). Our Women's Circle data indicates that the problem of abuse is even more extreme: of the women surveyed, 86 percent responded that they had been physically abused, 92 percent had been emotionally abused, and 69 percent had been sexually abused in their lifetime (figure 17.1).

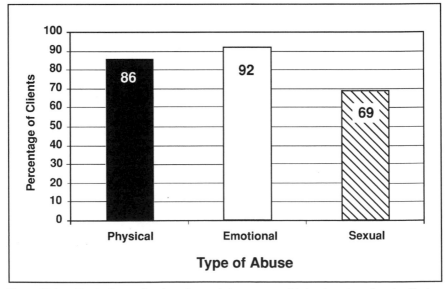

Figure 17.1.   Physical, emotional, and sexual abuse among Native American female clients.

Counselors report that many female clients come to the clinic with depression and posttraumatic stress disorder (PTSD), often associated with extreme sexual abuse and domestic violence issues. "A lot of women are totally shut down" (Beauchamp 2002). Of the women who participated in the Women's Circle, 59 percent of those surveyed reported being coerced or forced to have sex. Three percent of the women who reported being forced to have sex experienced this coercion within the past thirty days.

The California Area Indian Health Service reported that 26 percent of American Indian women tested positive for illicit substances during pregnancy, compared to 11.35 percent for all women in California (Epstein 1996). The fetal alcohol syndrome rate among American Indians is one in fifty, significantly higher than that of the general population. Fetal alcohol syndrome (FAS) and prenatal substance abuse are major concerns within Indian communities. Indian organizations have led the way in FAS prevention, using health education, awareness, and clinical assessment to change perceptions and behavior regarding this issue (May and Hymbaugh 1989).

Of the women we served through the Women's Circle, 57 percent had used alcohol to the point of intoxication in their lifetime. Five percent of the women reported that they injected drugs, and 24 percent reported they had unprotected sex with a drug-using partner in the past twelve months. In addition, 21 percent said they had unprotected sex with someone high on substances, putting themselves at high-risk for HIV infection. Native American women are one of the fastest-growing groups of people infected by HIV/AIDS. Although a large percentage of HIV-infected women acquire the virus through injection drug use, heterosexual contact with an HIV-infected man is the most rapidly increasing transmission modality. In San Francisco, American Indians had the third-highest rate of chlamydia among all ethnic groups, the second-highest for gonorrhea, and the highest for syphilis (DHHS 2000). These high rates of sexually transmitted infection (STI) indicate that Native women are frequently engaging in unprotected sex. STIs may be an indicator of HIV risk for women who have not yet been screened for HIV. Furthermore, women with HIV/AIDS often develop gynecological conditions before they develop other symptoms. Elevated local STI rates imply that the HIV virus is spreading very quickly in the San Francisco Bay Area Native population.

Core Program Elements of the Women's Circle

Holding on to traditional ways in an urban environment can be challenging and difficult. For urban Indians, there is pressure to live in both worlds, that is, to live within the dominant culture while trying to maintain a traditional identity and live in a way that is true to the teachings of the elders. Needless to say, these worlds do not always coexist easily. Blending different worlds is an art, a learned skill. Clients and staff at the Native American Health Center's Family and Child Guidance Clinics (FCGC) in Oakland and San Francisco talk about an implied need to try to fit into an unnatural mold, to conform to a preferential set of values determined by the dominant culture. Such standards of acculturation are a real element of the shared cultural currency that ethnic minorities constantly face.

A Mandan/Hidatsa/Arikara social worker says,

> Because of the way acculturation has worked, lots of women have to get past the shame of being Indian. You must learn how to be white. All of our people live with that. Our parents thought 'we have to teach you to be white.' That didn't work for my parents: they went to boarding school. So there is that deep shame. The spirit piece that is so important to our people has been cut off, has been lost (Beauchamp 2002).

At the FCGC, counselors work with clients to establish a different set of standards, those of respect and awareness of one's own history and culture, often reckoning with the trauma that comes with that history and attempting to grow from it.

The Women's Circle grant allowed the FCGC to enhance services by adding a number of important new elements, including a nurse case manager. Research and local experience have indicated that in therapeutic residential and community settings where the clinical management and staff are predominantly male and where treatment often uses aggressive confrontation as a therapeutic approach, women can feel isolated and have trouble progressing in their treatment (Brown et al. 1996).

Residential settings often lack an outlet for women to discuss sexuality issues, medical concerns, or past or present domestic abuse issues. The nurse case manager provides necessary medical and psychosocial assessments and makes appropriate referrals for medical treatment, dental care, mental health care, and social services. She also provides the liaison necessary for a woman to feel comfortable about transitioning to outpatient counseling once residential treatment is completed. Having a female nurse case manager on staff to run topically focused women's groups has been a consistent and important component of the program. Introducing a women-only group option in a treatment plan provides a non-threatening entry point for addressing some of the deeply rooted issues that may be contributing to substance abuse. Mental health issues are a central focus in this work, as are domestic violence, positive parenting skills, and community-oriented, participatory activities such as beading class or art therapy group.

Another central component of the Women's Circle has been a perinatal social worker on staff. The perinatal social worker coordinates with both the medical and mental health departments to teach skills concerning self-care, birthing, avoidance of substance use during pregnancy, breastfeeding, and parenting, in both individual and group contexts. Throughout the life of the project, parenting skills were brought to the forefront. The Community Relations Coordinator (Lumbee) says:

> Clients need guidance on how to deal with dysfunctional families. How do you be a parent and honor culture, work, take care of your kids, all while being separated from extended family? A lot of that care falls on the woman (King 2002).

Single-parent families are relatively common, which puts additional pressure on women as they attempt to care for their children and extended family. Family instability and domestic violence are huge issues for women coming into the clinic (Mallory 2002). For this reason, concerted focus has been placed on providing parenting skills training and domestic violence groups to all clients: female, male, and transgender.

Developing a strong cultural component has been a central focus of the Women's Circle program as cultural affiliation and identity are understood to be protective factors against high-risk behavior. Cultural involvement can be both community and individual assets in a woman's life (Zahnd et al. 2002).

Since our clinical approach combines Western psychotherapeutic practice with cultural ceremony and ritual, a major challenge has been the logistics of a holistic model in day-to-day practice. One important factor in discussing traditional healing is that "traditional" means many different things to people, and the personal subjectivity of this term is further complicated in an urban Indian clinic because the people come from many different traditions. Women's Circle clients represent ninety-five different tribal affiliations. This cultural diversity necessitates providing a variety of traditional, cultural options to clients. Native healers from different cultural backgrounds and traditions are brought in for several days at a time to work with clients. American Indian cultural healing activities include prayer, singing, drumming, sweat lodges, smudging, herbs, and tobacco. Talking circles are held regularly at the clinic for clients and staff. However, the way cultural interventions often occur is on the individual level, with counselors assessing a client's desire or readiness to work with traditional ways. A counselor's initial clinical assessment contains spiritual/cultural domains that allow her to gauge a client's cultural affiliation and identification, which in turn helps direct the development of the treatment plan. Sage, cedar, or sweetgrass smudges are often incorporated in a counseling session, and some counselors pray with clients at the client's request. Other clients are Christian, which is another important element in the spectrum of Native American cultural and spiritual identity. Counselors must be constantly aware of the subtle factors that each client brings: "You've got to really listen with your spirit, with everything you've got, to go to that spiritual piece" (Beauchamp 2002).

During the three-year period of the CSAT Women's Circle project, data have been collected from clients when they first enter FCGC for services and then at six and twelve months afterwards. Over the course of this project, 783 client interviews were conducted. This data allow us to look at changes over time in clients' behavior, attitudes, and living situation. Substance use decreased significantly after treatment, as indicated by reductions in use by the women who reported using substances at intake: Some 33 percent reported drinking alcohol in the thirty days preceding intake, compared with 29 percent at follow-up; 17 percent of our female clients used marijuana during the thirty days before intake, a figure that decreased by 3 percent after treatment; 5 percent used heroin, which decreased to 2 percent post-treatment; and 8 percent reported using methamphetamines or cocaine, a figure that fell by 3 percent. Benzodiazapine use decreased from 5 percent at intake to 1 percent after treatment. And while 5 percent of the women surveyed injected drugs at intake, only 2 percent reported injecting drugs at the twelve-month follow-up. See figure 17.2.

The limitations of self-reported data concerning illicit drug use are recognized and are perhaps exacerbated in a therapeutic clinical setting, where a client may desire to please the counselor with whom she has developed a relationship over six months (and thus say what the counselor wants to hear regarding a decrease in substance use). Another bias of self-reported data pertains to the residential treatment facility's strict rules about drug or alcohol use, so that if a client reports substance use while in the treatment environment, she risks being terminated from the program. Despite these reporting biases, all of these substance use trends move in a positive direction for our clients.

There is not a direct correlation between a decrease in drug or alcohol use and reduced sexual activity. Women's Circle data reveals that the clients' total number

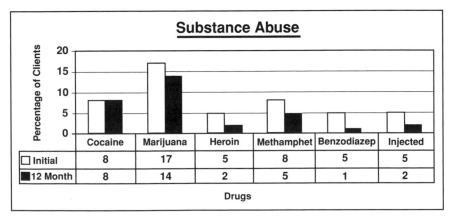

Figure 17.2.   Substance abuse among Native American female clients.

of sexual partners increased by 12 percent from intake to the twelve-month follow-up interview. However, with reduced substance abuse and with HIV prevention education, one would anticipate a decrease in unprotected sex. From the onset, a large majority of Women's Circle clients stated that they had not had unprotected sex with a drug user (76 percent) and had not had unprotected sex with an HIV-positive partner (100 percent). At the follow-up encounter, we observed a 2 percent decrease in unprotected sex with a drug user and 3 percent decrease in unprotected sex with someone high on substances.

Comparison of intake data with that collected at clients' twelve-month follow-up interviews indicates that the program has also effected improvement in the women's lives. For example, at the twelve-month interview, the rate of full-time employment had increased from 8 percent at intake to 27 percent (a 19 percent increase), and the percentage of clients who were employed part-time increased by 6 percent. Positive changes in clients' living situations have also resulted, as indicated by a 9 percent decline in the number of clients having spent one or more nights in jail or prison within the past month. In addition, client enrollment in school or job training programs increased 8 percent.

An important measure of the way a client's mental health has improved is the frequency with which the client accesses health care, whether inpatient, outpatient, or emergency room care. Positive trends move away from the use of emergency or inpatient care, which are more intensive and expensive treatment modalities, and toward consistent outpatient care. After receiving mental health care from the Women's Circle project, 13 percent of clients reported a decrease in seeking inpatient mental health services, and 2 percent decreased their emergency room visits for mental health care. In terms of substance abuse care, clients reported a 23 percent decrease in seeking additional inpatient substance abuse services, which may indicate that they had not relapsed and did not need additional residential services. Data support this interpretation as 67 percent of clients reported abstinence from alcohol at intake, and this rate rose to 72 percent at the six-month encounter and 71 percent at the twelve-month follow-up. This represents a 4 percent increase in abstinence among our female clients after treatment.

Self-reported health status also improved significantly through the course of the program, with increases in the percentage claiming good health and decreases in responses of "poor."

Clients were asked whether they experienced discrimination based on their race or ethnicity. At intake, 67 percent said yes; at twelve-month follow-up, only 46 percent felt that discrimination was based on race or ethnicity, a decrease of 21 percent. When clients were asked about their experience with discrimination during various social encounters, clients expressed a significant reduction in feelings of discrimination in the following arenas: from community or neighbors, a 26 percent reduction; from job, 19 percent; from family, 13 percent; from social service agencies, 13 percent; from police, 33 percent; and from the criminal justice system, 19 percent. Furthermore, clients reported very low discrimination from their current treatment program, whether FCGC, Friendship House, or the Friendship House Lodge, at intake (2.4 percent), and this number fell to 0 percent, or no discrimination, at the follow-up encounter. Furthermore, clients were asked about their response to discrimination: Those responding that they felt "hopeless" decreased by 18 percent, "ashamed" decreased by 15 percent, and "strong" increased by 21 percent. When clients reported how they reacted to or coped with discrimination, physical aggression decreased by 20 percent, using drugs decreased by 16 percent, and seeking help increased by 8 percent. These changes reflect very positively on clients' changing attitudes and sense of empowerment, which is one goal of behavioral health services.

Finally, the role of culture has been an important factor for female participants. When asked at intake how important their tribal affiliation is to them, 77 percent responded "very important," which increased to 100 percent at twelve-month follow-up (an increase of 23 percentage points). When clients were asked how much they knew about their culture, responses increased from intake to follow-up by 6 percent.

Family is an integral part of Native American culture and its approach to recovery and healing. When female clients were asked if their family was supportive of their treatment, the responses for "supportive" increased by 18 percent and "not supportive" decreased by 22 percent over the course of the program. When clients were asked whether their family was supportive of a healthy way of life for them, "somewhat supportive" increased by 7 percent, "very supportive" increased by 4 percent, and "not supportive" decreased by 7 percent from intake to twelve-month follow-up.

Part of actualizing and implementing a holistic model is understanding and braiding together elements of Western psychotherapeutic practice and Native healing. This process usually does not occur as an official process but rather as part of an individual counselor's personal clinical approach. Counselors also share a strong belief in meeting the client "where he or she is at." "Each women who walks in here is on her own path. This is very intuitive work. It makes a big difference being Native. But that is not to say that a non-Native can't have an equally strong connection with a client" (Beauchamp 2002).

Many of the FCGC clinicians are Native, and they come into the treatment environment from myriad tribal and ethnic backgrounds and with a wide variety of personal experiences that inform their approaches. Simultaneously, there is a constant learning process among non-Native FCGC staff about cultural appropriateness and jurisdiction, and there is an asking-and-teaching dynamic about ways to better serve clients. Nuances of administrative and staffing decisions affect how the Women's Circle program runs, and these decisions inform the way that a holistic approach is actualized and affect what the term comes to mean in an organizational environment. Being respectful and open to the diversity of clients and staff thus becomes a key component in a holistic model. Culture, as a "complex ensemble of emotions, beliefs, values, aspirations . . . that together make up behavior" (Fabrega 2002), is constantly in flux. Strong cultural identification and affiliation are multidimensional reflections of a person's investment in a social environment. While it is generally understood that the positive influence of culture on drug and alcohol use is indirect, involving Native cultural components as a central mental health and substance abuse intervention has been an important and successful programmatic element of the Women's Circle.

Notes

This three-year project was funded through a Center for Substance Abuse Treatment Targeted Capacity Expansion TCE/HIV Initiative, Substance Abuse and Mental Health Services Administration grant # TI 12205.

"Aiming to Balance: Native Women Healing in an Urban Behavioral Health Care Clinic" is an abridged version of "Women's Circle Comes Full Circle," by Karen Saylors, Ph.D., which appeared in the *Journal of Psychoactive Drugs* 35 (1). Reprinted by permission of Haight-Ashbury Publications, 612 Clayton Street, San Francisco, California.

Beauchamp, Sandra "Beau," Family Services coordinator and counselor, FCGC. Interview. August 13, 2002.

Brown, V. B., S. Sanchez, J. E. Zweben, and T. Aly. "Challenges in Moving from a Traditional Therapeutic Community to a Women and Children's TC Model," *Journal of Psychoactive Drugs* 28 (1996): 1, 39–46.

Center for Substance Abuse Treatment (CSAT). *Cultural Issues in Substance Abuse Treatment.* Rockville, Md.: DHHS, 1999.

Department of Health and Human Services (DHHS). *Healthy People 2010: Understanding and Improving Health.* Washington, D.C.: DHHS, 2000.

Epstein, M. *National Health Objectives for Year 2000: Summary of Health Data for American Indians in California: A Report of the California Area Indian Health Service.* Rockville, Md.: Indian Health Service, 1996.

Fabrega, H., Jr. *Disease and Social Behavior: An Interdisciplinary Perspective.* Cambridge, Mass.: MIT Press, 2002.

King, Janet, Community Services Coordinator, FCGC. Interview. August 13, 2002.

Klein, D., D. Williams, and J. Witbrodt. "The collaboration process in HIV prevention and evaluation in an urban Indian clinic for women," *Health Education and Behavior* 26 (1999): 2, 239–249.

Klein, D., D. Williams, J. Witbrodt, and B. Kolody. *The Women's Circle: Toward Healthier Relationships: Final Report to the University of California, San Francisco, and the California AIDS Office, A Project of the Native American Health Center and Public Health Institute.* Berkeley, Calif.: Public Health Institute, 1997.

Mallory, Erin, MSW. Native Youth Circle coordinator and counselor, FCGC. Interview. August 14, 2002.

May, P. A., and K. J. Hymbaugh. "A Macro-Level Fetal Alcohol Syndrome Prevention Program for Native Americans and Alaska Natives: Description and Evaluation," *Journal of Studies on Alcohol* 50 (1989): 6, 508–518.

Moran, J. R., and P. A. May. "American Indians in CSAP Cultural Competence Series," *Cultural Competence for Social Workers* 4 (1995): 145-179.

Walters, K., and J. Simoni. Trauma, Substance Use and HIV Risk among Urban American Indian Women, *Cultural Diversity and Ethnic Minority Psychology*, 5(3) (1999): 144–165.

Zahnd, E., S. Holtby, D. Klein, and C. McCain. *American Indian Women: Preventing Violence and Drinking, Project Final Report, National Institute on Alcohol Abuse and Alcoholism and Office for Research on Women's Health.* Bethesda, Md.: NIAAA.

Zolbrod, Paul. *Diné Bahane': The Navajo Creation Story.* Albuquerque: University of New Mexico Press, 1984.

Substance Dependency among Homeless American Indians in Oakland and Tucson

18

SUSAN LOBO AND MARGARET MORTENSEN VAUGHAN

THIS CHAPTER BRINGS together the results of in-depth, long-term ethnographic research among American Indian people in the San Francisco Bay Area and in Tucson, Arizona. Both research sites are similar in having large and long-standing Indian communities, and each has a considerable number of Indian people who are homeless. Like most Native American communities in an urban area, in both Tucson and the Bay Area a single Indian district or neighborhood does not exist, but rather the Indian community is dispersed throughout the city and is characterized as a network of relationships. There are also locational nodes on this network, such as the social service agencies (both Indian-run and non-Indian), the parks where homeless Indian people spend time, and the events and activities that draw Indian people together. This type of community may be more abstract than one that is primarily geographically situated.

In both the Bay Area and in Tucson, the Indian community is characterized by a dispersed population with a great deal of community-wide fluidity as well as individual mobility (Lobo and Peters 2001; Lazar 1998). Homeless men and women and their children live in this network of relationships, from which they draw resources necessary for survival. It is important to emphasize that the focus here is on one subset of the overall urban Indian population. The implication is *not* that all American Indian people living in urban areas are homeless or that all homeless suffer from substance dependency.

Tucson is situated in close proximity to both the Tohono O'odham and Yaqui reservations. In fact, one Yaqui community—Old Pascua—is within the city limits of Tucson. A number of other tribal homelands are within a few hours' drive of Tucson, and this close presence to tribal communities is one factor that shapes the multitribal Tucson Indian community. In contrast, Oakland, San Francisco, and San Jose were sites of the federal relocation program initiated in the mid-1950s. This program drew Native people from throughout the United States, and was the catalyst that created a very tribally diverse Indian community, with the majority of its people distant from their homelands.

The exact number of homeless American Indians is not known. However, estimates by the authors strongly suggest that the number of urban Indian people exceeds census figures, especially when the "hidden homeless" are taken into account. They include those who live in vehicles or in short-term hotels and motels, those who are residing temporarily in treatment centers or other institutions (for example, in jail or transitional housing), and those who are moving frequently, staying temporarily on the sofas and living room floors of family and friends. Many combine these varied forms of homelessness, interspersing them in a patterned and cyclical manner with other, more anchored residence (such as short-term rentals), periods of return to their home reservations, or seasonal moves to other cities. These often complex survival strategies by homeless Indian people warrant the need to move from culturally biased definitions of homelessness based on European models of what constitutes "home" or on stereotypes based on the more visibly homeless.

Background

The few studies that exist on substance abuse and homeless Native Americans emphasize the overwhelming use of alcohol as a favored drug by homeless Native Americans. Kramer and Barker (1996) found heavy alcohol use among elderly homeless Native Americans in Los Angeles. Native Americans, out of all the ethnic groups in Kasprow's (1998) study of homeless veterans, had the highest rates of alcoholism and alcohol-related hospital visits. Sugarman and Grossman (1996), in a study on the rates and nature of physical trauma among urban Native Americans in Washington State, found that American Indians needing trauma care were more often homeless than Anglo or African-American patients. A study on the rates and nature of physical trauma among urban Native Americans in Washington State found that American Indians needing trauma care were more often homeless than Anglo- or African-American patients. Koegel and Burnam (1987) found that Native American homeless individuals more often have a single addiction to alcohol than to any other drug. They conclude that alcoholism itself correlates with long-term homelessness. In a Chicago study, Bogue (1963) found more than one-half of the Indians were classified as chronic alcoholics.

Lobo (2001) focused on what have been termed "highly mobile" American Indian individuals, many of whom live on the street or are situated either permanently or serially in ways that could be defined as homeless. Mortensen (1998) studied the homeless American Indian population of Tucson to explore their perception of home and homelessness.

Methodology

Research in the Bay Area and Tucson was carried out from 1997 to 2001. The data from both sites were then collaboratively analyzed for this article. Both sets of research are strongly qualitative and utilize ethnographic methodologies including participant observation, extensive field notes that were revisited and refined over time, and in-depth, open-ended interviews, both formal and informal. The research in the Bay Area carried out by Lobo (who is coordinator of the Community History Project there) has been ongoing since the late 1970s. The research in Tucson was carried out by Mortensen-Vaughn in 1997 and 1998 as the basis for her Master's thesis at the University of Arizona, in which she focused on homeless American Indians. In Tucson, in-depth interviews were conducted with ten homeless men in soup kitchens and parks. Additionally, in Lobo's research in 2000, twenty-seven homeless individuals kept daily journals for a period of six to eight weeks, and their journals provided the basis for extensive interviews. Methodologically, this extensive involvement in a community creates the opportunity for understanding those aspects of community dynamics that shift and those aspects that persist over time—sometimes stretching across generations.

Results

Homelessness is a complicated circumstance requiring endurance, strategy, and knowledge on the part of the person facing it. Alcohol use indirectly factors into peoples' stories of how they became homeless, while for many it also serves as part of the strategizing for survival in daily street life. Yet alcohol use and abuse should not be viewed as either the one precipitating factor in creating homelessness or as the result of homelessness. Instead, it is in many cases but one factor—though a crucial one—in the constellation of interwoven factors and life processes that are a part of the overall picture of homelessness.

Varying Forms of Homelessness

Through their journals and interviews, participants told of their experiences of being homeless, describing a pattern that Jojola (1999) refers to as "episodic homelessness." Many interviewed in the Bay Area research described years of episodic homelessness, in which they moved through different forms of homelessness: (1) staying in the homes of a rotating set of family and friends, either in one area or over an expansive region; (2) living on the streets and sleeping in parks, under bridges, and in other places; (3) living in a vehicle; (4) staying in shelters; and (5) cycling in and out of institutions such as treatment centers or jails.

Many of those living long-term on the streets or alternating among the streets, shelters, and friends' homes suffer from the multiple effects of substance abuse and severe chronic health problems. One of the participants in the Bay Area research, a man in his mid-thirties, has lived most of his life on the streets since leaving foster care as a teenager. He endured several stints in jail for petty theft and drug offenses. His current drugs of choice are alcohol and crack. He also has many unmet health needs and is always on the move. He maintained, "To survive you have to know how to cover your tracks and never leave a trail." In one day, it was not uncommon for him to go from a homeless shelter, a friend's house, or an outdoor sleeping spot in Oakland into San Francisco for lunch at a particular soup kitchen, then return to Berkeley in the East Bay to spend the afternoon at a downtown park and have an afternoon meal at another church, and later return to Oakland for the night. Another participant, a middle-aged woman with chronic alcohol dependency and drug problems, lived on and off the streets of San Francisco for many years.

During the spring of 2000, she was with her husband on the streets, and occasionally they stayed at a "pay by the day or week" hotel. Then her husband stopped drinking and began staying consistently at a hotel. He urged her to join him, but she decided to remain living on the streets and deal with her longstanding alcohol and drug problem with counseling and visits to a methadone center. She had a woman friend who was in a wheelchair; they protected one another and found relatively secure places on the street to stay at night. She preferred this to staying in shelters because "really terrible, terrible things happen there."

"Jim" and "Cindy's" lives are burdened by both homelessness and substance dependency. They have lived since childhood in the Bay Area. They are members of an extended family household with a continually shifting composition that uses one apartment in a variety of ways. At the time of the research, Cindy was in her mid-thirties. In April of 2000, five of her and Jim's seven children had been taken from them and placed in foster homes. The other two were staying temporarily with an uncle. Cindy and her husband had an apartment on and off until six months before the research began, when a combination of things (not enough income, a rent increase, problems with alcohol and illness, and some legal matters) forced them to leave their apartment and find places to stay as best they could. Jim's sister had been staying with them and their children, so she also had to leave. Since then, there has been no steady income, although Cindy received General Assistance. Jim worked as a day laborer when he could. They tried collecting cans, but this did not raise enough money, and Cindy was then on crutches due to a knee injury, making it almost impossible for her to help. They had been able to get free food from various social service agencies and churches. Shelters could not deal with such a large family, and Jim said that in other ways they found shelters to be unbearable on the few occasions they tried staying in them.

From time to time during the spring and summer, Cindy and Jim stayed overnight at his cousin "Janet's" apartment in Oakland. Jim calls this apartment "our home base." At the least, they went there to shower a few times a week and use the kitchen. Their children slept there regularly, while most nights Jim and Cindy slept outdoors in a nearby park. The small, two-bedroom apartment rented by Janet for her household housed her own three children under ten, Cindy and Jim's children, and Janet's current boyfriend, who stayed on and off. Janet had two teenaged children, who stayed with their father but who joined her household about half the time. Also in the apartment was her aunt "Annette," a woman in her fifties who had grandmotherly responsibilities for a number of children of nieces, nephews, and friends, and some of these children stayed overnight from time to time. Annette also had a boyfriend, who was there more often than not, bringing along his four children during the times his ex-wife was homeless and living in a nearby park.

Until five of Cindy and Jim's seven children were placed in foster care, all seven children slept at the apartment. Two of their children suffered from fetal alcohol syndrome (FAS) and had serious health problems, necessitating frequent stays in health-care institutions. Jim's sister, who had been staying with Jim and Cindy and their children before they were evicted in the winter of 1999, also slept in Janet's apartment when she could not find any other place to stay. Grandma Annette has a sister, "Mira," who had been living in her van with her teenage daughter "Kelly." When the van broke down and could not be repaired, Mira and Kelly stayed in the apartment during the month of June before deciding to return to their reservation in Montana. Some nights as many as eighteen people stayed in the apartment, but never the same set of people in any given week.

During the summer, after her children were taken into foster care, Cindy decided to enter a ninety-day residential alcohol treatment center. An opening became available in August 2000, so she left the park and started treatment. In November she delivered another baby and extended her stay at the treatment center. Jim and a buddy, another Indian man, had constructed a hidden shelter in the bushes in the far reaches of the park. He still used his cousin's apartment to shower and cook, and he slept there from time to time. He was also considering entering a residential alcohol treatment program. Also, in September the apartment management began eviction proceedings to vacate Janet's apartment, and everybody staying there had begun to worry about what to do next. One of the reasons for the eviction cited by the apartment management was that the number of people using the apartment far exceeded the legal limit.

It is noteworthy that the many people who circulated through Janet's household turned consistently and through preference to the Indian-run social service agencies in the Bay Area. Likewise, the service providers in these agencies, encouraged by Indian community values of mutual support and sharing as well as by their professional mandate, extended strenuous efforts to assist with the burden of multiple problems facing this multigenerational extended family and others like it.

Substance Dependency from Participants' Perspectives

Drinking and drug use occur in a variety of settings and for many different reasons. One participant in Tucson said that the first thing he did when he first realized he was homeless was get drunk. Another participant there described his drug habit as being so large at one time that it was "the size of Nova Scotia." Some of the reasons reported in Tucson for drinking included to become comfortable or brave enough to panhandle, to handle harsh circumstances such as cold weather, to self-medicate for mental or physical stress, to provide recreation, or to provide a tool for metaphysical insights or spirituality. These participants reaped the rewards of memories of fun moments, friendship and solidarity, and positive spiritual experiences. However, these men were aware of the drawbacks of heavy alcohol and drug use. One drawback mentioned was that when using drugs, a person is then no longer "clean" to pass drug tests to obtain certain jobs in the labor force beyond the day labor scene. It is hard enough to get a job without a permanent address; drug testing makes it even more difficult. In both Tucson and Oakland, drinking on the street was frequently described as making one more vulnerable to crime, such as theft of personal belongings or bodily attack. Some other negative aspects of drinking on the street mentioned by those in the Tucson study included feelings of guilt and other emotional drawbacks, as well as hangovers, other illnesses, and vulnerability to accidents of all types.

History of Institutionalization

Some of the Indians involved in the studies have spent the better part of their lives institutionalized—from foster care to boarding schools, the military, long-term hospitalization, substance abuse treatment programs, and incarceration. This is what Fleisher (1989) refers to as "street-to-system cycling." For those who have had an institutionalized life, getting out and living on the streets may be part of a cycle that eventually takes them back in. The heavy influence of institutional regulation on the life course of the homeless, particularly those who are alcohol dependent, remains to be studied thoroughly. Likewise, the rejection of formal institutions and the role this reaction may play in accessing drug treatment is also a question for further study. As children, some faced heavy regulation and institutional control through unfriendly educational establishments and systems of punishment. As adults, they continue to rely to some extent on institutions such as shelters and soup kitchens that can be unfriendly and rule driven.

Life on the outside can seem strange and unsettling. One man, now in his mid-thirties, spent all of his youth in the Bay Area. He was first incarcerated at the age of twelve and had already started drinking. He was sent to the California Youth Authority (CYA), and until he was eighteen, he was at CYA or in foster homes. As an adult he served terms in nine different prisons, primarily for robbery-related offenses. He had been diagnosed with both substance abuse and mental health problems, as well as a number of associated physical health problems. At the time he participated in the study, he was under medication. He said that in some ways the rigid regimentation of prison was reassuring. "You knew you had a roof over your head, square meals and what was coming up the next day . . . same ol' same ol'."

One woman in the Bay Area study led a highly institutionalized life. Out on parole from prison, she started keeping a journal, in which she graphically told of her depression and severe physical symptoms while she received methadone treatment and worked on overcoming a long-standing alcohol habit. Sometimes she would stay on the street or in an inexpensive hotel conveniently located for her mandatory visits with her parole officer. She also spent time visiting with old friends and relying on the generosity of men friends and new male acquaintances. In her journal, she reminded herself to stay away from friends who might get her into trouble. Her journal ended abruptly when she went back to prison on a parole violation.

Institutions noted in the studies that helped alleviate homelessness were soup kitchens, shelters, and drop-in centers. Soup kitchens are often places not only for food but for socialization as well. Shelters were seen as places of last resort because they were dangerous and uncomfortable places where belongings might be stolen and other crimes committed. Most crimes against homeless people are committed by other homeless persons (Snow, Baker, and Anderson 1989). One participant said, "They [the shelters] are too crowded and everyone is getting on each other's nerves." Drop-in centers, particularly at Indian centers and other Indian organizations, were appreciated and provide a mailing address and a place to store belongings for a short period of time. They exemplify the more positive aspects that institutions can have.

Foster Care and Adoption: Metaphorically or Culturally Homeless?

Foster care and adoption played a large role in the early lives of many homeless Indians. The placement of children in foster care implies that their natal families are "in trouble" to the extent that a bureaucratic system such as child protective services must step in to enforce the children's removal from their parents. Often the children of those homeless adults who were raised in foster care are now also in foster care.

In Tucson, three of the ten men were adopted away from their birth families into communities where few Native people lived. Two of the adoptees had remained on good terms with their families; the third had not. All three openly related that non-Native families adopted them. One recounted a search for his biological family that ended in disappointment. His search for what it meant to be "Indian" was part of his travels that led to his homeless situation and also part of a metaphoric homeless condition. Two of the adoptees perceived that non-Indians or even other Indians expected them to know and share their backgrounds and tribal traditions. One participant explained that he began traveling because "I was sick of it. I was tired of people coming up to me [and asking] 'What do you know of your traditions?' I'm still searching. I'm trying to find out about my past." Another, when asked if he could be interviewed, asserted, "I grew up white," as if that piece of biographical information lessened his qualifications to be a participant in the study.

One more common choice for dealing with substance dependency is to enter into an inpatient or outpatient treatment center. In Tucson, a participant mentioned use of the Veteran's Administration detoxification program. Another spoke of being in the "County Hotel" (county hospital) to recuperate from intoxication. Another option mentioned was a Native American support group called the Red Road. A participant explained, "There are a lot of Indian brothers out there who don't drink. They try to get you on the Red Road, which is a sobriety group. It is a different way of tackling alcoholism. I've been to churches and meetings where there are no Indians there. The Red Road is ways you can help better understand it."

As noted by Jojola (1999), informal and casual networks serve many of the basic survival needs of Indians in Albuquerque who are homeless, either by choice or economic circumstances, and who prefer to maintain their anonymity rather than bear the scrutiny of non-Indians at social service agencies. The same was found to be true in the present research. The participants often discussed the system of reciprocity and social networks that exist among themselves. They indicated that this was a more common source of help with housing than friends or family with homes. In fact, family ties were often severed or haphazard.

One man in Tucson explained, "I chose to be homeless. I was living with my sister. She was demanding money. I cooked, cleaned, and everything, but she did work two jobs. Her son would get really mad when I came home drunk. I guess he seen [in] me . . . his own father. . . . I just say, 'Wait till he takes a drink and can't stop.'" This man was part of a larger group of homeless Native American men, all from the same tribe, who associated with each other as a group. One of them explained their relationship: "We all watch out for each other. Native people know each other and hang out with each other." If they are separated, they meet at the soup kitchen or return to the same place at night. "Leonard" remarked, "Since my divorce and I left my kids, I don't want to be alone." Many of the men in this homeless group are also Native language speakers, and they notice when another person is a nonspeaker or a less proficient Native language speaker. "Seth," the youngest participant in the research, described camping in another city and state with men from many different tribal backgrounds. Together, in his words, they "talked about Native American issues and tried to find out about their own cultural lives." Having been adopted into a non-Native family, he found this exploration aided him in discovering other Native cultures as he wondered about his own.

In the Bay Area, some of those who most consistently lived on the streets, and who often most persistently and customarily used alcohol and drugs, lived together in groups. Often these groups possessed an extended-family aspect, either consanguineous or figurative. One group or "household" of five people in the Bay Area had lived together, with some coming and going, for more than ten years. They were chronic alcoholics, and they stuck together as a group whether coming to one of the Indian organizations for the free dinners or walking along the street with their shopping carts filled with their belongings. Indian people living on the streets are often abused and assaulted by other street people, especially of other ethnicities, who see Indians as having low status or being easy prey, or by police. One reason this particular "street family" stayed together was to protect one another. They knew that alone, they would be more vulnerable.

This extended family included "Grandma," a woman in her mid-sixties, her son, her son's girlfriend, and two congenial men. Grandma's son, "Larry," has a son, "Larry Jr.," who was nineteen in 2000 and was raised on the streets. The Indian community remarks on how Larry Jr. miraculously escaped being taken by "the System," that is, placed in foster care. Larry Jr. now circulates among a number of his friends' houses, has had some brushes with the law, and spends only a few nights a month with his father on the street.

Others prefer a more solitary existence on the street and feel safer sleeping out when not in a group. "Antelope" and his brother were forced to leave the house after their father died because their mother began living with a non-Indian. Antelope has been on the road or on the street ever since. Now in his mid-forties, he sleeps on the street, rotating between two secret spots, or occasionally stays at the homes of a friend or of an older woman, a longtime friend of his family. Here he helps out where he can. He staunchly refuses any non-Indian institutionalized assistance or service delivery programs for the homeless, preferring the freedom to make his own way, drinking with his street buddies, doing odd jobs, and participating in Indian community gatherings and activities.

Another means of coping with homelessness is reliance on "key" or "anchor" households that provide a degree of permanence in the constant swirl of shifts and changes in the Bay Area American Indian community (Lobo 2001). These are similar to what Ackerman (1989, 1988) referred to on the Colville reservation; they are found on many other reservations throughout the United States. These are households headed almost exclusively by mature women of long-standing respect in the community who have become homeowners or have arranged for secure long-term inexpensive leases. Many people float or circulate through these households, knowing they will be welcomed with a place to sleep, if only on the floor, and a meal and shower. One participant pointed out that these urban households are like clan mothers' homes. One woman who was the head of such a household commented that "every morning I've got my alligator farm to look at when I get up," referring to the number of people rolled up in blankets on her apartment floor. Temporary visits by those who are considered "couch surfers" may become permanent, or at least as permanent as any living arrangement in the Bay Area Indian community.

Discussion

Key or anchor households informally serve the basic and necessary survival and cultural needs of many in the San Francisco Bay Area Indian community through the largesse of the women and their families who head them. These households demonstrate Indian values of extending hospitality not only to extended family members but also to others in need and to those traveling through town.

The most commonly utilized services are often Indian-run organizations in the Bay Area and mainstream services in the Tucson area with low levels of regulation and which can be used at an individual's discretion. Ironically, many in both studies said that they used alcohol and other drugs as part of a strategy to get by on the streets, a strategy that can also make it even harder to survive street life. At the individual level, the diversity of their lives and life experiences, their tribal affiliations, and their cultural expectations indicate the need for individualized services, resources, and options.

Both these studies from the two research sites describe and include the participants' perspectives regarding the circumstances of homelessness and the associated patterns of substance dependency. These studies are intended to make clear, in a summary and personal way, the range of types of homelessness and substance abuse, as well as some of the possible precipitating factors and coping strategies. It cannot be taken for granted that there is one form of homelessness or one motivating cause for substance dependency. There are, however, some common experiences in the lives of those in the study. Poverty, lack of affordable housing, childhood trauma, accidents, and the complications of substance abuse and other health-related issues were indicated as strong underlying factors in many cases. Some of the participants also experienced disrupted childhoods that included foster care or out-adoption. A prominent role was played by a range of institutions throughout their lives, and they experienced an early introduction to the use of alcohol or drugs.

The qualitative results from interviews, participant observations, and participants' journals in both Tucson and the San Francisco Bay Area indicate a strong association between substance abuse (particularly alcoholism) and homelessness. The results indicate possible precipitating factors including foster families, adoption into non-Native families, different types of involuntary institutionalization during youth and adulthood, and the personal impact of accident, trauma, and loss.

The emphasis in this study has been on the lives and perspectives of those who are both homeless and dealing with substance dependency. It suggests a few of the mitigating steps that some participants have taken regarding both housing and substance dependency. Other research efforts are greatly needed to assess the outcomes of these steps. The participants in the research told of many changes throughout their lifetimes, as well as the interaction of many factors, in regard to both homelessness and substance dependency. Attention should be paid to what those experiencing these life circumstances have to say.

In order to understand overall community dynamics and to interpret contextual and subtle cultural meanings, this study has stressed the value of ethnographic methods and techniques, with a resulting emphasis on qualitative data. The authors strongly believe that more research and more contributions to the literature on homeless Native Americans and substance dependency from the point of view of the participants in the research are needed in order to eradicate stereotypes, humanize statistical work, and better inform both the homeless and the housed, as well as social services and academics.

Notes

Dr. Lobo's research was funded through a grant (contract #43-YA-BC-030121) from the Statistical Research Division of the United States Census Bureau. Her previous research that provided much contextual background in the same area and with many of the same participants has been funded by the California Council for the Humanities, the LEFF Foundation, the Rosenberg Foundation, and the American Friends Service Committee. Ms. Mortensen's research was carried out as a part of her thesis, *I Relate to the Sense of Not Belonging: Native American Perspectives of Homelessness*, in American Indian Studies at the University of Arizona. Please address all correspondence to Susan Lobo, Ph.D., Slob0333@aol.com.

"Substance Dependency among Homeless American Indians in Oakland and Tucson" is an abridged version of "Substance Dependency among Homeless American Indians," by Susan Lobo, Ph.D., and Margaret Mortensen Vaughan, M.A., which appeared in the *Journal of Psychoactive Drugs* 35 (1). Reprinted by permission of Haight-Ashbury Publications, 612 Clayton Street, San Francisco, California.

Ackerman, L. "Residents or Visitors: Finding Motives for Movements in an Indian Population." Paper presented at the Society for Applied Anthropology, Santa Fe, New Mexico, 1989.

———. *Residential Mobility among the Colville Indians.* Washington, D.C.: Center for Survey Methods Research, Bureau of the Census, 1988.

Bogue, D. J. *Skid Row in American Cities.* Chicago: Community and Family Center, University of Chicago, 1963.

Fleisher, M. *An Ethnographic Evaluation of Street-to-System Cycling of Black, Hispanic and American Indian Males.* Washington, D.C.: Center for Survey Methods Research, Bureau of the Census, 1989.

Jojola, T. *Urban Indians in Albuquerque, New Mexico: A Study for the Department of Family and Human Services.* Albuquerque, N. Mex.: University of New Mexico, 1999.

Kasprow, W., and Veterans Affairs Connecticut Health Care System. "Substance Use and Psychiatric Problems of Homeless Native American Veterans," *Psychiatric Services* 49(3) (1998): 345–350.

Koegel, P., and M. A. Burnam. "Traditional and Nontraditional Homeless Alcoholics," *Alcohol Health and Research World* 11(3) (1987): 28–34.

Kramer, J., and J. C. Barker. "Homelessness among Older American Indians, Los Angeles, 1987–1989," *Human Organization* 55 (1996): 4, 396–409.

Lazar, D. "Selected Issues in the Philosophy of Social Science." In *Researching Society and Culture,* ed. C. Seale. London: Sage Publications, 1998.

Lobo, S. *American Indian Urban Mobility in the San Francisco Bay Area.* Washington, D.C.: United States Census Bureau, 2001.

Lobo, S., and K. Peters. *American Indians and the Urban Experience.* Walnut Creek, Calif.: AltaMira Press, 2001.

Mortensen, M. "I Relate to the Sense of Not Belonging: Native American Perspectives of Homelessness." Unpublished Master's thesis for the Graduate Interdisciplinary Program of American Indian Studies, University of Arizona, 1998.

Snow, D. A., S. G. Baker, and L. Anderson. "Criminality and Homeless Men: An Empirical Assessment," *Social Problems* 36 (1989): 5, 532–549.

Sugarman, J. R., and D. C. Grossman. "Trauma among American Indians in an Urban County, " *Public Health Reports* 111(4) (1996): 321–327.

American Indian Involvement in the Criminal Justice System

19

CHRISTINE DUCLOS AND MARGARET SEVERSON

I love a people who are honest without laws, who have no jails and no poorhouses. . . . I love a people who have never raised a hand against me, or stolen my property, where there was no law to punish for either.

—GEORGE CATLIN

D AILY OVER TWO MILLION ADULT Americans are in jail or prison—that's 1 in 147 U.S. residents (Harrison and Karberg 2003). The most troublesome aspect of this grim statistic is that our society is doing so little to change it. Additionally, the percentage of jail detainees—both male and female—with mental disorders is substantially higher than among the general population (Steadman and Veysey 1997). Kupers (1999) states that "prisons and jails have become the largest mental asylums and providers of psychiatric services in the United States." However, providing for appropriate treatment of inmates with mental and substance disorders is a task for which most facilities are ill equipped and underbudgeted (Lamb and Weinberger 1998). This situation merits elucidation because of its immediate and potentially long-term, intergenerational impacts.

Increasingly, mainstream and Indian local jails are perceived as appropriate alternatives to inadequate community-based mental health and substance abuse services. Historically, violative behavior was rare in traditional Indian communities (Armstrong et al. 1996b). Conformity to tribal norms was strongly instilled among all members and constantly reinforced by one's kinsmen. Misconduct, if it occurred, was generalized across the wider kin group (group blame versus individual blame). Help was offered to make amends and restore self-respect through purification and the restoration of balance and tribal harmony. Jails and prisons are mainstream institutions that were imposed on Indian communities. Jails and prisons were built to *punish* those who did not conform, based on Euro-Western values. Native societies, on the other hand, considered the individual good indistinguishable from the community good. The values of respect and kinship, not the imposition of rules and laws, defined societal justice and structure. Adaptations of the imposed justice practice are evident in Indian communities (Duclos 1999). For example, in one reservation community the Indian court and jail were seen as coercive gatekeepers to services, extended family, and respite. Recognizing reform is needed, tribes are now experimenting with more flexible and inclusive approaches that combine Indian historical customs with Western legal system elements (Armstrong et al. 1996b).

The overrepresentation of racial minorities in the criminal justice systems in the United States has been commented upon for many years (Devine et al. 1998; Pope et al. 2002). These racially disproportionate arrest and incarceration rates have been seen as threatening the survival of the distinct cultures associated with each ethnic and racial minority group (Alvarez and Bachman 1996). The few Indian studies completed found that arrest and incarceration rates of American Indians are also disproportionately higher than the percentage of American Indians in the general population (Poupart 1995; Silverman 1996; Armstrong et al. 1996a). Because of their disproportionate representation in jails and prisons, minorities are also the hardest hit by failure to provide treatment and ancillary services during and after involvement with the justice system (NCASA 1998).

After an extensive review of the criminal justice literature, Alvarez and Bachman (1996) concluded that Indians are among the most oppressed minority groups in the United States and are subjected to negative and degrading stereotypes (e.g., "the drunken Indian") that likely perpetuate and encourage continued discriminatory and adverse applications of the law against them. Complicating matters even further, various treaties, federal and state laws, and court rulings have created an assortment of jurisdictions over Indians who commit crimes—on or off the reservation. This jurisdictional complexity results in Indian detainment in facilities operated by tribes; the Bureau of Indian Affairs; and city, county, state, and federal authorities (Duclos et al. 1994).

We do know that most of the Indian offenders detained in jails are detained on alcohol-related offenses (Greenfeld and Smith 1999). In fact, Indians have a rate of arrest for alcohol violations (driving under the influence, liquor law violations, and public drunkenness) more than double the national rate. Compared to jail inmates of all races, Indians are less likely to have been jailed for a violent or drug offense. It is important that these statistics do not perpetuate the myth of the "drunken Indian." The majority of American Indians do not drink, drink to excess, or get arrested. However, there are a minority that do seem to follow the mainstream pattern of having emotional or substance-use problems and find themselves visible enough to come into repeated contact with justice officials, leading to repeated arrests and incarcerations (Jordan et al. 2002).

Jails as Fail Safe

The jail is the most important of all criminal justice institutions since almost all those arrested are processed through the jail, and two-thirds to three-fourths of all convicted criminals serve their sentences in jails (Steadman, McCarty, and Morrissey 1989). In the past, the primary function of the jail was simply to protect the community by detaining persons awaiting trial and to punish by incarcerating certain short-term criminals. Safety and security concerns were paramount, and treatment and rehabilitation were never an issue. Times have changed. Given the increasing seriousness of crime, the demonstrations of the interrelatedness of emotional disorders with delinquency and antisocial behavior, and the overrepresentation in our justice system of both minorities and people with mental and substance use disorders, increased collaboration between justice and other organizations within community systems of care is essential. In fact, local justice systems are called upon as a "service of last resort" when attempts to place an adult or juvenile into adequate treatment during a crisis have failed. Additionally, rigid eligibility requirements associated with many programs place adults and youth at risk for arrest and incarceration. For some Indian communities and reservations, adequate alternative services are just not available, especially where inpatient confinement is necessary, such as in cases of suicide ideation (Duclos 1999; Duclos et al.1994).

It has been shown that during the first day of incarceration, a detainee is at greater medical and mental health risk than at any other time of imprisonment (Hayes and Rowan 1988). For example, the risk of committing suicide is highest within the first three hours of incarceration; alcohol withdrawal also carries a significant mortality rate (MacDonald et al. 1996). With high arrest and subsequent incarceration rates, Indians are being placed at very high risk when placed in detention on or off the reservation for relatively minor crimes.

The Current Role of the Court and Jail in Indian Community Service Systems

A 1999 study of Northern Plains reservation-based detained Indian adolescents found that adolescent offenders were significantly more likely to receive alcohol, drug, or mental health services (ADM) than a nondetained sample (Novins et al. 1999). Court orders involved in the adjudication process appeared to be a key factor leading to treatment for youths on the reservation with substance use problems. Service provider comments and program statistics confirmed that the vast majority of clients, if not all, were court ordered.

Similarly, we conducted an adult study in 2000 in a Northern Plains border jail facility that showed Indian detainees approximately twice as likely to report prior hospitalization and past-six-month service utilization than their non-Indian counterparts (Duclos and Severson, in review). Jail recidivism was strongly associated with prior hospitalization, although this finding did not hold for past-six-month (prior to arrest) use of services. Our findings support once again what Jordan et al. (2002) concluded for the mainstream experience: There is a subgroup of troubled persons who receive ADM treatment services and who are also repeatedly incarcerated.

In a qualitative reservation-based juvenile detention study, Duclos (1999) found the role of detention to be less a matter of punishment and more of a "brokering service," "parenting service," "shelter," and "baby-sitting." These roles suggested that the facility and courts have stepped in to provide what in certain situations the extended families or groups cannot but traditionally had provided for the "family." Tribal council members have identified the loss of "the family" structure as an important contributor to this practice. Here is a quote from one of the council members. "I think the family structure should be put back in place. The loving and caring . . . should be put back in place. . . . It's more restoring the balance structure, more loving and caring, having society accept the fact that the family is the problem now."

Being in a detention facility also served as a form of family discipline, a parental threat of discipline, or even a replacement for discipline. This parental threat of banishment from the home to the facility was thought to keep the youth "in line." A detention officer remarked, "If we didn't provide it [discipline]. . . . A parent finds their child comes home, smells of being away. . . . The first thing they do is call the jail, instead of trying to talk, sit down . . . right away they call us."

These remarks were confirmed by service providers' comments, such as this one: "I think a lot of parents use it . . . as a tool to help them correct their kids. They threaten their kids and say 'I'm sending you to detention, I want you [the detention officer] to set them back there for two weeks.'"

Comments from the parent group suggested that "turning in" their own children might have been motivated out of a sense of desperation. They did not know what to do with their children and thought that going to jail not only might "straighten them out" but might also get them help. One mother admitted: "My kids go to detention a lot. Whenever I bust them for alcohol, I turn them in to detention. And I used to think I was real cruel about that, but they needed help."

Whether due to lack of parenting skills or out of desperation, this action resulted in a detention stay and in some cases court referral to services; it also applied a labeling of delinquency. We can argue that these actions are not appropriate, but without alternatives, they will continue. It is important to note that the majority of the community's parents do not threaten detention. However, some do, and this indicates detention performs an important purpose that is currently acceptable to the community. Interestingly, when asked, youths did not see detention as a punishment but just "some time out." This perception then also places the facility in a "safe haven" role where one can go to get respite from life stress and troubles.

The Reality

The failure to use any local justice system to get nonviolent alcohol-abusing offenders into treatment and training is irresponsible. Releasing alcohol-abusing and addicted inmates without treatment is irrational public policy. To address this illogic in service policy planning, communities must examine the current roles each of their services actually play and include all cultural nuances as medicine for wellness.

For Indian and mainstream communities, the local justice system serves important roles for the community, especially for those suffering from ADM disorders. Although this system may not be the most appropriate or efficient entry to services, it is unlikely to change if uncoordinated and fragmented services continue. However, the current reservation experience with lack of money and other resources and the "politics" of living in a small community with strong family loyalties hamper courts' effectiveness. Moving the court into a more authoritative role independent from tribal government interference might provide a comprehensive driving force for service provision, not only in a gateway fashion, but also in a policy-making capacity.

Accepting the important roles justice plays and then including these roles in a reexamination of the community's response to adult and youth needs and subsequent care might result in a redistribution of scarce community resources and a more coordinated and integrated system of care while increasing availability of services. This paradigm shift calls for a fundamental change in service delivery policy.

Traditionally, sociopolitical entities at local, state, and national levels have established discrete programs to meet discrete needs. While discrete programs may reduce the potential for duplicative services, it has failed to solve the problem of the duplicative client. Every help-giving community system—including the jail system—should acquire knowledge and understanding of the other local service resources and the ability to conceptualize, coordinate, integrate, and deliver comprehensive, culturally appropriate services to people in need (Sauber 1983).

It is a particularly crucial time to study the impact of these conditions on the American Indian population. Rising incarceration rates, troubling rates of substance abuse, suicidal behaviors, complex physical health problems, and the

ongoing migration from reservation lands into racially biased and culturally ig-
norant social justice systems demand studies that will result in service communities' coming together to organize around the myriad of health challenges
posed by indigenous peoples. The local jail system is one component of the
larger service community, and despite some of the difficulties associated with
jail-based assessment and treatment, it, too, must be a player.

Notes

Prisons generally hold inmates who have been convicted of felony offenses and sentenced
to two years or more of incarceration (state or federal). Local jails, on the other hand, generally house individuals convicted of misdemeanors and sentenced to two years or less and
individuals awaiting trial. Since jails are an integral part of the local community structure
and are generally short-term facilities having more direct impact on the community, this
chapter concentrates on their role, and not the prison's role, in service planning.

Alvarez, A., and R. D. Bachman. "American Indians and Sentencing Disparity: An Arizona
    Test," *Journal of Criminal Justice* 24 (1996): 549–561.
Armstrong, T. L., M. H. Guilfoyle, and A. P. Melton. "Native American Delinquency: An
    Overview of Prevalence, Causes, and Correlates." In *Native Americans, Crime, and Justice*, ed.
    M. O. Nielsen and R. A. Silverman. Boulder, Colo.: Westview Press, 1996a, 75–88.
Armstrong, T. L., M. H. Guilfoyle, and A. P. Melton. "Traditional Approaches to Tribal
    Justice." In *Native Americans, Crime, and Justice*, ed. M. O. Nielsen and R. A. Silverman.
    Boulder, Colo.: Westview Press, 1996b, 46–51.
Devine, P., K. Coolbaugh, and S. Jenkins. *Disproportionate Minority Confinement: Lessons Learned
    from Five States.* Washington, D.C.: U.S. Department of Justice, Office of Juvenile Justice
    and Delinquency Prevention, 1998.
Duclos, C. W. "Factors Associated with Alcohol, Drug, and Mental Health Service Uti-
    lization among a Sample of American Indian Adolescent Detainees," Ph.D. diss., Uni-
    versity of Colorado at Denver, Denver, Colo., 1999.
Duclos, C. W., W. LeBeau, and G. Elias. "American Indian Suicidal Behavior in Detention
    Environments: Cause for Continued Basic and Applied Research," *Jail Suicide Update* 5
    (1994): 4–9.
Greenfeld, L., and S. Smith. *American Indians and Crime.* Washington, D.C.: Bureau of Jus-
    tice Statistics, 1999.
Harrison, P., and J. Karberg. "Prison and Jail Inmates at Midyear 2002," *Bureau of Justice
    Statistics Bulletin*, NCJ 198877 (2003).
Hayes, L. M., and J. R. Rowan. *National Study of Jail Suicides: Seven Years Later.* Alexandria, Va.:
    National Center on Institutions and Alternatives, 1988.
Jordan, B. K., E. B. Federman, B. J. Burns, W. E. Schlenger, J. A. Fairbank, and J. M. Cad-
    dell. "Lifetime Use of Mental Health and Substance Abuse Treatment Services by In-
    carcerated Women Felons," *Psychiatric Services* 53(3) (2002): 317–325.

Kupers, T. *Prison Madness: The Mental Health Crisis behind Bars and What We Must Do about It.* San Francisco: Jossey-Bass, 1999.

Lamb, H. R., and L. E. Weinberger. "Persons with Severe Mental Illness in Jails and Prisons: A Review," *Psychiatric Services* 49 (1998): 483–492.

MacDonald, J., E. M. Twardon, and H. J. Shaffer. "Alcohol." In *Sourcebook of Substance Abuse and Addiction*, ed. L. Friedman, N. F. Fleming, D. H. Roberts, and S. E. Hyman. Baltimore, Md.: William and Wilkins, 1996, 109–137.

The National Center on Addiction and Substance Abuse (NCASA). *Behind Bars: Substance Abuse and America's Prison Population.* New York: NCASA, 1998.

Novins, D. K., C. W. Duclos, C. Martin, C. S. Jewett, and S. M. Manson. "Utilization of Alcohol, Drug, and Mental Health Treatment Services among Anerican Indian Adolescent Detainees," *Journal of the American Academy of Child and Adolescent Psychiatry* 38 (1999): 9, 1102–1108.

Pope, C. E., R. Lovell, and H. M. Hsia. "Disporportinate Minority Confinement: A Review of the Research Literature from 1989 through 2001." OJJDP: *Juvenile Justice Bulletin.*

Poupart, L. M. "Juvenile Justice Processing of American Indian Youth." In *Minorities in Juvenile Justice*, ed. K. K. Leonard, C. E. Pope and W. H. Feyerherm. Thousand Oaks, Calif.: Sage Publications, 1995, 179–200.

Sauber, S. R. *The Human Service Delivery System.* New York Columbia University Press, 1983.

Silverman, R. A. "Patterns of Native American Crime." In *Native Americans, Crimes, and Justice*, ed. M. O. Nielsen and R. A. Silverman. Boulder, Colo.: Westview Press, 1996, 58–74.

Steadman, H., and B. M. Veysey. "Providing Services for Jail Inmates with Mental Disorders," *National Institute of Justice Research in Brief*, NCJ 162207 (1997): 1–10.

Steadman, H. J., D. W. McCarty, and J. P. Morrissey. *The Mentally Ill in Jail.* New York: Guilford Press, 1989.

American Indian Public Charter School

Why Is It a Model School for Students?

BEN CHAVIS

⌐⌐

> *AIPCS is a very structured school. We do not have the chance to goof off in school. The teachers make sure we know the rules and we don't want to break them. The teachers are strict and keep us on task. We know what is going to happen every hour of the school day. At AIPCS, we are a big family. It was not like this at my old school.*

—NATHAN ROBLES, 7TH GRADE NAVAJO INDIAN STUDENT

COULD IT BE THAT many students know how a school should be structured to ensure they are prepared with the academic and social skills to be productive members of society? Students and parents are interested in a school that provides structure and discipline. Students are more at ease when they know what is expected of them in a school. It allows them to focus on what they must accomplish in school. When students are aware of what is going to happen each day in class, they have more stability in their lives. In a public school, stability and structure are important factors that lead to successful student development. With the structure comes discipline. Students expect a consequence when they do not follow rules. If they are not disciplined, students will not respect their teachers or administrative leadership (Chavis 1986). Effective learning cannot occur in such an environment! Those students who want to learn are held hostage by the class clowns. The teachers have three options: They can (1) take control of their classroom, (2) let the students take control, or (3) choose another profession. The American public is repeatedly informed that there is a teacher shortage. Could it be that many of the teachers have chosen to leave the public schools because they will not allow themselves to be disrespected? A successful public school must provide a structured learning environment where students, educators, parents, and community members are committed to quality education.

The American Indian Public Charter School (AIPCS) is considered a model school for students. The school has a structured environment that focuses on preparing students to be productive members of their community. First and foremost, the school has committed itself to sound fiscal accountability. AIPCS is sponsored by the Oakland Unified School District in Oakland, California. This is a case study of AIPCS that is presented in three parts: (1) a brief history of the California charter school movement and AIPCS, (2) the creation of a positive school culture at AIPCS, and (3) collaboration and the community. This chapter provides an internal perspective of this unique urban middle school designed around a productive theoretical educational model that has produced positive academic results for students who are traditionally labeled *at risk*.

The California Charter School Movement and AIPCS

In California in the early 1990s, the passage of charter school legislation grew out of the school choice movement. Republicans, Libertarians, and many minority parents supported the movement as an alternative to the traditional public school system. The minority parents did not have the financial resources to send their children to private schools. Those who supported the school choice movement were accused of being racist or trying to undermine public schools. This was a very strange accusation, considering that as late as 1970, American Indians were not allowed to attend a public school with white students in North Carolina and other parts of the United States. Why? Because God made them American Indians and the public school boards prohibited Indians and blacks from attending school with whites. How can anyone accuse American Indians or other minorities for undermining the public school system? Where is the logic? A review of the educational statistical data maintained on American Indian students clearly shows that the public school system has dug its own grave (Thomas 1984).

In 1992, the California state legislators passed charter school legislation. The school choice movement became less of an issue for many people. In 1993, the California Department of Education Charter School Division supported the funding of fifty new charter schools in various parts of the state. The charter schools were funded based on the number of students enrolled and their Average Daily Attendance (ADA) for the school year. In 1994, a group of American Indian parents and community members started the process to create the American Indian Public Charter School as one of the goals of the Community Mobilization Project. This group created a committee and decided by consensus that the school should focus on serving the educational needs of American Indian students enrolled in Oakland public schools. This was done because American Indian students had the highest dropout rate, lowest school attendance rate, lowest standardized test scores, and lowest graduation rate in the Oakland system. In short, they were not succeeding in the public school system.

During the 2001–2002 school year, 40 percent of the students at AIPCS were American Indian, 35 percent were of Hispanic origin, 24 percent were of African American descent, and 1 percent were Filipino. Some 97 percent of the students qualified for free or reduced-price lunches. Friedman (2000) has noted that poverty has a staggering negative effect on the Academic Performance Index (API) scores of students. Student attendance is over 98 percent, test scores continue to increase, and the suspension rate has been less than 1 percent during the past two years. What brought about this amazing transformation?

Creating a Positive School Culture

The school culture at AIPCS is based on high expectations of the staff and students. Student achievement is accomplished through hard work and dedication. Excuses are not accepted from those not putting forth their best effort in school (Chavis 1998). The staff, students, family members, and school board have embraced this philosophy of education. The success of AIPCS is directly related to a competent school board, a simple fact. School board members are recruited based on their commitment and contributions to enhance the education of students. The board represents a unique group of individuals who have diverse experience in the public sector. The chairman of the school board is a parent, educator, and attorney. The treasurer of the board has a strong business background. Two AIPCS board members are employed at the university level, have a sound grasp of public education, and are aware of what it takes to succeed in higher education. Two other board members are parents and actively involved in the community. All board members are required to complete at least sixteen hours of course work on charter school governance and school finance. In addition, school board policy prohibits any board member or relative of a board member from being employed by AIPCS.

The school board members have established sound policies and procedures that all employees of the school must follow. The principal reports directly to the board, and the staff reports directly to the principal. This is reflected in the policies and flowchart of the school. It is very important for board members and employees to know their responsibilities within the school structure of AIPCS. The following is the mission statement authored by the school board, administrator, staff, families, and community members:

> The American Indian Public Charter School serves inner-city students in 6th through
> 8th grade. The focus of AIPCS is to meet the academic needs of American Indian

students and others interested in attending our school. We will provide them with a structured education to enhance their academic skills in reading, writing, spelling, mathematics, science, business and humanities in order to be an educated person in the 21st century. This will be a collaborative effort between the school, students, families and community members.

A list of measurable student outcomes was created to ensure these goals were met. It stated that students would be competent in each of the following areas after completing their school experience at AIPCS:

1. Ability to attend school daily.
2. Ability to read and respond accurately and analytically to test questions.
3. Ability to write critically.
4. Ability to compute and solve math problems.
5. Ability to comprehend and apply scientific knowledge.
6. Ability to comprehend the role of history in our society.
7. Ability to comprehend the role of business in our society.

The following criteria were utilized in measuring students' progress: (a) student attendance would be a minimum of 95 percent each year, (b) the expulsion and suspension rate would be reduced to 1 percent by the next year, and (c) sixth-through eighth-grade students would achieve a minimum of 5 percent above AIPCS's results on the 1999–2000 STAR testing for each of the next five years. To ensure that the goals were accomplished, a stable environment was designed to enhance the learning process. AIPCS adopted the concept of a self-contained classroom for sixth through eighth grade. The focus of the curriculum is language arts, math, science, and social studies. This correlates directly to the California Department of Education's state standards for these grade levels. AIPCS teachers spend a minimum of seventy minutes each day on reading, writing, and spelling. Research has indicated that students with strong language arts skills are more likely to achieve academically in school. Therefore, the staff participates in ongoing language arts in-service training that continues throughout the school year.

Teachers with a strong academic background in the core subject areas are recruited. The teachers who do not have a Multi-Subject Teaching Credential are enrolled in the Cal State TEACH program and receive an emergency teaching certificate. In the self-contained classroom, teachers spend the whole day with the same students. The teachers have a planning period while their students are with the physical education teacher. At AIPCS, each year teachers move up to the next grade level with their students until the students graduate from the eighth grade. Then the teachers move back down to the sixth grade and repeat the looping process. This practice provides the teachers a more personalized environment that offers them the opportunity to focus on addressing each student's academic and social needs during a three-year period.

The AIPCS board, administration, staff, students, families, and community members have embraced student assessment as a positive tool to assist the school in achieving established goals (Chavis and Duffie 1997). Frequent monitoring of students' homework and weekly testing is used to diagnose students' strengths as well as weaknesses. Through ongoing assessments, students are able to apply their knowledge and know when they are successful and why. The student assessment serves to stimulate and reinforce good instruction. The testing data reflect significant improvement at AIPCS during the past two years (tables 20.1 and 20.2). Katz and Tucker (2002) noted:

> At the American Indian Public Charter School, Stanford 9 test scores went through the roof. . . . In math and language almost half of American Indian's seventh-graders were on par with the national average. That's compared to two years ago, when none of the school's seventh-graders met the average in math, language or reading. The school improved its standing in some areas more than any other Oakland public school this year.

The academic gains that have been made by the students are evidence that American Indian students can successfully compete at a national level with other middle school students. The socialist Indian "experts" who say American Indians are not competitive are perpetuating a racist ideology based on their

Table 20.1.   Percentage of Students Scoring At or Above the 50th Percentile, Oakland Unified School District 2000–2002

	Reading			Math		
	2000	*2001*	*2002*	*2000*	*2001*	*2002*
Grade 6	22 percent	22 percent	24 percent 2 percent gain	29 percent	30 percent	33 percent 4 percent gain
Grade 7	24 percent	24 percent	25 percent 1 percent gain	28 percent	30 percent	29 percent 1 percent gain
Grade 8*	26 percent	26 percent	26 percent Even	26 percent	25 percent	31 percent 5 percent gain

*These data represent the percentage of students at or above the national average. The gain is the total percentage of improvement for each grade level at the end of the three years of testing. It should be noted that all the 8th grade students at AIPCS take the algebra portion of the STAR 9 test; however, the majority of the 8th grade students enrolled in the Oakland Unified School District take the general math portion of the test.

Table 20.2.   Percentage of Students Scoring At or Above the 50th Percentile, American Indian Public Charter School 2000–2002

	Reading			Math		
	2000	*2001*	*2002*	*2000*	*2001*	*2002*
Grade 6	8 percent	33.6 percent	44.2 percent 36.4 percent gain	0	29.5 percent	39.2 percent 39.2 percent gain
Grade 7	0 percent	43.4 percent	47 percent 47 percent gain	0	31.8 percent	41.4 percent 41.4 percent gain
Grade 8*	17 percent	46.4 percent	48.5 percent 31.5 percent gain	0	29.5 percent	34.1 percent 34.1 percent gain

*These data represent the percentage of students at or above the national average. The gain is the total per-centage of improvement for each grade level at the end of the three years of testing. It should be noted that all the 8th grade students at AIPCS take the algebra portion of the STAR 9 test; however, the major-ity of the 8th grade students enrolled in the Oakland Unified School District take the general math por-tion of the test.

own ignorance. Could it be they prefer to see American Indian people as vic-tims and that allows them to assume the paternalist role toward American In-dians? What would these individuals do if they did not have some ethnic group to save? Throughout the United States, American Indians are participating in competitive activities (Chavis 1993).

Collaboration and the Community

There is a great deal of rhetoric in the United States of America regarding edu-cational excellence and public education. The two most common themes, in-creased parent involvement and more money for schools, have been repeated so many times by the teachers associations (unions) that they have now become ce-lestial excuses. The issue of parent involvement has been whooped up as the main ingredient to successful public schools. This is regurgitated by educational re-searchers, teachers, school administrators, politicians, the National Education As-sociation, which boasts of over two million paying members, and pig farmers. These guardians of education believe that if parents are visiting the school, serv-ing on the PTA, and raising funds through candy sales for their children's school, education will improve. The candy sales do increase the PTA's bank account and cavities in the mouths of minority students. They also contribute to the devastat-ing sugar diabetes problem among minorities. More money is not the answer! AIPCS receives an average of $5,000.00 per student, and Oakland Unified School District (OUSD) receives over $7,000.00 per student (Friedman 2000). The students at AIPCS outperformed their peers who attend OUSD on each of the standardized tests used to measure student achievement.

The problem is with the structure of the educational system and the general public's definition of parent involvement. In the United States, parent involvement refers to and focuses on the nuclear family. This preempts the importance of an extended family. The extended family is the heart and soul of the majority of people living on American Indian reservations, in ethnic communities, rural communities, urban ghettos, and so forth. How can poor parents afford to take time off from work to volunteer in schools? They are barely surviving financially to support their families. Where is the logic of more minority parent involvement in schools?

AIPCS refuses to add to the economic and social burdens these families already have in their lives. Instead, AIPCS focuses on creating a family and community environment at the school. This environment does not cost a great deal of money. It requires commitment to our job as educators, hard work, and a willingness to stop blaming parents for the school's problems. At AIPCS, the family is responsible for getting their children to school on time, with a lunch and ready to work. Families are not required to raise funds or volunteer for the school. Aunts, uncles, grandmas, grandpas, and other extended-family members are encouraged to participate in family activities at the school. The school works very closely with the American Indian Child Resource Center that has a very good Indian Education program. The program, designed to provide after-school tutoring and culture services to American Indian students, is a wonderful resource for the students.

Each year, after their eighth grade graduation, students and teachers go on a trip to a place they have studied during the school year. For the 2001–2002 school year, the students chose Washington, D.C., and got a chance to tour the White House and Capitol Hill. For the 2002–2003 school year, the eighth grade students went to Mexico City. The trip did not cost the students as it was a reward for their hard work and dedication to giving their best effort at AIPCS. When an event is held at the school, a minimum of 300 family members attend the function. This is a major accomplishment considering that the household income of most of the students attending AIPCS ranks below the poverty level. The aunts, uncles, parents, grandparents, friends, students, and staff are part of an extended family at AIPCS (Holm, Pearson, and Chavis 2002). Therefore, the gatherings are seen as a family celebration of student achievement. The school has created an excellent reputation for high academic achievement. The students have embraced the concept of being respectful to others and maintaining a clean school and positive family environment (Cobb 2002). This has transformed AIPCS into a model school. Last year, the school had the highest API increase of all secondary schools in California. We have high expectations of our AIPCS family every second, minute, hour, day, week, month, and year. We are "A School at Work!" and expect to be the BEST!

Notes

Nathan is a 7th grade Navajo Indian student at AIPCS. After scoring 970 on the SAT, he was awarded a scholarship to attend the Johns Hopkins University during the summer of 2002. He was the only seventh grader in the Oakland Public Schools to qualify for the program based on SAT test scores.

Chavis, B. "The Teacher-Student Relationship as Perceived by Lumbee Indians." Ph.D. diss., University of Arizona, Tucson, Arizona, 1986.

———. "All Indian Rodeo: A Transformation of Western Apache Tribal Warfare and Culture. Research Findings," *Wicazo Sa Review* 9 (I) (1993): 4–11.

———. "What is Lumbee Indian Culture? Does It Exist?" In *A Good Cherokee, A Good Anthropologist*, ed. S. Pavlik. Los Angeles: American Indian Studies Center, University of California, 1998.

Chavis, B., and M. Duffie. "American Indian Studies and Its Evolution in Academia," *The Social Science Journal* 34 (4) (1997): 435–445.

Cobb, P. "American Indian Public Charter School Prepares Students for Colleges." *Post*, August 28, 2002, 1B.

Friedman, D. "The Economic Root of Low Test Scores." *Los Angeles Times*, March 26, 2000, M6.

Holm, T., D. Pearson, and B. Chavis. "Peoplehood: A Model for the Extension of Sovereignty in American Indian Studies," *Wicazo Sa Review* 18 (I) (2002).

Katz, K., and J. Tucker. "Student Test Scores Stay below U. S. Average." *Oakland Tribune*, August 30, 2002, 1, 15.

Thomas, T. *Lecture on American Indian Education*. Tucson: University of Arizona. 1984.

Index

progress measurement, 202–3;
teachers, 202–3
American Indians and Alaska Natives
(AI/AN): alcohol dependence among,
1, 127–28; community awareness of,
142; cultural activities of, 113–14;
cultural values, separation from, 113;
drug dependence among, 1;
HIV/AIDS concerns, 149, 160–62;
HNI for, 20–28; incarceration of, 152,
192; jurisdictions over, 192; Native
Circle program for, 140; population
statistics, 58; post-traumatic stress
disorder incidence in, 7, 12–13, 15,
162; sexually transmitted diseases
among, 160–61; sovereign status of,
47, 159; stereotypes about, 52, 192;
stressors on, 162–63; substance abuse
among, 19 (see also substance abuse);
traditional health practices use,
109–11 (see also traditional health
practices [THP])
Angelica, 122
Antonovsky Life Crisis Scale, 12
anxiety, 162; of urban Indians, 46
Arikara, 67–73
arts and crafts in aftercare projects, 21
art therapy, 143
Ashley, Hanson, 144
Asian Pacifica Islander Wellness Center,
141
assimilation, 65, 68–71
awareness-raising interventions, 82

balanced integration, 118–19
Bay Area American Indian Two Spirit, 141
Bay Area Red Road (BARR) project, 100;
collaboration of care, 102; continuum
of care, 101; culturally relevant
database, 104; data system mapping
and adaptation, 102; project needs and
database design, 103
Bear, 122–23

behavioral health treatment: traditional
healing in, 57–62; Village Sobriety
Project, 57–62
bicultural identity, 6; of C/Yup'ik,
57–58
Bien, Melanie, 143
binge drinking, 127–28. See also alcohol
use and abuse
Blessing Way ceremonies, 128
boarding schools: abuse in, 72;
assimilationist policies of, 69; death
and illness in, 70; indoctrination by,
68; language loss caused by, 68–70;
religious instruction in, 69–70; trauma
caused by, 10–11
body-centered therapy, 143–44
border towns: substance abuse in, 87;
substance abuse policy in, 88
Bowen Family Systems theory, 143
bózhó, 169
Bureau of Indian Affairs relocation
programs, 46

California charter school movement,
200–201
Callicum, Andy, 43
capacity in HNI-sponsored activities,
enhancing, 22, 24–26
CARE Act, 150, 155–56; AI/AN
initiatives, 150–54
Case, Harold, Reverend and Mrs., 70, 72
case management, integrated, 153
Catlin, George, 67–68
Center for Mental Health Services
(CMHS), 14; Circle of Care initiative,
48
Center for Substance Abuse Treatment
(CSAT): Village Sobriety Project
funding, 57; Women's Circle funding,
170
Centers for Disease Control and
Prevention HIV/AIDS prevention
funding, 149–50

About the Contributors

Ruthie Alexius is currently the clinical supervisor for the Fort Defiance office within the Navajo Nation's Department of Behavioral Health Services (DBHS). She has been with DBHS for eighteen years, first as a secretary, followed for fifteen years as a substance abuse counselor. Ms. Alexius has been a Peacemaker for the entire Window Rock District for eleven years, where she has officiated peacemaking cases for individuals, families, and organizations. Those cases have involved alcohol and drug use and abuse, child abuse and neglect, divorces, family disharmony, probate, and small claims. For her, the most challenging cases are those involving probate of land, where verbal agreements are different from legal documents. The most rewarding cases are when she is able to help a family come back together in harmony.

David D. Barney, Ph.D., received his MPH from the University of California at Berkeley, his MSW from San Diego State University, and his Ph.D. in social work from the University of Kansas. Previously, as director of research at the National Native American AIDS Prevention Center, he conducted evaluation activities for a network of twelve Special Projects of National Significance throughout the United States that served American Indians, Alaska Natives, and Native Hawaiians. He has made more than twenty-five presentations on HIV/AIDS at national conferences, published two articles on HIV-care evaluation methods, and published four articles on HIV/AIDS case management.

Sandra Beauchamp, M.S.W. (Mandan, Hidatsa, Arikara), began her career late in life after losing her parents and siblings to diseases associated with alcoholism, and her son to a drunk driver. She is devoted to being a part of the process of healing in her native community. She is a published writer of poetry and articles relating to the Indigenous Nations of the United States.

Maria Yellow Horse Brave Heart, Ph.D., L.C.S.W. (Hunkpapa/ Oglala Lakota and member of the Wapaha Ska), is the president/director/cofounder of the Takini Network and is an associate research professor at the University of Denver Graduate School of Social Work. She specialized in trauma work for indigenous communities and is a very well-known author on intergenerational transfer of indigenous traumatic history.

Martha Burnside, B.A. (Sac and Fox), is a research associate at the Tri-Ethnic Center for Prevention Research at Colorado State University. She is from Oklahoma and serves as the field coordinator for a nationwide project that tracks American Indian adolescent substance use as well as field coordinator for a project to prevent delinquency in tribal communities. She is also a member of the Community Readiness Technical Assistance team.

Ben Chavis, Ph.D. (Lumbee), is the director of the American Indian Public Charter School in Oakland, California. He is a member of the Lumbee Indian Tribe, located in southeastern North Carolina. He completed his doctorate at the University of Arizona. He has been employed as a public school teacher, counselor, principal, superintendent, and university professor.

Rose L. Clark, Ph.D. (Navajo), was born and raised in Albuquerque, New Mexico. She received her B.A. in psychology and Ph.D. in clinical psychology with an emphasis in multicultural community clinical issues. She sits on numerous boards at the local, state, and federal levels and advocates on American Indian issues. She is involved in administration, program development, research, teaching, and direct services for the American Indian community.

Nalini Daliparthy, M.S., M.P.H., is currently an evaluation assistant reporting on quantitative process and outcome evaluations for program components in the mental health department of the Native American Health Center, Oakland. She is an epidemiologist trained at the University of Massachusetts, Amherst, and has also worked for the Disease Control Unit of the San Mateo County, California, Health Services Agency, responsible for data analysis of Hepatitis C infection in high-risk populations.

Christine Duclos, Ph.D., is an assistant professor in the Department of Family Medicine, University of Colorado Health Sciences Center. Her research and intervention development include the intersection of medical or health and justice systems, community-integrated health system development, and minority health issues—especially American Indian.

Betty E. S. Duran, M.S.W. (Pojoaque Pueblo), has more than nine years of experience in research and HIV/AIDS program administration. Her experience includes five years working with AI/AN and Native Hawaiians living with HIV, two years conducting multisite evaluation of HIV/AIDS services for the United States/Mexico border population, and two years in American Indian aging, including ethnographic interviews of tribal elders at Pojoaque Pueblo and comprehensive health assessment surveys to establish Title III medical services. She has coauthored publications on case management and mental health issues with American Indians.

Ruth W. Edwards, Ph.D., is a senior research scientist and director of the Tri-Ethnic Center for Prevention Research at Colorado State University. For over two decades, Dr. Edwards has conducted research on the prevention of social problems in rural and ethnic minority communities. Her work includes epidemiology and etiology as well as the development and evaluation of prevention and intervention efforts. Dr. Edwards is a member of the Community Readiness development team.

Yvonne Edwards, Ph.D., is a family therapist and did her graduate work in clinical psychology at the California Institute of Integral Studies. She became licensed as a marriage and family therapist in 1988. She met Helen Waukazoo when she spoke at a meeting on cultural sensitivity, and subsequently volunteered as an art therapist at Friendship House for nine years and witnessed the healing transformation of many Friendship House clients.

Bernard H. Ellis Jr., M.A., M.P.H., is principal researcher, Bernard Ellis and Associates, Inc., Santa Fe, Tennessee. He has studied community mobilization to reduce substance abuse in McKinley County, New Mexico, and Fremont County, Wyoming.

Candace Fleming, Ph.D. (Kickapoo/Oneida/Cherokee), raised on the Northern Cheyenne Reservation, is the associate director for the Circles of Care Evaluation Technical Assistance Center of the Center for Mental Health Services. Dr. Fleming's interests are in the areas of individual, family, and community resiliency and the use of culture and history in the restoration of balance within the Indian community.

Robert Foley, B.A., is a research associate for the Tri-Ethnic Center for Prevention Research at Colorado State University, where he works as the technical assistance coordinator for the Community Readiness Model and the project field coordinator for a grant exploring domestic violence and men. He has a B.A. in political science and is currently pursuing a master's degree at Colorado State University.

J. Phillip Gossage, Ph.D., is a senior research scientist at the University of New Mexico's Center on Alcoholism, Substance Abuse, and Addictions (UNM/CASAA). Over the past twelve years, he has been involved in evaluating the effectiveness of treatment modalities for substance abusers; the effectiveness of driving-while-intoxicated prevention programs; the interrelationships of alcohol, other drugs, and crime among American Indians of two reservations in the northern plains; and the epidemiology and prevention of fetal alcohol syndrome (FAS) in the United States and in South Africa.

Nelson Jim, M.A., MFTI (Dineh), is the clinical director for the Family and Child Guidance Clinic of the Native American Health Center in San Francisco. He has worked in the areas of HIV/AIDS, mental health, and substance abuse for twelve years. He oversees the *Native Circle*, a program funded through the Mental Health HIV/AIDS Services Collaborative Program of the federal Center for Mental Health Services. He has developed an innovative program that incorporates traditional Native American culture in an integrated approach to well-being and mental health.

Pamela Jumper-Thurman, Ph.D. (Western Cherokee), is a senior research scientist with the Tri-Ethnic Center for Prevention Research. She has worked in mental health and substance abuse research, treatment, evaluation and in the provision of direct services. She is a member of the Community Readiness development team.

Janet King, B.A. (Lumbee), has worked in the San Francisco Bay Area Native American Community for twenty-five years. As a community relations coordinator, she provides cultural awareness and educational training on mental health and Native Americans for hospitals, health clinics, and Bay Area university and college social work programs.

Susan Lobo, Ph.D., was trained as a cultural anthropologist; is a consultant emphasizing research, advocacy, and project design; and works primarily for American Indian tribes and community organizations in the United States and Central and South America. Her books include *A House of My Own: Social Organization in the Squatter Settlements of Peru*; *Native American Voices: a Reader*; *American Indians and the Urban Experience*; and *Urban Voices: The Bay Area American Indian Community*.

Spero Manson, Ph.D. (Pembina Chippewa), is professor, and head, Division of American Indian and Alaska Native Programs, Department of Psychiatry, at the University of Colorado Health Sciences Center. Dr. Manson directs the National

Center for American Indian and Alaska Native Mental Health Research. He has published extensively on the assessment, epidemiology, and prevention of alcohol, drug, and mental disorders across the developmental life span of Indian and Native people.

Philip A. May, Ph.D., is a senior research scientist and associate director of the University of New Mexico's Center on Alcoholism, Substance Abuse, and Addictions (UNM/CASAA) and a professor of sociology. Dr. May has worked collaboratively with American Indian communities for over thirty years. He has written extensively about alcohol policy, alcohol use and abuse and its prevention, suicide and its prevention, and fetal alcohol syndrome (FAS). He is the principal investigator for two very large FAS epidemiology and prevention studies in the United States and in South Africa.

Phoebe A. Mills, M.S.W. (Yup'ik), is originally from Fairbanks, Alaska, and is Yup'ik, English, and Danish. She received her master's in social work in 1999 and worked as the village Clinician in Bethel, Alaska, with the Yukon-Kuskokwim Health Corporation. She also worked as a perinatal clinician in Oakland, California, at the Native American Health Center, and currently works in Portland, Oregon, as a community development specialist at the National Indian Child Welfare Association.

Pamela G. Monaghan-Geernaert, Ph.D., is a research assistant professor at the Institute for Ethics, Health Sciences Center at the University of New Mexico. She received her Ph.D. from Case Western Reserve University in Medical Sociology and Gerontology. Her interest lies in utilizing culturally attuned methods in caring for Native Americans. Dr. Monaghan-Geernaert believes that gathering qualitative data through story telling and dialogue is a necessary venue for understanding people.

Larry Murillo, M.P.H., Dr.P.H., is Shoshone from Fort Hall, Idaho, and graduated from the doctoral program at the University of California, Berkeley, School of Public Health. His research interest is cultural health practices and how they contribute to public health. He has written a position paper on Native American Cultural Health Care for the National Center for Complementary and Alternative Medicine. "Native American Public Health Issues" is a course he currently teaches in the school of public health at Berkeley. He has worked for more than twenty years with various Native American communities, mostly as a public health educator and community organizer. He organized regional traditional gatherings with the assistance of spiritual leaders in California to educate Native American people about public health issues.

Ethan Nebelkopf, Ph.D., is director of the Family and Child Guidance Clinic of the Native American Health Center in Oakland and San Francisco. He is principal investigator for several projects funded by the federal Substance Abuse and Mental Health Services Administration and Health Resources and Services Administration in the areas of substance abuse, mental health, and HIV/AIDS among Native Americans. He has worked for community-based nonprofit organizations for thirty years and is a licensed family therapist in California.

Sarah Nebelkopf, B.A., is the evaluator at Friendship House, responsible for the management of the MIS/IT Team and, for the past four years, she worked in data collection, data management, and research. She received a B.A. in sociology from California State University, Long Beach, in 1998 and is currently a third-year graduate student in the M.P.A. program at California State University, Hayward.

Tim Noe, M. Div., is deputy director for the Healthy Nations National Program Office, Center for American Indian and Alaska Native Mental Health Research, Department of Psychiatry, University of Colorado Health Sciences Center and is currently in graduate school in a Ph.D. program in public administration at University of Colorado.

Otis Parrish, M.A., is a member of the Kashaya Pomo Tribe in northern California. He is a traditionalist and follows the old ways of his culture. He earned a bachelor's degree in Californian Indian Histories and minored in anthropology at Sonoma State University, graduating in 1977. He earned a master's degree in anthropology from the University of California, Berkeley, in 1997, and now works as the cultural attaché for the Phoebe Hearst Museum of Anthropology NAGPRA Program at the University of California, Berkeley.

Mary Phillips (Omaha/Laguna, Pueblo) has experience in program coordination, managed information systems development, evaluation, and community assessment for the Native American community, and works for United American Indian Involvement, Inc. She has participated in several publications on mental health and Native Americans and received her bachelor's degree from Nebraska Wesleyan University.

Barbara A. Plested, Ph.D., is a research scientist with the Tri-Ethnic Center and has worked extensively in providing direct services to special populations. She has experience in both administrative and therapeutic services in both mental health and substance abuse. She has also been involved in the evaluation of treatment and prevention programs for the past twelve years and is a member of the Community Readiness development team.

Caitlin Rosenthal is an undergraduate at Rice University in Houston, Texas. Her major is political science. Other interests include sociology, intellectual history, and mathematics. Her primary focus has been on education, health, and the intersection of migration and child health.

Karen Saylors, Ph.D., was trained as a medical anthropologist in Montréal, Québec, where she worked on women's health issues in bilingual, multicultural settings. She has worked with state, tribal, and local nonprofit organizations on collecting both qualitative and quantitative substance abuse data for statewide need assessments and evaluation purposes.

Margaret Severson, J.D., M.S.W., is associate professor, University of Kansas, School of Social Welfare. Professor Severson's research and practice focuses on suicide prevention and mental health intervention in local and state correctional facilities, intimate partner violence among incarcerated and ethnically diverse populations, and on strategies for successful offender reentry.

Antony Stately, Ph.D. (Ojibwe, Oneida), is a licensed clinical psychologist and the associate director of AIDS Project Los Angeles. He is involved in administration, program development, teaching, training, research, and program evaluation.

Margaret Mortensen Vaughan, M.A., is visiting scholar, University of Arizona, Tucson, and coordinator, Community History Project at Intertribal Friendship House, Oakland, California.